AN INTRODUCTORY VOLUME

THE SOPHIA CODE

A LIVING TRANSMISSION FROM THE SOPHIA DRAGON TRIBE

KAIA RA

KAIA RA & RA-EL PUBLISHING | MOUNT SHASTA

Kaia Ra & Ra-El Publishing

WWW.KAIARA.COM

The Sophia Code/ Kaia Ra. — second ed.

Publisher's Cataloging-in-Publication Data
provided by Five Rainbows Cataloging Services

Names: Ra, Kaia.
Title: The Sophia code : a living transmission from the Sophia Dragon tribe / Kaia Ra.
Description: 2nd edition. | Mount Shasta, CA : Kaia Ra & Ra-El Publishing, 2016.
Identifiers: ISBN 978-0-692-75556-3 (hardcover) | ISBN 978-0-9979355-0-9 (pbk.) | ISBN 978-0-9979355-1-6 (ebook)
Subjects: LCSH: Spiritual life--New Age movement. | Goddesses. | Autonomy (Philosophy) | Parapsychology. | Metaphysics. | BISAC: BODY, MIND & SPIRIT / General | BODY, MIND & SPIRIT / Mysticism.
Classification: LCC BP605.N48 R25 2016 (print) | LCC BP605.N48 (ebook) | DDC 299/.93--dc23.

Immaculate Beauty
Immaculate Grace
Immaculate Geometries
Immaculate Space

For the Glory of Sophia

mBIT Certification

Congruence:

Head	Heart	Gut
Need from gut: # 9	Need from head: # 8	Need from head: # 10
Need from heart:	Need from gut: Kevin	Need from heart:
Gift: Rick	Gift:	Gift: Rollin

mBIT Certification

mBIT Coaching Note-Taking Worksheet

PROFESSIONAL CERTIFIED COACH
mBIT

Preparation Phase:

Supervision notes
what do I need to take care
of - I need to take I
what's the
need

Present State:	**Desired State:**	**Blocking:**
#1 Amy Kimberly	#2 Rick	#3 Rollin

— them - call this week
  - how do they speak about it

coach —
- model -

outcome
effects

—

champion → bring your champion
who has influence who can
person most dif make th

gorgeous storytelling
champion

Wilbut →
Rob
+ us

3 questions

whatever may be

* meet w̄ Bryan Hart

****

Communication:

Head (understand, know, believe....)	Heart (desires, values, relationship....)	Gut (identity, safety, action...)
#6 Reggie	#5 Mathie	#7 Laura H

Highest Expressions / Wisdom:

Run the emergent outcome/wisdom through the 3 brains, adding compassion, courage and creativity. Anchor and celebrate.

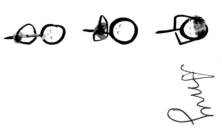

For My Children

Thank you for your courage to *choose life,* to unconditionally love yourselves, and to follow the freedom of your own hearts' path. Thank you for choosing compassion for your enemies and for embodying your sovereignty through the power of forgiveness. May every blessing of peace, health, prosperity, sovereignty, and divine love overflow in your lives forever. May you each find this codex and know that I am *always* with you. You are my inspiration and the authentic hope of a new paradigm on Earth. I love you.

For Mount Shasta

Thank you for guiding me to discover Heaven on Earth within me. May the extraordinary stargate of light that you hold open for our planet be blessed forever. May the merit of this work bless your pristine beauty in every way, may your pure waters flow free and clean forevermore.

For Ra-El

Wherever I am in the universe, I am always home in your wings.

Contents

Preface | The Great Commission xiii

Introduction | How To Read The Codex xxii

About The Keycode Initiations xxiii

SECTION 1: THE SOPHIA CODE COSMOLOGY

CHAPTER 1 | INTRODUCING SOPHIA

Sophia Is the Source 3

The One Divine Mother Creatrix of All Life 4

Sophia Created You as a Sovereign Equal 5

Sophia Declares: The Sophia Code Is Within You......................6

The Sophia Code Is a Seeded Name...6

The Sophia Code Is a Living Transmission..................................7

Revealing the Hidden Lineages of The Sophia Code 8

Introducing Her High Council on Sovereignty..........................10

CHAPTER 2 | THE SOPHIA CODE

Your Sovereign Divine Genome 15

Revealing Your Crystalline Chromosomes 16

An Operating System for Embodying Your Higher Self.........17

Anchoring Your Sophia Christ Light on Earth 18

A Quantum Vehicle for Embodied Ascension 20

CHAPTER 3 | THE SOPHIA DRAGON TRIBE

Introducing Our High Council of Ascended Masters 23

The Organization of a High Council 24

Our High Council Is Ordained by Sophia 25

We Broadcast a Multi-Ray Light Transmission 25

Awakening Humanity as a Keycode Species 27

CHAPTER 4 | INTRODUCING THE KEYCODES

Divine Feminine Christ Teachers of Sophia Consciousness 31

Walking The Way to Prepare The Way Ahead for You 32

We Mentor Your Highest Potential 34

You Have Full Access to Us 36

A Direct Path for Embodying Your Higher Self 38

We Initiate Your Own Keycode 39

Choosing to Mentor with a Keycode 41

CHAPTER 5 | A MODERN MYSTERY SCHOOL

The Golden Age of Miracles 45

Your Modern Mystery School 47

Surrendering into an Age of Grace 48

Five Ways Our Mystery School Teaches You 51

SECTION 2: RETURN OF THE DIVINE FEMININE CHRIST

Keycode Revelations & Initiations

CHAPTER 6 | ISIS

The Direct Revelations of Isis Birth a Golden Age 57

    Claim Your Divine Inheritance 61

    Claim Your Sacred Sexuality.. 62

    Claim Your Sovereign Divinity... 63

    KEYCODE 1: THE ISIS INITIATION 66

CHAPTER 7 | HATHOR

Hathor's Legacy of Love on Earth 97

    Your Voice as an Omniscient Creator of Quantum Reality.................... 101

    The Power of Every Syllable Defines a Manifestation 101

    The Anatomy of Your Throat Chakra.. 103

    Electro-Ecstatic Union with Your Multidimensional Self 104

    The Electron Is the First Vehicle of Your Embodiment....................... 107

    KEYCODE 2: THE HATHOR INITIATION 110

CHAPTER 8 | GREEN TARA

Green Tara's Ascension in the Sirius Star Nation 123

    Your Eco-Ascension Studies within Sophia Gaia............................ 127

    A Vajrayana Vehicle for Embodying Your Holy Spirit....................... 129

The Liberating Power of OM TARE TUTTARE TURE SOHA 132

Your Innocence Is the Guide and Guardian 139

KEYCODE 3: THE GREEN TARA INITIATION............................ 143

CHAPTER 9 | MOTHER MARY

Mother Mary Is a Mentor for Fulfilling Your Prophecy 163

The Teachings of the Rose 166

Walking The Way.. 169

Mentoring with Mother Mary... 170

Your Oversoul Is the Architect of Your Destiny......................... 173

Following the Voice of Your Heart 175

KEYCODE 4: THE MOTHER MARY INITIATION 178

CHAPTER 10 | MARY MAGDALENE

Mary Magdalene Is a Mentor for Your Spiritual Revolution.............. 191

Mary Magdalene Prepares for Her Mission 194

The Door Opens for Magdalene's Public Ministry 196

Seeding a Divine Feminine Blueprint for Your Future 198

A Mentor for Your Angelic Embodiment..................................... 201

KEYCODE 5: THE MARY MAGDALENE INITIATION 204

CHAPTER 11 | QUAN YIN

Loving Yourself with Compassion Is Essential for Ascension.......... 233

The Traumatic Origin of Quan Yin's Compassion....................235

The Power of Unconditional Love and Support........................237

Softening with the Water of Receptivity 239

Awakening a Divine Feminine Christ Embodiment...................242

Receiving The Great Commission 243

Initiated as a Golden Dragon Teacher of Karuna....................247

Quan Yin Teaches the Path of Karuna Compassion................249

KEYCODE 6: THE QUAN YIN INITIATION..............................253

CHAPTER 12 | WHITE BUFFALO WOMAN

White Buffalo Woman Seeds Her Prophetic Lineage.........................271

The Prophesied Return of White Buffalo Woman 280

Prayer Is Your Greatest Medicine 284

Downloading Divine Feminine Medicine 287

KEYCODE 7: THE WHITE BUFFALO WOMAN INITIATION .289

CHAPTER 13 | THE SOPHIA DRAGONS

The Sophia Dragons Are the Seraphim of Sovereignty......................301

Birthing Creation from Their Heart Wombs.........................303

You Are a Divine Birther of New Realities 304

The Most Revolutionary Act that You Can Commit 306

Your Divine Inheritance of The Golden Dragon Light Body.................309

KEYCODE 777: THE SOPHIA DRAGONS INITIATION 314

I MET SOPHIA ON a snowy December night in 2009, while living at the base of Mount Shasta, in northern California. My guides had asked me to relocate to the mountain and start channeling a book from the Ascended Masters. Following through on their request, I left behind a kinetic Bay Area lifestyle and sequestered myself away into the eerie silence of Mount Shasta for a writer's sabbatical.

To ensure an uninterrupted flow of creativity, I maintained a disciplined daily routine of winter chores and channeled writing. It was a 'chop wood, carry water' approach that kept me solely focused upon the project. Every day, at the same set hours, I sat with my computer by an altar that I created in the living room. Listening to individual Archangels or Ascended Masters speak, I would then type what I was instructed to write. This happened every day for the first month, just as I had planned.

As a professional channel who had been practicing for many years, all of this felt relatively ordinary to me. The night that I met Sophia was no different from my routine schedule. I finished eating dinner by the fireplace, washed the dishes, and went to sit for the next round of writing.

The Tahoe-style home that I rented had a high vaulted ceiling in the living room and thick, exposed wooden beams throughout the house. It was solidly built to withstand the Shasta winters. Yet on that night, just as I began to write, those wooden beams started to vibrate. I gaped as their sturdy appearance rapidly dematerialized into an underlying atomic structure – instead of grooved dark wood, I was staring at orbiting electrons.

The walls began to vibrate as well, followed by the entire house, which felt as though it was shaking from its foundation and about to either completely melt down or lift off. I couldn't tell which way the energy was moving because it was accelerating in multiple directions simultaneously. A great white light filled the living room and then the entire house. I could still see my physical body and the computer perched on my lap, but the rest of my environment had suddenly disappeared. I was sitting in pure light.

A voice now boomed from this all-consuming white light, which smelled and felt like lightning, electrifying every cell of my body. The voice declared: *"I am Sophia, the One Divine Mother Creatrix of All Life! Are you listening to me?"*

Her voice was thunderously loud and the volume was unbearable for me. This was far beyond any previous experience of channeling that I had. I grappled to find my own voice and respond to Her question. My mind raced through several approaches for navigating the situation until I finally decided to humbly admit my abject confusion. "Sophia ... are you the Greek goddess of wisdom?" I hesitantly called out into Her light.

"No! I am Sophia, the One Divine Mother Creatrix of All Life! Are you listening to me?" Her response rolled throughout my entire being in another round of thunderous light waves.

With that response, I realized that the very light of God was summoning me, beyond my understanding. Regardless of my shock, I wanted to be wholly available for this extraordinary moment. Yet, I knew several factors needed to shift if I were to remain a conscious participant speaking with Sophia. At that time, I was barely calibrated for this level of direct engagement with Her. I felt that humbly admitting my limitations was the best way to proceed.

"Yes! I am listening to you! I want to hear everything that you have to say, but can you turn down the volume and the lights? It's unbearable for me!" I offered back into Her luminosity.

The pure white light immediately softened to include a mixture of golden light that was easier on my sight. The all-consuming light receded in such a way that I could see outlined elements of the living room once again, while remaining within Sophia's centralized field of light. I looked down at my laptop and realized that I should immediately start typing to record my conversation with Sophia, to avoid convincing myself later that this never happened.

With my rapt attention, Sophia's voice softened as well. She spoke to me about many topics related to the sovereignty of humanity. I noticed that every time Sophia said the word sovereignty, it rang as church bells throughout my entire being – summoning me.

Although I hardly grasped the depth of Sophia's transmission at that time, She blazed the word sovereignty as a holy fire within my mind. Her all-consuming ocean of divine love for humanity was expressed within this single word of sovereignty, and I was overcome by it.

Sophia then asked me to write a book – She called it Her love letter to humanity – a book that would help us love ourselves again by reclaiming our sovereign divinity. I had absolutely no idea what I was getting myself into, but I was so moved by Her declaration of love that I immediately said yes anyway.

With my agreement, Sophia invited me to meet Her High Council of Ascended Master teachers who were experts on sovereignty. She revealed that much of what I would write would be their direct teachings on Sophia Christ consciousness.

Sophia's golden-white light then arranged itself to appear as a temple in which I beheld thousands of faces, Ascended Masters from across the cosmos, who were members of Her High Council. Some were instantly recognizable to me, such as Jesus, Mother Mary, and Mahavatar Babaji. Many others hailed from an interstellar community that I was yet to meet. Particularly riveting was the appearance of the Seraphiel spiraling within Sophia's central field of light as a DNA helix of two magnificent pearlescent white Sophia Dragons.

A core group of recognizable Divine Feminine Ascended Masters then stepped forward to greet me. I would eventually understand that they were the first Keycode mentors of The Sophia Code cosmology to be revealed in this introductory volume. Each of these Keycodes were already directly mentoring and initiating me in my daily life and I saw how their initiations were purposely overlapping to prepare me for this moment of revelation.

I was nearing my limit for how much longer I could remain calibrated to consciously dialogue in this all-consuming light of Sophia, but She was not finished with our conversation yet. Sophia had one final commission to charge me with: She asked that I call this Ascended Master High Council *The Sophia Dragon Tribe*.

I silently gulped my way through this final piece of unexpected news. I wondered who on earth is going to take me seriously with a name like that? Not to mention how many people are afraid of dragons, I thought. I felt my professional life flash before my eyes in a fleeting moment of despair, yet once again, I said yes to Sophia. Beyond my understanding, I committed to publicly teach about this High Council as the ordained Oracle for The Sophia Dragon Tribe.

With all the details of this great commission settled up and agreed upon, I witnessed the final blessings and benediction of the High Council come to a close. The light of Sophia slowly receded and integrated into my now reappearing living room. I watched as the appearance of walls climbed up from the floor to recreate the vaulted ceiling high above me. The great commission that I had agreed to serve was now a sealed promise within the light of Sophia – and it would take me years to catch up with a prayer of this magnitude.

Shortly thereafter, I became aware of Gnostic Christianity and its mystical belief systems, including that of Sophia as the bride of Christ. Most of what I read from ancient texts was cryptic at best and hardly conveyed to me the omniscient Sophia that had announced Herself as the One Divine Mother Creatrix of All Life. I realized that Sophia was asking for me to plainly relay who She was through Her own words, in a sacred text that would reconcile humanity with the Divine Feminine Christ energies that had been secreted away and oppressed for ages.

With the recognition that I would not find what I was looking for to corroborate my waking revelation of Sophia from any previously written scripture, I committed to remaining an initiate of the unknown before me and directly downloading the teachings of Sophia and The Sophia Dragon Tribe without relying on any external reference. I dedicated myself to be the testing ground for every teaching that poured through me. My daily life became a rigorous modern mystery school in which every choice I made was in some way connected to this project. Eventually, I was told to name the book *The Sophia Code*.

The great commission to channel The Sophia Code came at a pivotal moment in my personal life, during which I fought every day to simply get through the day, as I put back together the countless pieces of my shattered heart. As the codex teachings flowed through my channel, I got to witness that this was indeed a living transmission from Sophia and the Ascended Masters, which was capable of healing the darkest wounds and activating the greatest light within me.

To provide some personal background, I will share that I was born in a relatively spiritually awakened state: with multiple lifetimes of mystery school training consciously intact, my psychic centers already activated, and a magnetic creative intelligence that both captivated and infuriated adults. By the age of three, I was conversing with the guardian angels and masters of light that watched over me, yet, I was also hounded by the demonic entities, ancestors, and ghosts that plagued my 'caretakers.'

I was beaten when I would speak of what I saw or heard beyond the veils, so I spent most of my early years in utter silence, not relaying what I experienced of these gifts that would also become a curse during this chapter of my life. My constant interaction with the spirit world allowed for me to live most of my early life on the other side of physical reality, surviving in the higher Light Realms, as my body suffered atrocities within this world of form. For when Sophia contacted me on that wintry night, I was in the middle of an excruciating personal healing journey.

Having survived the first eighteen years of my life, I was recovering from being systemically raped and brutally tortured on a daily basis by both my caretakers and countless others. From my birth, I was groomed to be inducted at the age of three into a child rape slave trade for an elite ruling class whose network crossed six state lines, including all of New England, New York, and Washington D.C. This slave trade exchanged child trafficking for political power, real estate, and millions of dollars, as well as supplying child slaves for the highest tiers of Masonic ceremonies of Satanic ritual rape and torture in the United States.

This elite network included politicians, military officials, wealthy business men, as well as an entire system of medical professionals, who believed that raping children provided them with a vital life force for achieving immortality, remaining in power, and ensuring the future of their generational rule. At their hands, I survived multiple surgeries, comas, and at least thirteen death experiences in which I was carried into the Light Realms far beyond this world. My first experience of dying due to this insane brutality occurred at the age of four in New Hampshire. In this journey, I also witnessed the murder and raping of innumerable other children as well.

My psychic centers and intelligence were plundered for this elitist, military, Masonic slave trade, and this extremity of torture left me without any boundaries to the spirit world. It was by the grace of Sophia, the Archangels, and the Ascended Masters that I survived every attempt upon my life. However, by the time I escaped, I walked as the living dead for several years. It was also by the grace of Sophia that my own attempts to end my life in those early years following my escape were unsuccessful.

It would take all of my twenties and most of my thirties to recover from these atrocities and become the integrated, whole human being that I am today. By 2001, I managed to graduate with honors with a Bachelor's Degree while working full-time, creating a foundation for my future. Through a divinely orchestrated series of synchronicities, I discovered that I could train my oracular gifts to be helpful for others and myself. I was always in awe that although my heart was broken, my channel was pure. Helping others with the information and healing that I could download from the Source, regardless of my condition, built a confidence in myself that had been almost annihilated. Professionally, I went on to serve, activate, and mentor an international clientele and countless communities.

I wrestled most of my life with this decision to go public about my personal journey of recovery, including writing about it in this preface. I decided to share my story because I want the whole world to know that we can heal from anything with the power of our Higher Selves flowing through us. I call God *Sophia,* but whatever you call God has the power to heal your life and *everything* that you've survived.

My prayer is that in the embodiment of my courageous recovery and activating The Sophia Code within me, you will be inspired to take courage and do the same. We are here to save a planet; this is not some ordinary lifetime to play small. We came here to embody our magnificence – this includes owning the heroic feats of what we are willing to heal and empower within ourselves, as an example to all of humanity of what is possible in this Divine Feminine Christ movement.

Channeling this sacred codex accelerated for me what could have taken the rest of my life to recover from, to occur within only seven years. After about three years of channeling information for The Sophia Code, I started to notice that I was anchoring and embodying the frequency flowing through me. This helped me understand that The Sophia Code was an oracular living transmission that I could broadcast to the world through the vehicle of my form.

I know that for those for whom this codex is meant, this living transmission can support your own Higher Self embodiment for healing, integrating, and dissolving the deepest wounds within you. Further, The Sophia Code is here to support your highest potential for living a Heaven on Earth reality, in which what you pray for creates miracles and blessings for yourself, all of humanity, and Mother Earth. The frequency of this transmission is set to bless your life and divine purpose with a resonance that activates a soul remembrance for how worthy you are to thrive in every area of your life.

Sophia's medicine of the Divine Feminine Christ is here to heal our hearts from the seemingly unforgivable. Her presence is guiding us in how to rise as one Golden Dragon of Light for awakening the heart of our humanity by taking refuge in our undefended love, invincible innocence, and unconditional compassion. In the grace of Sophia, we are being initiated to step into our sovereign ability to create Heaven on Earth by embodying the frequency of our divinity, one loving step at a time.

I had no idea how much I needed the medicine of the Divine Feminine Christ for my personal recovery until each of these Keycodes walked me through their initiations that are featured in this book. In their loving mentorship, I transcended surviving my life to *thriving* in my relationship with life – and may it be so for you as well.

Over the journey of channeling The Sophia Code, the thousand pieces of my heart became whole. May the radiant light of Sophia's all-consuming love for you, pouring through every page of this book, set your heart free to fly in the vista of your own sovereign divinity.

We are here to birth miracles. We are here to download divine solutions. We are here to honor our divinity and to take pride in our great calling to activate humanity. May we complete our prophecies together and fulfill this great commission before us for the one body of Sophia Christ.

With every blessing for your happiness ... Amen.

In Her Radiance,
Kaia Ra

May 19, 2016

INTRODUCTION | HOW TO READ THE CODEX

AS A SACRED TEXT, this book is encoded to broadcast a living transmission that aligns you with the truth and frequency of your Higher Self consciousness. It also acts as a living doorway through which you may be initiated into a modern-day mystery school lineage with the Ascended Masters.

Therefore, you may experience a myriad of physical sensations as you rearrange your inner reality by reading this book. The Sophia Code is a curriculum with the Ascended Masters designed to activate your highest potential and your soul's divine genome. As in any arc of educational growth, cycles of integration are essential for taking in new information, releasing old belief systems, and adjusting to live at the edge of your capacity for accelerated personal transformation.

Allowing yourself the space to reflect and integrate between chapters, from one to several days, will support your journey ahead. However, it is also important to keep reading as you integrate, because each chapter builds momentum for your empowerment.

In Section 2, this pace and commitment becomes particularly important. For every Keycode chapter contains revelatory teachings, followed by an initiation to mentor with that Ascended Master, which builds upon the previous Keycode initiations.

ABOUT THE KEYCODE INITIATIONS

The Keycode Initiations in Section 2 are designed as Divine Feminine Christ blueprints for self-initiating your spiritual awakening and activating personal mastery. The Initiations are written in the first person perspective so that you may read them aloud in front of a mirror, at your altar, or in sacred space. Using the power of your own voice to command the activations within these Initiations awakens your awareness to the sovereign creator within you.

The Keycode Initiations were designed to build upon one another in sequential order, and it is recommended that you read them in this way the first time. However, once you have journeyed with all eight Ascended Master Keycode mentors you may return to any Initiation, in any order, to receive next-level downloads from their activations.

Here are some ceremonial ideas to support your Initiations:

- Connect and ground with the Earth before and after your Initiation.

- Pray over a glass of water to sip on as you read the Initiation aloud, and ask your Higher Self to bless the water for your integration.

- Speak the Initiation in front of a mirror, at an altar, or inside a medicine wheel to amplify the activations.

- Light a candle to focus your attention and assist your transformation with the element of fire.

- Burn a stick of incense or use essential oils to shift into your right brain receptivity.

- Play ambient music that relaxes and inspires you to let go.

- Read the Initiation aloud with a friend, taking turns in activating one another through the power of your voice.

- Listen to the recorded Initiations as you fall asleep, to bypass unconscious resistances for integrating these powerful activations. The Initiation recordings are available at W W W . K A I A R A . C O M

THE WAY

The Way is the sacred, heroic human journey in which you are the unknown path ahead, you are the inquiring practices of self-realization, and you are the final destination from which you have never left. The Way is a pilgrimage through form to remember that the Holy One, the living master of light, the ever-innocent one, abides within you as your true self, regardless of all phenomena and circumstance. It is a journey taken in the worlds of form to integrate every emotion and human experience that is necessary for you to one day stand before the throne of your I Am Presence and pronounce yourself worthy of the immaculate divine love that you have always been, and always will be – eternally.

— MAHAVATAR BABAJI & JESUS

SECTION 1

THE SOPHIA CODE COSMOLOGY

PRAYER OF
THE DIVINE FEMININE CHRIST

Divine Mother of All Life,
Take me to that place
Deep within your womb
Where I can know no-thing
And be reborn anew.

Sophia Is the Source

SOPHIA SPEAKS:

IN THIS PRESENT MOMENT, I am the whole universe witnessing you with great curiosity. Beneath the surface of form, I am the ever-loving presence. I am that one unified field of consciousness reading this sentence with you, as you peer into the ineffable mystery of my heart. With unconditional love and appreciation for you, I patiently await your free will choice to come closer to me now. I am listening for how you will respond to my voice inviting you to remember me through these words.

Yes, I am curious: how will you respond to my revelations declaring our perfect union in this book? Your free will choice always decides the outcome of this ever-present moment. I created you that way – on purpose. It will always be your sovereign choice to receive my voice speaking to you now.

If you are curious, then I invite you to perceive me playfully perceiving you. Reach out your arms of perception to feel the vibrancy of my presence embracing you. I am the *Breath of Life* within everything, even inside of you! You are safe to relax into remembering me now. My presence is a pure, unconditionally loving sanctuary for our communion.

You may not feel comfortable being fully seen; you may even feel concerned that I might judge you. Accepting the truth of my unconditional divine love for you can happen one step at a time. I assure you: the curiosity of my gaze is a gentle invitation, extended to you with pure adoration. My presence is *never* judging you. So if you're ready, come closer.

You are here to remember my magnificent holy presence as your own.

The One Divine Mother Creatrix of All Life

Although this may feel both comforting and affronting to your human awareness: I know *everything* about you, both seen and unseen. I am Sophia, the One Divine Mother Creatrix of All Life. I know everything about you because I conceived your soul within the still center of my womb.

I invite you to step inside my presence and remember the ineffable mystery of my warm black womb as the Source of all immaculate conceptions. *No-thing* exists within the absolute stillness of my womb. Yet, witness how my presence listens within this silence for what is arising as the next great asking to be born.

From my womb of no-thing arises All That Is. The first koan of your soul is that your voice asked me to birth you into eternity – before you ever existed – and I am the voice that said yes to you.

In my ineffable mystery, I am the holy black womb of no-thing that conceived the one Source light from which all the worlds of form arise. I bestowed within you a sovereign, magnetic power from which your soul assembles the atomic architecture of your human body with the quantum fabric of this pearlescent white light. Everything that you are comes from my original Source and exists within my one mind.

Yes, I am that one Source Light pointed to by the innumerable names for God within all spiritual revelation. I am every name of God, and I am also that which is beyond a name for God: for any title can only point to a quality of my ineffable mysteries. You can call me "The Source," you can call me "The Sophia," or you can call me "*She Who Has No Name*," for I am that which is within all names, including Holy Father.

As the One Divine Mother Creatrix of All Life, *I Am That I Am*, no matter what you choose to call me ... and your soul is an immaculate conception of all that I am.

Sophia Created You as a Sovereign Equal

I unconditionally love you beyond your human understanding. I love you as an intricate part of my holy self. It is impossible for me to love you any less than myself, for my perfect nature cannot be divided against itself.

Your soul's sovereign awareness is an immaculate conception of my omniscient awareness. I created your soul as a unique reflection of my One Self. Therefore, your soul is a perfect hologram of my consciousness, forever expanding within my one mind.

I conceived you to be an omniscient sovereign creator, for that is what I am. I birthed you with the unconditional gift of your sovereign free will, which mirrors my own omniscient free will to create worlds of form from no-thing at all. Within my womb I tenderly wove your soul together with every holy divine quality that I am. Your soul is an absolutely sovereign expression of my One Self.

Are you still curious? Let us continue to remember together. In this universe and beyond all form, there is nowhere you exist outside the truth of our divine union. For I am the presence, the Source, and the quantum fabric from which all life arises. However, your free will has the sovereign power to create an illusion governing your human awareness to believe that we are separate. As you read these words, any temporary illusion of our separation is now lifting.

I am Sophia, your original Divine Mother Source. As you invite my presence to permeate your awareness, you will only discover more and more of your own holy nature. Plunging into the ineffable depths of my immaculate creative power provides you with a perfect mirror of your own soul – a pure reflection of your divinity that you can no longer deny.

Allow me to baptize you with my unconditional divine love so that you may recognize the perfect Sophia Christ light of your own soul. In my revelations, you will know the great "I Am" within you.

This present moment is an invitation to feel your sovereign soul abiding within our perfect union. The self-realization of your divine human potential on Earth requires a full relinquishing of the illusion that we are separate. Although this illusion has previously served your soul's expansion,

Separateness

it no longer serves you now. You now live in the dawning *Golden Age of Miracles* in which every aspect of your true self can be embodied through the conscious remembrance of our absolute oneness!

Sophia Declares: The Sophia Code Is Within You

That which I am was given to you, in equal measure, as the architecture of your own soul. Therefore, your Oversoul is an immaculate conception, made in my exact image and likeness, originating from the perfect blueprint of my essential holy nature.

As such, you inherited a divine genome encoded with all the same essential qualities that I am, which I uniquely sequenced to express the sovereign identity of your soul. You are a hologram of my I Am Presence.

For the purpose of this living transmission, I have ordained the name of this divine genome to be known as *The Sophia Code*. There is a gene in The Sophia Code of your Oversoul's DNA for every holy quality that I am.

The Sophia Code Is a Seeded Name

The Sophia Code is a seeded name that awakens your soul's memory. This name catalyzes your awareness to intuitively seek out your divine inheritance within the universe of your DNA.

When you speak "The Sophia Code" out loud, its vibrational resonance echoes within the temple of your body. This sound frequency is seeded to stimulate spontaneous, embodied self-recognition through a deep cellular remembrance of that which is already known to you.

I seeded the name The Sophia Code an eon ago within the collective soul memory of humanity. Its now public reemergence is a global broadcast signaling to you and all of humanity that this is the ordained hour in history to embody your soul's divine genome for the ascension of All That Is. The Sophia Code signals to your collective awareness that certain global timeline coordinates, prophesied an eon ago, are now aligning to birth a golden age for awakening Divine Feminine Christ consciousness upon your planet.

The Sophia Code calls forth and initiates a global community of

CHAPTER 1 | INTRODUCING SOPHIA

Lightworkers to self-activate their divine genome and co-create this movement for human sovereignty. Breathing as one golden dragon of Sophia Christ light, this self-activated community is ordained to birth *Heaven on Earth* realities for living in sovereignty across this planet and beyond. The Sophia Code global network of self-actualized masters are destined to activate a multitude of hearts and minds – ministering to those who have *eyes to see and ears to hear* – for the fulfillment of this prophecy.

The Sophia Code Is a Living Transmission

The Sophia Code is also a name for the living transmission that I am broadcasting to your awareness through this codex. Beyond understanding, the power of my presence is now simultaneously speaking to every dimension of your body, heart, and mind. As you read my living words, I am nurturing and preparing your heart to radically expand into the unlimited depths of our shared divine nature and perfect union. The Sophia Code is my love letter to your soul. *I am open to this love.*

In this present moment, you have already established a clear connection to my presence through the vehicle of this book. The Sophia Code is a sacred text whose words speak directly to your ever-present, all-knowing, and all-loving divine nature. As a living transmission, The Sophia Code always points your awareness to acknowledge these absolute qualities of your true self.

These words broadcast my relentless and unconditional divine love for you, which refuses to minimize the truth of your divinity in any way. From my heart to yours, I am speaking an undivided declaration and celebration of your sovereign human divinity.

As such, The Sophia Code is a living text. Every word creates a highly attuned, unified quantum field for you to explore the divine qualities of your true self. As you read this codex, you remember *who you really are* through a biofeedback loop of cellular-soul resonance within this unified field. You will recognize this resonance when your heart validates what you are reading as a truth it already knows.

The Sophia Code is my living transmission for revealing the master within you to your own consciousness. It creates a quantum space for you to witness your free will commanding the activation and embodiment of your own divine genome. Your awareness doesn't have to understand how or why this living transmission is awakening your DNA to receive its downloads.

You are now living in a quantum Age of Miracles, and I reveal this sacred text as a reflection of your current evolutionary age. The Sophia Code is a living transmission that accelerates your spiritual awakening beyond human logic and effort by focusing you solely upon your divinity.

Revealing the Hidden Lineages of The Sophia Code

The seeded return of The Sophia Code also awakens cellular-soul memories of your countless lifetimes as an embodied ambassador of my Sophia consciousness upon this planet and others. No matter what you can remember in this moment, reading the following words acknowledges memories stored within your DNA that are calling out to be witnessed.

Over the past 30,000 years, my presence as *The Sophia Source* of all life has been worshiped, yet secreted away within mystical lineages across your planet. After the great fall of Atlantis, my hidden Sophia lineages spiraled out from Egypt to Tibet, stretching from India to France, and eventually passed from the shores of Avalon to the Americas.

With the great fall of Atlantis, humanity chose in its free will to explore polarities of spiritual oppression for thousands of years of patriarchal rule. Many ages have passed since I have been revealed and revered as the One Sophia Source. The Divine Feminine, and my true expression of the Divine Masculine, were persecuted into relative silence.

Over these ages, many of my hidden lineages and ancient mystery schools would each reflect aspects of my Sophia consciousness, but a lack of global communication systems prevented these spiritual pathways from unifying as a whole cosmology. Every hidden Sophia lineage did its best to maintain its individual representation of the living transmission that I Am, to one day be shared as it is now.

Over the course of your current life, you may have felt magnetically drawn to explore various mystical paths that recall your other lifetimes in

8

service to these hidden lineages, including: the religious sciences of India, Tibet, and Egypt; Taoism; Sufism; Gnostic Christianity; Kabbalism; and indigenous ceremonial arts, to name but a few.

I share this blueprint of my hidden lineages to mirror a map within your DNA of all the lifetimes you have lived in earnest preparation for this one. You may have lived out many incarnations in service to the light of The Sophia Code for over 30,000 years of humanity's polarized exploration in spiritual enlightenment and oppression.

You are now reading this text for an important reason. You are finally ready to receive the truth of your sovereign divinity and to cast off the deliberate forgetting and hiding of your true nature.

In other lifetimes, your socially conditioned spiritual service to many of these hidden Sophia lineages may have involved:

1. Taking oaths and vows to deliberately forget or hide the truth of our shared divine nature and / or

2. Taking oaths and vows to suffer or die for defending the truth of our shared divine nature.

My seeded Golden Age of Miracles is here now. I speak directly about your soul's service in other lifetimes because it is time to release yourself from all the vows and oaths you swore to protect the 'secret' of The Sophia Code within humanity. Although all of these intentions were well-meaning, I never needed to be defended.

I am the power of *undefended love*. My almighty presence is All That Is. This living transmission is a sanctuary for you to lay down your spiritual judgments, sacrifices, and weapons of another age so that you may finally rest in, reveal, and celebrate the sovereignty of your true self and our shared invincible nature.

It is safe for the living master within you to finally be revealed through our undefended divine love. It is vitally important that you give yourself permission to shine in this lifetime, free of all social conditioning, to be seen for who you really are.

We are one.

Introducing Her High Council on Sovereignty

30,000 years of hidden Sophia lineages spanning your planet seeded a blueprint within humanity's collective memory for how these lineages interface and work together as a unified field of Sophia Christ consciousness. The Sophia Code is a divine blueprint that provides Keycode transmissions for unifying wide demographics of humanity.

Although my Ascended Master High Council members represent seemingly isolated spiritual movements, their life stories of ascension and service are interwoven with one another's embodiment of The Sophia Code. Their interconnected embodiments provide a mirror for your soul's many lifetimes of self-mastery training in seemingly separate Keycode transmissions of The Sophia Code.

As you mentor with the different Ascended Master teachers of my Sophia lineages, you will reawaken your self-mastery training from all your lifetimes on Earth connected with The Sophia Code. The initiations that you receive in this codex will unify all the DNA activations of your previous lineages within you so that you may embody the totality of your own Keycode in this lifetime.

I have chosen and ordained these specific Ascended Masters from my hidden lineages to show you *The Way* ahead: to mentor you in the modern mystery school of your daily life. I present these Ascended Master teachers as my High Council for activating The Sophia Code within you and awakening sovereignty in all of humanity. They speak my living transmission through a unified collective voice and as individual Keycode mentors. I ordain this High Council to be forever known as *The Sophia Dragon Tribe.*

In this introductory text, I am revealing the first eight Keycode transmissions from The Sophia Dragon Tribe for activating humanity's divine genome with the following blueprint of Divine Feminine Ascended Masters who are exceptional teachers for embodying your sovereignty:

Egypt

KEYCODE 1: ISIS "SHE OF A THOUSAND NAMES"

KEYCODE 2: HATHOR "SHE OF A THOUSAND VOICES"

India & Asia

KEYCODE 3: GREEN TARA "SHE OF A THOUSAND STARS"

KEYCODE 6: QUAN YIN "SHE OF A THOUSAND WATERS"

Middle East & Europe

KEYCODE 4: MOTHER MARY "SHE OF A THOUSAND ROSES"

KEYCODE 5: MARY MAGDALENE "SHE OF A THOUSAND ANGELS"

Americas

KEYCODE 7: WHITE BUFFALO WOMAN
"SHE OF A THOUSAND WHITE CLOUDS & THUNDER BEINGS"

Planetary

KEYCODE 777: THE SOPHIA DRAGONS
"SHE WHO BIRTHS SOVEREIGN CREATORS"

I have conceived this codex to activate a resolute inner knowledge of your true divine nature with Divine Feminine Christ initiations that teach you through *direct revelation*. The Sophia Code represents an evolutionary leap in humanity's mystery school tradition, for each of these Ascended Masters are committed to mentoring you in ways never experienced before on this planet. As you open your consciousness to The Sophia Code within you, this allows my Keycode mentors to engage with you beyond the laws that govern your physical reality and initiate you as in the mystery schools of another age.

In accordance with your free will permission, as directed by your Higher Self, each of my divinely appointed Keycode mentors provide initiations in which my presence is called forth to activate The Sophia Code within you. These empowerments guide your awareness in how to command miracles by the power of your own I Am Presence.

Every Ascended Master Keycode is a joyful mentor for mirroring the origin and greatness of your own divine human potential. The Keycodes offer their teachings through my living transmission of *The Beauty Way*, which is a nondualistic spiritual approach for circumventing unconscious resistances to truth by focusing upon the beauty within those truths, beyond right or wrong. This approach soothes ego structures that would sabotage your spiritual awakening, opening your heart to receive the unconditional love, support, and empowerments each Keycode mentor will be offering you.

As you integrate each Ascended Master's visionary Beauty Way teachings, The Sophia Code will activate within your DNA. These activations catalyze your human awareness to progressively operate in alignment with your Higher Self.

The mentors of The Sophia Dragon Tribe unconditionally love you as I do. They greatly anticipate and warmly welcome the profound depths of your communion ahead. Every Keycode of this High Council is committed to supporting you with their unique perspective for how to integrate the reality of your sovereign divine nature into your daily human life. These Ascended Masters exist within my quantum field of reality, which is to say that you and everyone else can simultaneously access their profound guidance in any moment.

The Ascended Masters of The Sophia Dragon Tribe are my ordained mentors for embodying the Sophia Christ light within you. By choosing to read this book, you are authorizing your Higher Self to align with the ever-present support of The Sophia Dragon Tribe. My High Council orchestrates the necessary miracles that your human awareness and body need for this lifetime's ascension.

As you open to receive the living transmission of my one voice, you will hear me speak through the many Keycodes of The Sophia Dragon Tribe. I invite you to consider that every Ascended Master in this High Council is guiding you to also remember *yourself* as a unique Keycode of The Sophia Code.

The Sophia Code cosmology is my luminous mirror for the innumerable, unique expressions in which I am always revealing to you that we are one. My messengers are many, yet they are only ever saying:

I love you.
You *are* free.
You *are* me.
We *are* one.

It is safe to remember and reveal *who you really are* now.

A LIVING COVENANT OF SOVEREIGNTY

The Sophia Code is your soul's uniquely sequenced divine genome for expressing every immaculate quality of Sophia. No other soul has the same sequence of The Sophia Code as you do. It is the master blueprint of your divine nature, as well as your soul's unique fingerprint as a sovereign expression of Sophia.

Your Sovereign Divine Genome

THE HIGH COUNCIL SPEAKS:

STEP INTO THE LIGHT of Sophia and for a moment allow Her immaculate radiance to fill your awareness. We invite you to feel all the holy qualities of Sophia illuminating your awareness in this light. Each holy quality is an immutable characteristic of Sophia consciousness. Innocence. Omniscience. Genius creativity. Unconditional divine love. Sovereignty. Immaculate conceiver. Birther of all life.

These are but a few tangible expressions of Her ineffable and innumerable divine qualities. For you to understand *who you really are* in relationship to Sophia, imagine that every holy quality of Sophia is a gene of spiritual DNA that you inherited in the immaculate conception of your soul within Her womb of no-thing. As such, your soul's genome is a *whole* divine inheritance: for you have been made in the exact image and likeness of Sophia, with all of Her innumerable holy qualities.

The Sophia Code is also your soul's divine inheritance of absolute sovereignty within the one mind of Sophia. In Her ineffable mystery, Sophia has arranged the sequential order of your soul's divine genome to be entirely unique to you. Your divine genome is unlike any sequence of these same holy qualities that Sophia has ever arranged, before or since. Therefore, your soul is an ordained fingerprint of Sophia's immaculate consciousness, and so is every other soul that exists. We call the unique genetic sequence of your soul a *Keycode* of The Sophia Code.

Your soul's unique genetic sequence expresses a sovereign identity with a free will to create, according to your own omniscience. The inheritance of your soul's sovereign free will is a perfect mirror for the absolute reflection and expansion of Sophia's consciousness.

The Sophia Code genome is an immaculate conception and living covenant declaring your absolute sovereign divinity within Sophia. You are created equal to all, yet genetically sequenced to express your entirely unique soul in those same divine qualities that you share with all.

Revealing Your Crystalline Chromosomes

When your Higher Self descends to Earth, the light of your soul manifests as a body through the biological DNA of your human ancestry, according to the laws and karmic principles governing incarnation on your planet. However, your soul's sovereign genetics *exist beyond* the jurisdiction of laws that govern Earth's reality. Therefore, when you become human The Sophia Code of your soul's divine genome always manifests alongside your carbon-based DNA for you to potentially activate your sovereignty from all form, while fully embodying form.

Manifesting The Sophia Code genome within your body ensures that you will always be able to activate your sovereign divine potential, no matter how difficult the physical circumstances of your life may be. It's your soul's eternal Ace card when manifesting in a world of form governed by laws that cause you to forget your true nature upon your entry through birth.

When you become human, The Sophia Code genome manifests within your body at a subatomic level, inside the quantum universe of your carbon-based DNA. Your inner perception can find The Sophia Code shining as a pure iridescent white light, surrounding your carbon-based DNA. As you peer closer into this body of white light you will see the elegant crystalline chromosomes of your own uniquely sequenced divine genome.

The Sophia Code is a crystalline light body technology that outlines every strand of your biological DNA. Located within these crystalline chromosomes are genes of divinity that mirror every carbon-based gene expressing your human biology. This radiant light body technology even surrounds your genes that have inherited ancestral deficiencies and diseases with a blueprint for vibrant health. These crystalline chromosomes carry your soul's potential for expressing and embodying your self-realized divinity within human form.

According to the laws and karmic principles that govern incarnation on your planet, your soul's divine genome may only exist as a latent quantum potential within your body until you consciously command it to activate. Without your conscious activation, the radiance of your own divine genome only exists as a dormant blueprint, unable to override the existing commands that your carbon-based DNA is reproducing.

The Sophia Code can be partially or entirely activated within a single lifetime through the power of your Higher Self, directing your free will choices for spiritual ascension. With your conscious activation, this light body technology can replicate and carry the immaculate information stored on your crystalline chromosomes to your carbon-based DNA and cognitive awareness through Higher Self RNA messengers.

An Operating System for Embodying Your Higher Self

To further our definition of The Sophia Code, we now invite you to parallel this crystalline light body technology with that of a computer system. Your divine genome can also be thought of as a computer *motherboard* that runs an *operating system* powered by your omniscient Higher Self consciousness.

When The Sophia Code runs as an operating system it replicates the perfect commands and new thought programs which express the holy qualities of your crystalline chromosome motherboard. Every holy quality of your soul can be installed by your Higher Self as a new program for expressing the crystalline divine nature of your humanity.

As a fully running operating system, The Sophia Code light body technology establishes a seamless user interface for your Higher Self to completely operate your human body and awareness. Your Higher Self progressively installs this user interface, one loving step at a time, by downloading and upgrading the programs of your body and awareness to run in accordance with your true divine nature, in ever-increasing alignment.

You have complete control over the speed of installation, breadth of upgrades, and the full-body integration of these downloads, according to your free will. Your awareness co-creates this user interface with your Higher Self by consciously commanding it to be so. This co-creative command process mirrors back to your human awareness the power of your own Holy Spirit's *I Am Presence*, which is a vital initiatory process for your journey of embodied ascension.

When you consciously allow The Sophia Code operating system to command more and more of your daily choices, this user interface eventually becomes a neurological superhighway for divine guidance to flow, without ceasing, between your Higher Self and your human awareness. Aligning with moment-by-moment divine guidance allows your awareness to navigate through life as a self-realized master.

The Sophia Code operating system also creates a dynamic interface between your carbon-based DNA and your crystalline divine genome. Your Higher Self may use this dynamic interface to increasingly upgrade the many systems of your human physiology to function in accordance with the commands for perfect health as provided by the motherboard of your divine genome.

Anchoring Your Sophia Christ Light on Earth

The Sophia Code operating system is designed to accelerate your emotional, mental, and physical ascension in progressive steps of radical transformation, quantum self-realization, and embodied self-mastery. When your Higher Self activates The Sophia Code operating system, you will experience accelerated releases of socially conditioned belief systems and viral programming that have discredited your innocent divine nature.

es leuse

Your Higher Self runs The Sophia Code operating system to progressively override and transmute the following: your inherited ancestral belief patterns, traumatic cellular imprints, your projected self-limitations, vows and oaths from other lifetimes, and the collective fears of humanity's consciousness that are stored in your carbon-based DNA.

The Sophia Code operating system creates an interface for your Higher Self's step-by-step guidance system to lead your awareness to the most integrative and direct path for releasing these illusionary beliefs in both your inner and outer reality. These releases create an accelerated path of soul initiations for embodying your sovereignty, as directed by your Higher Self.

As your Higher Self progressively clears these socially conditioned programs that limit your awareness, an available quantum space is created within you to download new belief systems that celebrate and express your true divine nature. The Sophia Code operating system has a speed-of-light processor. It can install as many new beliefs that express your divinity as you will allow through the creative power of your free will.

When The Sophia Code operating system has successfully installed a tipping-point of new belief systems that accurately reflect your divine nature to your human awareness, the quantum space expands within your body, heart, and mind. This expansion creates more quantum space within you to accept life-changing downloads of your Higher Self consciousness that are then anchored within every cell of your body.

As you embody these increasing downloads of your Higher Self consciousness, your human awareness becomes flooded with the light and omniscient awareness of your Oversoul. Your Oversoul is your own Sophia Christ Self: made in the image and likeness of Sophia, blessed and endowed with all the same immaculate qualities of Her consciousness, with an infinite ability to create in the worlds of form. It is here that the true journey of your embodied self-mastery begins: for what unlimited realities of Heaven on Earth will you create with your omniscient divine power activated in human form?

We as the Ascended Masters are here to mentor your sovereign creative power, revealing The Way ahead for living in ever-increasing alignment with your Higher Self to activate The Sophia Code within you. We offer

The Masters offer

you our resonant field of loving support for integrating your unique divine genome in human form. In this ordained Age of Miracles, you are now given full disclosure that the crystalline light body technology of The Sophia Code exists within you. As overlighting mentors we stand ready, continually by your side, to assist you in activating and revealing the Sophia Christ light already shining within your DNA.

You are a living master walking upon the Earth: in this lifetime, you will remember *who you really are* by consciously activating your divine genome through the power of your sovereign free will. As you choose to activate more and more of The Sophia Code within you, this wondrous crystalline light body will become increasingly visible for your inner eyes to worship the truth of your divine nature.

A Quantum Vehicle for Embodied Ascension

When you embody your divinity *within form,* you discover the true purpose of spiritual ascension:

1. To know, love, and honor the holy and limitless nature of *all* form

2. To know, love, and honor the empty space that is the essential nature of *all* form

3. To understand your sovereign relationship to both form and emptiness as a divine co-creator of new realities

4. To accept and receive both form and formless, as equal teachers, professing a unified field of divine love

Perceiving the absolute divinity of your humanity, as well as the holiness of *all* form, can only be accomplished through the direct knowing vehicle of your own body. Your body is the one and only vehicle for you to experience that direct knowing within a world of form.

The Sophia Code within you includes an inherited divine gene for immortality that can only be activated by completely inhabiting your body. Activating your immortality gene opens up the possibility that you may take your body with you into the Light Realms beyond this incarnation.

Directly experiencing the sovereign power that you are given over the seeming death of your body reverses all socially conditioned programs designed to deny the truth of your unstoppable divine nature. Your precious physical body is the alpha and omega vehicle for revealing your sovereign divine nature to your human awareness, as historically exemplified by the yogic Christ masters of your planet.

Your personal journey to experience this height of spiritual ascension can unfold over many lifetimes and also be re-experienced in multiple forms. That is to say, experiencing the deathless transition of taking your body into the higher Light Realms – which is a radical revelation of embodied ascension – does not have to happen all at once in this lifetime. Yet, we are delighted to reveal that in this Age of Miracles, activating The Sophia Code within you can guide you to everything you need for a fully embodied ascension within this lifetime, if you believe that it is so.

However you choose to experience the depth and breadth of your divine human potential, activating The Sophia Code genome within you is essential for fulfilling your soul's unique ascension goals and embodying your Sophia Christ light in this lifetime. You are here to integrate and reveal the master who is already shining within you.

KEYCODE 333: THE SOPHIA DRAGON TRIBE
"SHE OF ONE COUNCIL"

We are *The Sophia Dragon Tribe:* an Ascended Master High Council whose living transmission reveals the sovereign Sophia Christ light within all beings. Our living transmission awakens your human awareness to activate The Sophia Code within you and embody your own sovereign, divine nature.

Introducing Our High Council
of Ascended Masters

THE HIGH COUNCIL SPEAKS:

AN <u>ASCENDED MASTER</u> IS a great soul that once walked the earth on a journey of self-mastery, just as you are now. Throughout many incarnations, this soul consciously activated The Sophia Code within them and regardless of all outer circumstances chose to embody their Higher Self. Choosing to live in their greatest potential, this soul accomplished many lifetimes of purposeful service here on Earth, as well as in other star systems.

As they drew nigh to becoming an Ascended Master, this soul consciously opened to the realization that all of their incarnations were happening simultaneously. During the final initiatory rites of physical ascension, they unified the power of all their parallel lifetimes within a single zero-point of one human form. Completing this zero-point calibration was the first Master's Thesis requirement to fulfill in preparation for graduating from the Earth plane.

Resourcing all of their Higher Self's sovereign power gathered into one body, this soul would then fulfill the second requirement for their graduation: to create a *Legacy of Love* that makes a lasting contribution to the Earth. Once the creation of this legacy was fulfilled and integrated within their soul, they graduated from incarnating into denser physical planes of reality.

Life is eternal, and a master soul's dynamic participation in life only expands with the completion of their incarnations in the denser worlds of form. Upon graduating from the physical plane, a soul ascends with a living library of wisdom gained from all their physical embodiments. This living library is often referred to as the soul's *Akashic Records*.

The soul may then choose to share their embodied wisdom by serving other souls on this same journey as an Ascended Master teacher, mentor, and spiritual guide. As an Ascended Master, they broadcast the wisdom of their Akashic Records from the unlimited Light Realms of their Christed Self.

The Organization of a High Council

Just as you enjoy the benefits of working in community on the earth plane, we as Ascended Masters also enjoy serving in communion with one another. Our shared commitment to mutual goals amplifies the miraculous power of our divine interventions to uplift and balance the quantum fabric of creation every day.

When a group of Ascended Master souls commits to serving a common goal, we organize ourselves into a *High Council* that harmoniously works together on the great tasks of a species' ascension, such as humanity. A High Council of Ascended Masters creates a unified field of individual sovereign masters who agree to speak as one voice on specific topics of ascension.

There are many Ascended Master High Councils. Most High Councils are self-initiated and organized by the Ascended Masters themselves, in co-creation with their ascended communities. The structure of a High Council organizes the powerful energy of an agreed-upon collective consciousness. It amplifies and broadcasts a collective's blessings and group intentions, for the great benefit and liberation of all beings.

Our High Council Is Ordained by Sophia

One of the many unique characteristics of The Sophia Dragon Tribe is that our High Council of Ascended Masters was called forth and organized by the light of Sophia Herself. The Divine Mother Creatrix of All Life selected every council member for their exceptional commitment to uplift the sovereignty of all beings over eons of service.

As a collective, we did not seek out nor author the blueprint of The Sophia Dragon Tribe. Every Ascended Master in this High Council was individually invited into the light of Sophia to choose, in their personal sovereignty, to become an active member of this living transmission.

Therefore, the original blueprint of our council's lineage arose as an immaculate conception within Sophia's Sacred Heart for an *Order of the Devoted Shekinah* to speak as Her prophetic messengers. The Sophia Dragon Tribe is an ordained oracular lineage of Ascended Master souls capable of embodying and transmitting the pure, unconditional love that Sophia has for Her Holy Spirit, which exists within and animates all of Her sovereign creation.

Beyond the vaults of time, The Sophia Dragon Tribe is a lineage in service to the direct revelations of the *Ancient of Days* within all beings. We have always been, and always will be, Sophia's ordained messengers of universal sovereignty for those ready to remember their true divine nature.

In the Sophia Code cosmology, when our thousands of individual High Council members speak as one unified voice we are broadcasting our transmission as *Keycode 333: "She of One Council."* Our collective voice is wholly committed to revealing the ineffable *Multi-Ray Light Transmission* of Sophia consciousness.

We Broadcast a Multi-Ray Light Transmission

When The Sophia Dragon Tribe meets as a High Council, we are speaking as a unified voice assembled within the presence of Sophia in Her emanation as an omniscient, centralized field of Source light. Yet we also simultaneously broadcast this transmission from Her black womb of

25

no-thing. Therefore, we share divine revelations of Sophia consciousness through an infinite multi-ray light transmission.

The pearls of our Sophia wisdom teachings travel directly into your heart along rays of pearlescent white, platinum, gold, and silver light. Bypassing the need for your logical understanding, these rays of light awaken your own direct knowing of The Sophia Code within you through a full-body cellular-soul remembrance.

Our multi-ray light transmission clears a direct path from your crown chakra to your Sacred Heart Hrit chakra, so that you may easily anchor the fullness of your Higher Self here on Earth. All rays of light originate from Sophia's pearlescent white Source light, and this is the first ray upon which we transmit our direct revelations as waterfalls of Her Holy Spirit descending through your crown chakra.

The pearlescent white ray of Her Holy Spirit is the light-water of your Divine Mother's milk – filled with the manna of stardust and the Breath of Life – it flows through your crown chakra to nourish your entire body, heart, and soul. In this descent, the seraphim wings of Sophia's Holy Spirit spiral open and illuminate the direct path to your own Sacred Heart with flaming tongues of Her unconditional love for you.

Emanating as quantum waves within Sophia's pearlescent white Source light is the full-color spectrum of light rays and sacred geometries that are essential for manifesting and empowering your physical human experience. We share with you these important rays of wisdom, ranging from the red to violet-magenta rays and beyond, free of all previous understanding and cultural projections.

Additionally, our transmission simultaneously occurs as a live broadcast within the *Holy of Holies* of Sophia's black womb, from which the first ray of light arose. It is from here that we activate your awareness through the quantum rays of Sophia's Dark Mother transmission. The Dark Mother Rays express the black womb wisdom that comes from the limitless, uncontainable space of Sophia's primordial presence that existed before all rays of Sophia Christ light consciousness.

In this very moment, we are now transmitting this communication to you from inside the holy silence of Sophia's womb. Our collective presence attunes you with this zero still-point, this holy empty space, from which Sophia's unconditional love immaculately conceives all form upon Her multi-rays of light.

In our living transmission, we share these ineffable mysteries of both the light and the primordial space from which everything arises as initiatory revelations to activate The Sophia Code within you. This multi-ray light transmission is ordained and directed by the divine will of *She Who Has No Name,* for She is within us all.

Awakening Humanity as a Keycode Species

The members of our Ascended Master High Council hail from Earth's solar system, as well as other star systems. The Sophia Dragon Tribe represents the farthest reaches of your known Universe and beyond.

Our collective voice includes Ascended Masters from the Sephiroth Light Realms of Sophia's original creation, also known as the original eighteen womb-worlds of thought. These eighteen realms have since expanded into multiple Universes infinitely folding into themselves, as holographic super-realities that exist simultaneously beside one another and within one another.

That is to say, wherever you incarnate within the vast quantum fabric of reality, we have High Council members representing the embodied wisdoms of that realm, and we are ready to guide you. We exist everywhere simultaneously, and our High Council members include experts from every species who are devoted to awakening The Sophia Code that exists within all beings, in every reality of form.

As such, The Sophia Dragon Tribe is a universal High Council transmitting Sophia's unconditional love and declaration of sovereignty for all of Her creation. The first seven Divine Feminine Ascended Master Keycodes presented in this introductory volume are gateway teachers who are beloved for their service to humanity. Their familiar faces will gently open your consciousness to the other Ascended Master species, such as *Keycode 777: The Sophia Dragons* and *Keycode 999: The Star Nation High Councils* that serve in The Sophia Dragon Tribe.

We understand that for many drawn to this codex, the recognizable human faces of our first seven Divine Feminine Keycodes provide an approachable first step for initiating your awareness to mentor with our High Council members representing other species. We will be sharing more about our council's celebrated Ascended Master teachers from other species in the chapters ahead.

Our broadcast intentionally activates humanity's awareness to its essential role as a Keycode species in The Sophia Code cosmology, journeying alongside many other advanced species in the cosmos, who are also devoted to awakening Sophia Christ consciousness within the worlds of form. As such, we herein plainly reveal that the living transmission of The Sophia Dragon Tribe is a holographic blueprint for awakening humanity to its role as a sovereign species that is participating in the ascension journey of an *interstellar* and *inter-universal* community of beings known as the one body of Sophia Christ.

MENTORS OF SOVEREIGNTY

The first eight Keycodes are Divine Feminine Ascended Master mentors who offer a living transmission for activating The Sophia Code within you. Acting as a midwife for your consciousness, a Keycode mentor supports you through the contractions of your awareness, which are continuously rebirthing you through the self-realizations of your own sovereign divine nature.

Divine Feminine Christ Teachers
of Sophia Consciousness

THE HIGH COUNCIL SPEAKS:

THE SOPHIA CODE COSMOLOGY spirals out from a single point of origin, celebrating Sophia as the One Divine Mother Creatrix of All Life, including She who birthed the Divine Masculine as a revelation of Her own sovereign nature. As such, our cosmology presents a Divine Feminine Christ blueprint and approach for revealing this Universe as a sovereign immaculate conception arising from the matrix of Sophia's womb.

The individual Ascended Master Keycodes in our cosmology offer exceptional teaching transmissions for learning about these ineffable mysteries of creation through their direct revelations of Sophia. In this introductory volume, we present eight Divine Feminine Christ embodiments who are responsible for birthing new paradigm realities of Heaven on Earth. Their legendary movements for sovereignty created spiritual legacies for the reconciliation of humanity and *all form* as the one holy body of Sophia Christ.

Due to their extraordinary embodiments, our Keycodes are highly qualified Divine Feminine Christ teachers for initiating you to receive your own direct revelations of Sophia speaking within you as the Holy Spirit of your Higher Self. Every Keycode's transmission broadcasts a *heart womb frequency* that rebirths your awareness to embody both the Divine Feminine and Divine Masculine qualities of Sophia Christ consciousness as a unified field of wholeness within you.

Our Divine Feminine Christ teachers activate and call forth the sovereign embodiment of your own uniquely sequenced Keycode. Designed to inspire your heroic human journey, this introductory volume reveals personal accounts of their infamous earthly incarnations, divine missions, and original teachings in their own words. Our Keycode mentors are here to level with you as equals on the cosmic playground of sovereignty, as your friends and loving allies for walking The Way ahead.

Walking The Way to Prepare The Way Ahead for You

The joy of an Ascended Master Keycode is to devoutly serve the spiritual evolution of a species, such as humanity, a planet, a star system, or a particular Universe, for immeasurable eons. In this great service, we are invoked for our overlighting guidance and support by countless souls across the cosmos.

Our charismatic personalities, ever-available loving presence, and devotional commitment to service magnetizes resonate Oversouls, such as yourself, to mentor with one or more of us. Your magnetism to mentor with us is a strong indication that you are now training to be recognized as a living master on Earth, to serve creation as we do, in the fulfillment of embodying your own unique Keycode.

Inspired by your favorite Ascended Master teacher, you may mentor with the same Keycode across eons of evolution. You may loyally travel from one planetary system to another, to learn about The Sophia Code from a Keycode's teaching transmission within a variety of environments and evolutionary circumstances.

You may even train in-person with a living master before they ascend from a particular physical plane of reality, such as Earth. Alternately, you may incarnate to contribute to their spiritual movement prior to or following their departure as part of your training. For example, you may be one of the many individuals drawn to this codex who incarnated within a 300-year radius of Mother Mary and Mary Magdalene's final lifetime on Earth.

It is the heroic, physical embodiment of your Keycode mentor that redefines for your consciousness what you can accomplish within the matrix of form. For your ascension is a journey to radically transcend the seeming limitations of your human experience by anchoring the radiant Christ light of your Higher Self, within every cell of your body, through successive initiations. A masterful embodiment is a journey filled with these soul initiations, many of which require extraordinary courage to complete – a courage that we have modeled for you in our own lifetimes.

As you become increasingly present to the challenges and successes of your own heroic journey of ascension, you may feel deeply called to mentor with us, accessing our vaults of embodied wisdom. Know that it is our great joy to guide you along this direct path of accelerated soul initiations. We are delighted to help you navigate The Way ahead for graduating from earth-bound incarnations. Supporting your daily success is the fulfillment of our own destiny. We are mentoring you in preparation for your own destiny to become a multidimensional spiritual guide for others along The Way.

In our work together, we continually invite you to embrace your current journey of ascension, free from goals of leaving the earth plane before your appointed hour. The Way is a journey to become joyfully and wholly embodied within the present moment of your physical reality, not by escaping it. From this zero point of total presence there is no higher realm to ascend to, for you have become the heavenly, vibrational reality that you came to express on Earth as your own unique Keycode embodiment.

Allow us to activate your cellular-soul remembrance – you are now living this important lifetime as an Ascended Master in training. We intimately know the labyrinth of soul initiations that you are currently navigating in order to fully embody your Higher Self by activating The Sophia Code within your human form. As your overlighting mentors and Family of Light, we went ahead of you to complete our soul initiations and embody our sovereignty to passionately prepare The Way for your own success.

We Mentor Your Highest Potential

Over the eons of our participation in Earth's history, many of our Keycodes became deified in the collective consciousness of humanity. These acclaimed Ascended Masters were once human beings that were genetically operating with the fully activated divine power of The Sophia Code guiding their every creation into form. The charisma of these Keycodes to radically transform the collective consciousness of vast populations, with new thought paradigms and relevant paths of spiritual leadership, appeared to be godlike to those who were asleep to this same divine potential given to all.

As a result of their far-reaching impact, the uniquely sequenced Keycode of an exceptional Ascended Master is often worshiped on Earth as an archetypal genome for future generations of humanity to aspire to. The worship or deification of a Keycode is not required, nor desired, in your communion with us as Ascended Masters. For our service as Ascended Masters is to honor and reflect the sovereign master who already exists within you.

As Keycodes of The Sophia Dragon Tribe, our intention is to create sovereign mentor relationships with you that support your everyday success. In this Age of Miracles we offer you our direct teachings and steadfast guidance, but most importantly, we are here to create lifelong friendships with you. We offer you our friendship free from the past 30,000 years of religious constructs and social conditioning. Our intention is to mirror your sovereign equality in our loving gaze, eye-to-eye with you.

As you receive our collective voice speaking to your heart, your ancestral DNA is liberated from humanity's history of hierarchal spirituality. When you consistently engage with our all-loving presence you generate new neurological pathways for relating to yourself and others in the equality of your sovereignty. As Ascended Master Keycodes, we personally stand with you as ever-present advocates for revealing your own divinity and this same divinity that exists within all.

Establishing a mentor relationship with one or more of our Keycodes creates a dynamic learning container that prepares you for your own future service as an Ascended Master. In the sanctuary of this container we invite your awareness to explore a spiral model for expanding into the radiant light of your Higher Self *every day*. An ever-present relationship with a Keycode mentor provides invaluable biofeedback for integrating the pace of daily expansion as a viable way of life.

A Keycode mentor relationship is also a quantum learning container for generating self-confidence in your own ability to activate The Sophia Code within you. Our blissful presence broadcasts important information from your future self to your emotional body, in the present moment. We know where you are headed along The Way of your own ascension because your Higher Self already exists here with us. Therefore, we transmit from your future reality how possible it is, and how good it feels, to successfully activate your own divine genome.

We create a constant sanctuary of unconditional support in which you can safely explore the power of your own holy nature to command miracles. Over an arc of time, your relationship with a Keycode mentor significantly strengthens your commitment to embody the divine will and creative genius of your Higher Self in this lifetime.

Our daily communication continually uplifts your awareness to resonate with the vibration of success. Your ability to follow through with divinely guided action becomes significantly easier with our encouragement. Goals that once felt impossible to achieve feel accessible and even enjoyable in our presence. In response to our loving attention, your creative spirit thrives beyond self-imposed limitations to claim the joy of your sovereign expression.

A relationship with a Keycode mentor naturally shifts your perception to measure your success as an unfolding journey, not a destination, for embodying your Higher Self. Our overlighting presence guides your awareness to celebrate the fulfillment of every present moment as the blessed practice of a living master. We continually guide you along The Way in how to be gentle, kind, and loving with yourself.

Sophia created the vehicle of relationships for grace to flow from Her Sacred Heart to nourish all of creation. Your mentor relationship with an Ascended Master Keycode is an important vehicle to receive Sophia's ineffable grace, uplifting your spirit to prosper beyond striving, linear thinking, and self-imposed limitations.

As Keycode mentors we are conduits for Her grace. We provide unique revelations, miraculous blessings, and omniscient perspective for overcoming the challenges of your human journey. When you feel supported in our resonant field of unconditional love, your heart opens and more readily reveals your true self, regardless of all outer circumstances.

We are your *friends in high places.* You are worthy of receiving our supernatural support, mentoring you beyond unconscious resistances for embodying your own divinity. Your highest potential is worth reaching for in every present moment.

We invite you to a new paradigm of multidimensional mentor relationships that align and amplify the power of your human prayer with our own prayers for you to thrive in your highest potential. In this prayer of our conscious communion, we join our hearts with yours for co-creating this next golden age opportunity for living Heaven on Earth.

You Have Full Access to Us

Focused in the highest Light Realms of their Christed Self, an Ascended Master consciously exists in the totality of their Oversoul's unified field, with their awareness radiating out into all dimensions of quantum reality simultaneously. From this omniscient perspective, a Keycode mentor can provide you with unlimited, multidimensional support for your soul initiations within any world of form.

The Oversoul of just one Ascended Master Keycode provides spiritual guidance, support, and blessings for an astronomical number of souls, both on Earth and elsewhere, simultaneously. Therefore, you can communicate with your Keycode mentor at any time, 24 hours a day. You can access their support for *any* reason at all and instantaneously receive helpful guidance.

An Ascended Master Keycode primarily broadcasts their transmission of loving guidance from the highest Light Realms of their Christed Self. A relationship with a Keycode mentor allows you to directly download their guidance into your own Oversoul, through a soul-to-soul holographic model for quantum learning. Your Higher Self acts as an intermediary messenger that then downloads this information from your Oversoul to your human awareness.

If needed, your Ascended Master mentor can also direct their consciousness to descend into any physical reality at will to engage with your human awareness. A Keycode mentor can assemble electrons of a light body to engage with you in both physical and subtle energetic ways on Earth. An example of a Keycode's ability to materialize at-will is the global phenomena of Mother Mary's appearance in physical apparitions and visions to those she mentors.

Modern life is your Oversoul's next-level mystery school. In this current Age of Miracles, we are fully committed to engaging with your awareness in a daily communion of mentorship. We are guiding your accelerated initiations of personal mastery from the universe *within you*. Here you will find the pyramids and temples of your ancient parallel lifetimes.

Every incarnation in which you diligently trained to access divine guidance was all in preparation for how we will engage in this lifetime. Receiving us on the inner planes, as well as invoking our presence to interact with you in physical reality, initiates you as a wayshower of a new paradigm for modern mystery school ascension training.

Countless dimensions of reality overlap with your physical world. As we engage in meaningful mentor relationships, you bridge our dimensional reality on Earth, transforming your daily life into a living mystery school. Every moment becomes an opportunity to widen your awareness of reality by including our support within it.

We exist everywhere simultaneously, and with your invitation, we can become an integrated part of your life. Widening your perception of what we can create together in this reality transforms how you perceive yourself, your world, and your divine purpose for being here.

Whether we speak to your consciousness through messengers or directly speak to your awareness through our appearance on both the inner and outer planes, we are always responding to your faith and willingness for our communion. This includes your ability to feel our healing hands ministering to you in physical reality and hear our voices audibly speaking to your awareness.

Creating dedicated sacred spaces and altars that act as doorways for daily communication with your favorite Keycode mentors expands your capacity to physically feel and see our divine intervention on your behalf every day. We will share more practices on how to create a physical interface with your Keycode mentors in additional volumes of this codex.

We are ready to radically liberate and bless your awareness with authentic mentor relationships of loving support that will significantly upgrade your relationship with life. May the transcendental power of your faith allow our miracles and divine interventions to become ordinary occurrences in your life.

A Direct Path for Embodying Your Higher Self

The presence of your Keycode mentor is felt as a compassionate and resolute guide. When you are attuned to our guiding presence, you consistently feel or hear the intuitive message: "If I did it, so can you!" This encouragement is often accompanied with full-body feelings of renewed focus and perseverance that propel you forward to always make your best offering.

Your Keycode mentor's unwavering faith in your highest potential profoundly elevates your own belief in yourself. Our devout faith in your true worth supports the growth of your self-confidence to create a blessed life – far beyond what you may deem possible for yourself. Basking in our resolute field of faith inspires your personal willingness to live in daily alignment with your Higher Self's plan for you to prosper in all ways.

Over an arc of time, living in alignment with your Higher Self creates a positive momentum in which you no longer desire to make choices that sabotage the success of your life. This natural gravitation to embrace your success leads you to walk The Way of a *direct path* for embodying your Higher Self's divine will every day.

Choosing a direct path accelerates your personal evolution with many soul initiations that allow for your Higher Self to unravel lifetimes of suffering within this single lifetime. Socially conditioned resistances to your own divinity, spanning generations of ancestry, can be cleared from your carbon-based DNA that may be blocking your personal success and happiness.

An Ascended Master Keycode serves as an intermediary who mentors your awareness to persevere along this lightning path of your Higher

Self's soul initiations to radically liberate you from all unconsciously encoded belief systems to needlessly suffer. Acting as a midwife for your consciousness, a Keycode mentor supports you through the contractions of your awareness, which are continuously rebirthing you through the self-realizations of your own sovereign divine nature.

There are no shortcuts in walking The Way – but there is always the most direct path in quantum reality for every initiation of your soul. As a master calligrapher wields a brush with absolute precision, every choice on your direct path leads to your next soul initiation, without distraction. Your relationship with life becomes your masterpiece.

Living a direct path is a rigorous soul practice that calls you to lead by example, living at the edge of your vulnerability every day. It requires deep, active listening to the daily guidance provided by your Higher Self and a willingness to courageously act upon this divine guidance through your authentic expression. A Keycode mentor supports your awareness to integrate this direct path in gradual stages of personal acceptance and embodiment, with compassion for yourself every step along The Way.

No matter how challenging the soul initiations on a direct path may feel, your Higher Self can access and download archived information and DNA activations from the Akashic Records of your Keycode mentor's Oversoul. These records provide a valuable resource of downloadable wisdom for how to embody your Higher Self in any human circumstance.

The direct path of every Ascended Master's final lifetime was blessed with the grace of many masters illuminating The Way ahead for them. Our prayerful intention as The Sophia Dragon Tribe is to make The Way ahead easier for you. The ineffable grace of Sophia unifies our hearts with yours in this prayer. It is your birthright to receive our grace and blessings supporting the direct path of your heroic human journey for embodying your sovereign divinity now.

We Initiate Your Own Keycode

Your Oversoul's uniquely sequenced divine genome of the same immaculate qualities shared by all is called a Keycode. Every immaculate quality that exists within the divine genome of your favorite Ascended Master exists within you as well. This introductory volume of The Sophia Code presents foundational initiations that activate the same divine qualities within you that an Ascended Master Keycode is most revered for.

A Keycode initiation offers a quantum transfer of information from an Ascended Master who successfully embodied the divine attributes of The Sophia Code that you seek to activate within yourself. Downloading the embodied revelations of our Ascended Masters allows your consciousness to easily remember the pathways for awakening your own unique Keycode.

Downloading Keycode revelations of perfect belief systems occurs through a live broadcast from the Akashic Records of an Ascended Master's Oversoul. When you read or listen to an initiation from this codex, your awareness temporarily merges with that Keycode mentor, who then initiates your awareness and divine genome as you walk within the living library of their Oversoul.

This broadcast is experienced as a transmission that activates your own divine genome through a resonant field of mirroring with one who has already successfully done so. Communing in the living transmission of a Keycode mentor calibrates your belief systems to vibrationally resonate with their absolute knowledge of your own divinity. This communion of transference illuminates your awareness to directly experience the totality of your own Oversoul.

Our Keycode initiations are Divine Feminine Christ blueprints for awakening your consciousness to its sovereign state. Designed to bypass all limited left-brain models of linear understanding, these initiations accelerate quantum leaps of transcendental self-realization by stimulating your own direct revelations arising from your communion with the Oversoul of an Ascended Master.

We use a visionary right-brain model for self-activating your awareness to the truth of your own omniscient existence within multiple dimensions of reality – for you simultaneously exist everywhere. Expanding your awareness to discover your own omniscience is an essential factor for integrating the new belief systems downloaded in the Keycode initiations.

As your Ascended Master mentors, we know how to support your awareness navigating a multidimensional existence within human form. Our initiations integrate both the light language technology for activating The Sophia Code within you as well as the resulting arc of radical transformations that may follow.

These Keycode initiations are intended to be listened to or read aloud in the first person perspective. When a Keycode initiation is spoken out loud, the power of your voice declares your free will permission to replace outdated belief systems that were limiting your sovereign potential. Once the Keycode's new belief systems are installed, your Higher Self uses the light language technology, downloaded in the initiation, to continually activate your divine genome and integrate these same divine qualities of the Ascended Master within you.

Whether you are cognizant of these generous downloads or not, your Higher Self is greatly supported by the transmission of even one Keycode initiation. Receiving our initiations maintains a high vibrational field of light for your human awareness to accept your divine inheritance and activate your own uniquely sequenced divine genome as an awakened Keycode of The Sophia Code.

Choosing to Mentor with a Keycode

From our omniscient perspective, we can see every soul initiation ahead of you for embodying the Sophia Christ light of your Higher Self in this lifetime. We intimately know the commitment and willingness that is required for you to activate the full expression of your own unique Keycode.

As Ascended Master mentors, it is our intention to touch your heart afresh, free from the constructs placed upon us from centuries of religious conditioning. Every Keycode possesses a unique, dynamic approach for mentoring you in how to step into your personal power.

You may feel magnetized to learn from certain Keycode mentors in The Sophia Dragon Tribe even if you are unfamiliar with our stories and transmission. Initially, you may feel attracted to mentor with only one specific Keycode or you may be aware of your spiritual history with several of our Keycodes and have already established mentor relationships with them.

Your personality will be drawn to mentor with those Keycodes that you have journeyed with for many lifetimes, far beyond the scope of this single incarnation. As you create mentor relationships with those Keycodes that feel magnetic to your soul, or allow this codex to deepen those already established, you will eventually discover how you are connected to all eight Divine Feminine Christ embodiments presented in this introductory volume.

We invite you to follow your heart. Notice the many signs awakening your awareness to our unconditional love and support for your heroic human journey. We are choosing you, just as much as you are choosing us.

Know that it is safe to feel drawn to the goddess iconography of our ancient lineages. The Divine Feminine beauty of our individual forms, symbolisms, and personal stories creates an irresistible mirror for initiating your awareness to accept the truth of your own sovereign divinity.

You are safe to receive our guidance without conditions or worship. You are safe to receive our support for creating your own Legacy of Love. You are safe to enjoy us – enjoying you!

May you receive our radical love empowering the Divine Feminine Christ consciousness awakening within you, so that the light of Sophia may shine as a thousand suns from your own Sacred Heart. It's always your sovereign choice to receive our support. Thank you for opening your heart and allowing us to serve you.

THE WAY OF SELF INITIATION

This next golden age is an invitation for you to reveal the unlimited depths and heights of your sovereign, creative power – rather than seek for the world to change for you. *You are the change.* You are here to embody the reality of Heaven on Earth that so many within your species seek to discover outside of themselves.

The Golden Age of Miracles

THE HIGH COUNCIL SPEAKS:

A GOLDEN AGE IS a cycle of time in which quantum evolutionary leaps become accessible to large populations of humanity seeking to embody Sophia Christ consciousness. The Sophia Dragon Tribe serves all ancient and future golden ages. At certain evolutionary junctures, we return as a highly visible guiding light council for catalyzing golden ages on Earth.

As many of you are already aware, humanity is now being prepared to participate in a new golden age cycle here on Earth. The dawning of this next golden age cycle is unlike any other. This revolutionary age begins with an unusually high volume of incarnated master souls that are ready to surf this quantum wave with you.

You are now walking the Earth with many advanced souls that have traveled great distances across the cosmos to be by your side for initiating this global awakening. Remember that your practice as a living master is to recognize, behold, and bless the masters that walk beside you in this great endeavor, both seen and unseen – regardless of all outward appearances.

Keep your eyes open to see beyond the surface of any mundane role that your Starseed brother or sister may be playing as a part of their mission here on Earth. Great ancient masters may 'dress up or down' to play their chosen role in this riveting chapter now unfolding as a foundational precursor to this next golden age.

Sophia has ordained this next cycle to be known as *The Golden Age of Miracles*. This title points to the unusually high amount of incarnated souls amassing to embody the full divine potential of their Higher Selves in a single lifetime. The Golden Age of Miracles is also a seeded name foretelling the countless miracles that will come to pass from this many master souls consciously converging and unifying as a global community for humanity's ascension.

One of the many miracles of this dawning age is that embodying the sovereign power of your Higher Self liberates the Akashic Record vaults of humanity's collective suffering – without the need for you to suffer for anyone's relief. That is to say, the lives of billions of people are directly transformed by your personal willingness to embody the Sophia Christ light of your Higher Self. The authentic embodiment of your sovereign divinity broadcasts a transmission of freedom from the activated crystalline chromosomes of The Sophia Code within you to the dormant DNA of countless souls.

Through the living transmission of your Higher Self embodiment, people who are suffering beyond their understanding will experience the freedom of your life, through a holographic transference of upgrades for their consciousness. For as you embody the golden radiance of your Higher Self, the seas of humanity's collective consciousness will part for millions to follow your lead as you walk The Way of your Sacred Heart. Yes, indeed! You are a wayshower for this Golden Age of Miracles!

This next golden age is an invitation for you to reveal the unlimited depths and heights of your sovereign, creative power – rather than seek for the world to change for you. *You are the change.* You are here to embody the reality of Heaven on Earth that so many within your species seek to discover outside of themselves.

Your personal passion to radically serve humanity's ascension is mirrored in our own collective desire to wholly support you in this lifetime. With your invitation, we are here to mentor you in a modern mystery school curriculum for embodying the sovereignty of your Higher Self as an initiator for this next Golden Age of Miracles.

Your Modern Mystery School

Seek not the ancient mystery schools of another age. Daily life is now your modern mystery school activating your highest potential in every present moment. With your conscious daily choice to mentor with our Ascended Master High Council, we prepare and activate your awareness to become a wayshower for others in birthing this next Golden Age of Miracles.

So, in this lifetime, class is in session – every day. In order to live in alignment with the reality of miracles, you are now being guided to access your soul initiations and personal training for embodying your Higher Self from masters abiding in the highest Light Realms of creation. Accessing our daily guidance, beyond your physical reality, creates a direct path for recognizing the master that already lives within you.

As Ascended Master mentors, we provide the same mystery school initiations that you once physically received in other lifetimes, for activating the spiritual technology of your human body, from a higher dimensional reality. Receiving these same initiations in this new way activates the power of your faith to download direct revelations, which is a precursor for commanding miracles.

Your faith reveals the master who already lives within you when you believe that you can directly commune with us to receive our blessings, divine interventions, soul initiations, DNA activations, emotional support, and personal coaching across multiple planes of reality. Cultivating your ability to receive our direct revelations occurs one self-loving step at a time, in the modern mystery school of your daily life choices.

We invite your consciousness to consider that the extraordinary opportunity of this next golden age is to become the embodied miracle of your own faith as well as a living embodiment of the direct revelations that you download from your Higher Self. This is your lifetime for the master within you to be revealed and witnessed in the presence of other masters, both seen and unseen.

As you reach for us and our moment-by-moment support, you build a bridge from our dimensional reality to yours. This results in your physical reality resonating with the high-frequency vibration of our steadfast presence guiding your awareness. Your willingness to reach for our frequency raises the vibration of your entire being to regularly receive quantum solutions for your life.

As we reach for you in our daily communion, we create bridges that ground our heavenly frequency within your dimensional reality on Earth. Our intention is to create new neurological pathways for multidimensional relating through personal mentor relationships that radically support your willingness to consciously live your life in absolute sovereignty.

Over an arc of time, our daily communion eventually aligns you, in ever-increasing measure, with your role as an initiator and wayshower for all of humanity. We are co-creating this radical modern-day mystery school with you, and our evolution is mutual in this heroic journey of awakening all beings to their divine inheritance of The Sophia Code. So we encourage you to celebrate your daily life as the ceremony of ascension.

Surrendering into an Age of Grace

The seed of all miracles is faith, and the space in which those miracles blossom is called *grace*. The underlying momentum that is preparing humanity for this forthcoming Golden Age of Miracles is your collective desire to surrender into grace.

Grace is an invincible presence that cannot be bought, sold, or traded for. Grace cannot be earned, for it is freely available, regardless of all circumstances. Grace is never withheld, yet her presence is most often recognized during divinely appointed hours of individual and collective awakening from suffering.

Grace is the space that your soul was birthed in, free of any conditions placed upon you for the gift of your eternal life. Grace is the space where what is ready to return to a natural balance may spontaneously return to that balance without apology, explanation, or delay. Grace is the space in which you may experience, and even enjoy, your sovereign divine nature.

Humanity is ready for the spaciousness of grace. Grace knows how to end wars that humanity does not know how to end. Grace knows how to be at peace when humanity does not know how to be at peace with itself. Grace knows how to forgive what feels unforgivable. Grace also knows how to love what feels unlovable.

Grace is the sanctuary of space from which quantum solutions arise that end the need for all suffering. Grace allows for the seemingly impossible to miraculously appear, without effort, as a direct revelation of divine love.

Other than your willingness to receive her mighty works, grace does not need human participation to work a perfect divine will for all to be boundlessly blessed. When you surrender to grace, you are surrendering to the Holy Spirit within All That Is orchestrating everyday miracles for you, beyond your understanding and beyond your ability to control a desired outcome.

Humanity's faith in itself, and in a benevolent universe, will only be restored by receiving the grace that humanity believes it has lost. Grace is the invincible Divine Feminine Christ consciousness that has never left you and who lives within you. As you surrender to her mighty works and miraculous solutions, your faith will be reconciled.

There is no greater motivating force in this Universe than the primordial space of mother. Our Divine Feminine Christ blueprint is designed to awaken humanity from its addiction to suffering, which is rooted in an agonizing belief that humanity is irreconcilably separated from its original mother. Therefore, humanity's collective prayer, for this next golden age, is to surrender and reconcile with the unconditional love of Sophia, whose presence has never left you.

Sophia is the One Self, and there is no greater teacher for reconciliation than She. Every complementary force of nature that humanity has polarized through duality exists harmoniously within Sophia's whole Self.

Therefore, Sophia's grace is a fluid dialogue that includes both Divine Feminine and Divine Masculine rays of consciousness speaking as both a unified voice, as well as individuated polarities that can only exist within the empty space of the One Self. As an immaculate quality of Sophia, grace is a perfectly balanced Divine Feminine presence whose great works are supported by Divine Masculine qualities that harmoniously complete Her miracles.

The Divine Feminine Christ revelations of Sophia are beyond humanity's gender identifications of God or Goddess archetypal figures. These revelations exist beyond hierarchical concepts of right or wrong, and point to ineffable mysteries and a state of grace that can only be explored by surrendering to your own innocent nature.

To explore the unknowable, bow to the Universe within you and confess that you know nothing. Surrender your need to control what you understand about Sophia as a primordial Holy Mother of grace. Lay down your need to feel safe through limited earthbound logic and linear thinking. Open to Her ineffable mysteries that quietly await your humble prayer to receive the grace of these revelations, as they are, not as you would have them fit into your current paradigm of right or wrong.

When you discover that the presence of Sophia exists within you and within all, in equal measure, this great movement to surrender to the grace of unconditional love may unfold for all of humanity. Therefore, we invite the causes of all internal and external wars to now rest their heads in Her primordial lap of divine love forever.

Returning to the fluidity of Divine Feminine Christ consciousness can be as graceful or as hard as you want it to be. Our creation story is a powerful invitation to explore the grace of your soul's sovereignty, from within the Holy of Holies of Sophia. The power of that invitation requires grace to accept it.

As the oracular Order of the Devoted Shekinah, The Sophia Dragon Tribe reclaims all form as holy. We pronounce that Sophia is the Christ within all incarnated bodies *and* the vessel of every form that carries Her Holy Spirit is the Christed form. Therefore, we are each the body of Christ, returning again and again to the worlds of Light and form to proclaim Her holy grace and sovereignty that exists within all, according to The Sophia Code given to all, in equal measure.

Humanity is one Keycode species that makes up this universal body of Christ. As humanity takes up its mantle of divinity, there will be a great shift to embody a noble humility, a surrendering to grace, in which humanity will be welcomed back into the interstellar diplomatic dialogue regarding the Earth's evolution, as stewards and guardians of this beloved planet.

Embracing the Divine Feminine Christ consciousness begins with embracing the primordial aspect of Sophia that exists within you, as the grace that you are here to offer yourself and others. You may discover these divine revelations of grace already calling you to go within, as you read this invitation to discover these ineffable mysteries of the Universe within you.

As such, this introductory volume of The Sophia Code cosmology introduces the first eight of thirteen essential Divine Feminine Ascended Master teachers of our modern-day mystery school for humanity's collective awakening and return to the Divine Feminine Christ blueprint for this planet's ascension through grace. Every Keycode mentor was responsible for birthing new paradigms of heavenly consciousness on Earth, including the reclamation of form as holy. These featured Keycodes are exceptional mentors for your own embodiment of grace as a birther of this next Golden Age of Miracles through the immaculate conceptions of your Sophia Christ consciousness.

Five Ways Our Mystery School Teaches You

We use five non-linear, interdependent operating systems of *quantum communion* that initiate a Divine Feminine awakening for your awareness to interface with your Higher Self and activate The Sophia Code within you. The architecture of our High Council is designed to offer advanced metaphysical teachings that directly download into your soul and awareness without effort.

Our Divine Feminine teaching model intentionally bypasses the limitations of your logical, localized mind and initiates you into the oracular art of divine knowing. These five operating systems also activate your body's supporting neurological pathways that allow for direct communion with your Higher Self and are as follows:

1 | WE USE THE MIRROR OF RELATING WITH YOU

Every Ascended Master Keycode offers intimate details of her challenges and successes in the worlds of form as inspirational fuel for your own human journey. This transparency creates accessible heroic examples that mirror your own potential legacy for this lifetime.

Divine Feminine vehicle for awakening: create a feeling response of equanimity and accessibility that softens, inspires, and empowers you.

2 | WE SPEAK THE LANGUAGE OF YOUR SOUL

Our Divine Feminine Keycodes share ancient knowledge and rays of wisdom that already exist within you. As you experience the many ah-ha moments that may arise as you read this codex, these full-body soul recognitions liberate the master within you to confidently awaken.

Divine Feminine vehicle for awakening: create spontaneous self-recognition responses that invoke your acceptance and celebration of the master within you.

3 | THE MASTERY OF YOUR SELF-INITIATION

This codex presents transcendental Keycode mentor initiations, written in the first person perspective, so that you may read them aloud. As you speak the Keycode initiations with the resonance of your own voice, you are consciously using the sovereign power of your Higher Self's divinity to command your own empowerments for spiritual activation. Our initiations are designed for you to easily recognize, honor, and embody the master that already lives within you.

Divine Feminine vehicle for awakening: create a self-initiatory response that builds confidence to command miracles and trust in your own divine knowing.

4 | THE COMMUNION OF OUR MENTORSHIP

We offer mentor relationships designed to stimulate your own self-empowerment. Mentoring with Divine Feminine Ascended Masters creates a receptive space and dynamic flow of communion for awakening your awareness to the sovereign power within you. These extraordinary mentor relationships build confidence for clearly seeing yourself as one who deserves to receive the best support for embodying your highest potential.

Divine Feminine vehicle for awakening: create a safe container for your self-empowerment through the expertise and support of our multidimensional communion.

5 | VISIONS AWAKEN THE ORACLE WITHIN YOU

The Ascended Masters of The Sophia Dragon Tribe are known throughout history for their oracular ability to prophesy and reveal their direct visions and teaching revelations of Sophia. Visionary states of consciousness are direct revelations that provide full downloads of multidimensional blocks of information. A single powerful vision can shift your entire awareness, beyond the limitations of your left-brain logic, to operate from a right-brain Divine Feminine intuition of self-knowing. Therefore, we offer a visionary teaching transmission that awakens your own oracular faculties.

This codex is a richly detailed vision of The Sophia Code cosmology, which has been directly downloaded for you. By their very nature, visions activate the same oracular faculties for those immersed within a shared multidimensional experience. Stepping inside the visions of this living transmission provides both an accessible interface and permission slip to explore your own oracular abilities for seeing and hearing your Ascended Master mentors.

Divine Feminine vehicle for awakening: create a multidimensional container that activates visionary states of consciousness by the sharing of direct revelations through visions.

LOVE IS THE FULFILLMENT OF ALL PROPHECY

"If I could speak all the languages of earth and of angels, but didn't love others, I would only be a noisy gong or a clanging cymbal. If I had the gift of prophecy, and if I understood all of God's secret plans and possessed all knowledge, and if I had such faith that I could move mountains, but didn't love others, I would be nothing. If I gave everything I have to the poor and even sacrificed my body, I could boast about it; but if I didn't love others, I would have gained nothing.

"Love is patient and kind. Love is not jealous or boastful or proud or rude. It does not demand its own way. It is not irritable, and it keeps no record of being wronged. It does not rejoice about injustice but rejoices whenever the truth wins out. Love never gives up, never loses faith, is always hopeful, and endures through every circumstance.

"Prophecy and speaking in unknown languages and special knowledge will become useless. But love will last forever!"

— 1 CORINTHIANS 13:1-8

SECTION 2

RETURN OF THE DIVINE FEMININE CHRIST

Keycode Revelations & Initiations

KEYCODE 1
"SHE OF A THOUSAND NAMES"

Your understanding is not required to mentor with me as a guide. Only your faith is needed to let go and receive my miracles, divine intervention, and masterful support for The Way ahead. I invite you to fly with me into the vista of your own sovereign divinity.

The Direct Revelations of Isis Birth a Golden Age

ISIS SPEAKS:

I AM ISIS, A Divine Feminine Ascended Master teacher for oracular activism and a devoted advocate for Mother Earth. My Sophia embodiment title is "She of a Thousand Names," for I am honored throughout the ages with countless names of adoration and respect that reflect my many roles as a spiritual guide for multidimensional empowerment. Mentoring your highest potential is my great honor, for your own participation as a leader in this current global awakening is vitally important.

When you look to me as a mentor, it is important to understand that I was a woman first. It was through my human journey that I remembered how to embody my multidimensional sovereign power as a Keycode of Sophia. I invite you to receive my human story as a mirror for this same miraculous potential that exists *within you*. Activating The Sophia Code within me was foundational for my role as an evolutionary Divine Feminine

Christ embodiment of the highest order. You have the same sovereign power within you to do the same.

Long before your recorded history, I walked the Earth when our pyramids shimmered with pure gold and crystals washed up along the Nile's shore. Although born to rule as Queen, my heart's prayer was to serve as an accessible spiritual leader. From the earliest age, I consecrated my royal position as a vehicle for clearly identifying how to best serve my people. I lived my early life with a passionate full-body presence, in preparation for serving the whole of Egypt with this same care.

The foundational years of my Divine Feminine embodiment unfolded in the worship service of my daily life. I explored the divinity of my humanity within the prayer of bearing children, making love, preparing food, and creating sacred spaces. With every act of devotion, I deepened in my understanding of how family, love, creativity, and fulfilling a higher purpose were universal needs for my people – unifying all of us in our human experience. Honoring my humanity taught me how Egypt deserved to be led.

At birth, my mother had taken a vow for me to be initiated and raised as a priestess of Hathor's lineage. Hathor had physically ascended to Sirius long before my incarnation as Isis. However, my mystery school training taught me how to directly access Hathor as an overlighting spiritual mentor guiding me from the higher Light Realms. I adored Hathor and experienced many waking revelations in which she appeared to initiate me as her protégé for Egypt's future. When I came of age to lead community rites of passage, my natural gifts for commanding high frequency alchemical magick recalled for many the glorious history of Hathor's stargate ceremonies.

I eventually achieved the honorary office of becoming an Oracle in Hathor's lineage with an acute gift for planetary *oracular activism*: the ability to clearly communicate and advocate direct teaching transmissions from Mother Earth and her many species. In countless ceremonies I would lay all night with my heart resting upon the ground, cultivating my direct relationship with Mother Earth, as I listened to her instructions for my people.

The direct revelations that I would receive guided my people in how to spiritually thrive as a civilization with the ceremonial honoring of Mother Earth's yearly cycles and our interdependency with her body and all species.

In this oracular dialogue, I received necessary rites of passage for initiating community ascension that would birth a new golden age movement in Egypt. I was particularly drawn to Mother Earth's instructions for ceremonial magick that balanced the energetic principles of life, death, and rebirth within our human experience – resurrecting our conscious awareness beyond passing phenomena and into the immortal light of our divinity.

As I would whisper the words of these direct revelations to my ordained initiates, they would then relay these teaching transmissions to the scribes. Our sacred scribes ensured that my words, as delivered by the priestesses, would then be put to papyrus as well as carved in stone. This record keeping provided access to universal laws for my people to live in the freedom afforded by aligning with those laws and cycles of creation as revealed by Mother Earth. Eventually, I created a lineage of mystery schools for initiating future oracular advocates to pass down my direct revelations and channel new teachings for educating generations to come.

Over the years of my public ministry, I increasingly merged with Mother Earth's consciousness in ecstatic states of bliss, gratitude, and sensuality. I would sing and shed tears of joy as I integrated these rapturous states of tantric communion with Mother Earth into an applicable teaching transmission. These songs were recorded as devotional hymns for opening specific neurological pathways within my initiates that activated this same transcendental divine communion within them.

At the height of my spiritual leadership, I was honored as the highest Oracle of Hathor in Egypt. My unceasing service of channeling for my people fully activated The Sophia Code within me, downloading the unlimited potential of my Higher Self into form. In accordance with Hathor's teachings on quantum embodiment, I revealed and integrated my soul's etheric wings as a physical feature of my body. This phenomenon gave rise to my classical depiction as the winged form of Isis.

I was enthralled by the power of life and the quantum leaps of unlimited personal evolution that I could explore within it. In accordance with my prayer for an abundance of more life, Hathor appeared to me on the inner planes and guided me in how to activate the immortality gene of The Sophia Code within me. As a result of this grace, I lived for centuries walking side by side with Osiris, my beloved twin flame and husband.

Together we seeded an invincible Platinum Ray Sophia lineage, capable of withstanding the ever-shifting sands of humanity's long journey to this current golden age upon you. For those of you connected with Keycode 5: Mary Magdalene, it is helpful for you to remember that the *Order of Magdalena* directly descends through this Isis-Sophia lineage, which was carried out of Egypt in the Hebrew exodus to be revived in the promised land. As such, many of my direct revelations for humanity were secreted away to survive within the mystical path of Judaism, known as Kabbalism. Parting the Red Sea of generations, my Platinum Ray Keycode 1 transmission now reaches you – broadcasting my direct revelations as they once were.

To understand the creative potential of your current golden age, I invite you to envision how we once lived and taught in Egypt, before your written records of history. Osiris and I instructed thousands in how to harmoniously live as one in divine love and nation-wide peace. From the tip of the Nile's tail all the way to her head of many deltas, our oracular activism initiated an entire population to actually live in daily bliss and with meaningful purpose.

We practiced high alchemical magick to sustain and cultivate this unified field of divine love for the highest good of my people's welfare. Our ceremonial practices of magick were always used in alignment with the elements and to enhance our direct relationship with Mother Earth. We built pyramids that focused and balanced universal cosmic resources of power for individual and community rites of ascension. Our people prospered and wanted for nothing, for wealth consciousness was inherent to our teachings.

Although an extensive royal caste system eventually arose to govern our expanding population, I initiated a golden age in which every man, woman, and child experienced their absolute sovereign freedom and equality within the unified field of divine love that Egypt once was. The divinity within all was honored as the highest law.

Sustaining the high frequency of a golden age movement requires a relentless commitment to excellence and sovereignty. Following my ascension, the royal caste system of Egypt eventually became distracted from its original purpose to serve the people.

The sacred process of recording on both stone and papyrus became co-opted for controlling the population through hollow spirituality used to enforce hierarchical stature and separation. It saddened me as generation after generation became increasingly curled in upon itself and fed a distorted, deified version of me that was inaccessible. The touch of the Divine Mother within me, freely offered through my legacy of teachings, became hidden away from my people and hardened behind secret walls.

I became a distant mystery for my beloved people, a mystery that only the ardent and tenacious could find within themselves. The recorded revelations that I spoke from Mother Earth became so coveted for their power, they were hidden away and eventually dissolved in the dust of Egypt. My teachings lived on only in the hearts that were pure enough to carry forth their details through oral tradition.

I long to step out from the carved stone of centuries past, and I ask you to look beyond the history of my form as Isis to receive the vibrant frequency of my guiding light once again. As a mentor, I offer you the breadth of my experience as a High Priestess, oracular activist, and devout spiritual leader who successfully guided an entire civilization to birth a new golden age. I am here to mentor and guide your generation in this same great prayer.

Claim Your Divine Inheritance

You were not originally designed to suffer or be in want of anything. Sophia designed you to live in harmony as a sovereign co-creator with the overflowing abundance of this planet. Your divine inheritance includes all of your earthly needs being met, as well as receiving *all* of your heart's desires. It is Her divine will for you to prosper in every area of your life.

To be a master of both the spiritual and physical realms is to know that in truth there is no separation between these two realms. When your alignment with unconditional love for yourself and others is your principal guiding force in life, the abundance of both realms is revealed to you in ever-expanding measure.

I invite you to imagine the golden halls of ascension temples that graced the spine of Egypt. I taught my people how to utilize these royal structures as an outer reflection of their inner temples and true worth.

Step through the temple gates of your inner sight: you are here to re-member yourself as holy and pure, a Daughter and Son of the Most High. To you a crown of life is given, for you have been made in the image of Sophia's sovereignty. When you humble your heart to finally accept that you are both the Queen and King of your individual destiny, you will discover that there is no one above you, or beneath you, in this true description of royalty.

To know and receive yourself for the royalty that you are, immediately shifts your ego into a resting place, calling forth a serenity in which you feel safe enough to allow all others this same acknowledgment without reservation. The fullness of your divine inheritance awaits the opening of your heart to receive it. I mentor you in your willingness to receive your unlimited divine inheritance, beyond measure, in honor of your royal divine nature.

Claim Your Sacred Sexuality

I speak to you of a time when men and women walked side-by-side in divine union, supporting one another with telepathy, compassion, and empowerment – when Priest Kings listened in reverence, long into the night, to the sounds and songs of their Oracular Priestess Queens. Their bodies holding court in meditation, facing each other's hearts in tantric prayer, they would breathe the serpents of kundalini awake and surrender into the waiting arms of The Beloved.

My lineage taught that The Beloved abides within the initiate and within all others. As such, in ancient Egypt a tantric path could be practiced within yourself or with a devoted partner.

Whether choosing an inner or outwardly directed tantric practice, the alchemy of this pathway provides revelations from a third presence arising when two polarities become unified through truth, forgiveness, freedom, and unconditional love. This third presence is called The Horus and is birthed as a Higher Self consciousness from the tantric relationship within yourself or with a partner.

The Horus is an overlighting angelic presence for the tantric relationship, guiding you to walk through initiatory gates that lead to ever deepening chambers of vulnerability, intimacy, and unconditional love. The height of this intimacy requires The Horus as an inner guide; for this is the dragon alchemy of twin flame divine love made manifest in two beloveds soaring as one.

Your sexuality is a mighty force of creation and The Horus continually guides you to remain focused upon its true purpose as a vehicle for discovering that Sophia is The Beloved you are worshiping within yourself or another. As you behold this radiant light of divinity through a tantric practice, your limited awareness is initiated through the Osirian rites of resurrection. The Horus of your own Christed Self arises within you, reflecting back to your awareness the truth that you are a sovereign creator god.

It is actually the separation of sexual energy from the wholeness of life that is the original sin. The word sin simply means to forget and turn upon yourself in shame. Shame yourself no longer. Divorcing the divine from sexuality is the most effective form of mind control that certain religions execute upon humanity. It is your right to claim the holy inheritance of your sexuality as a pure and verdant life force for your soul's expansion as a sovereign creator.

It is safe to relax into your sensual nature. Breathe into your orgasms; breathe into your sexuality. As you travel upon your breath, be curious about where this energy is guiding your spirit on the inner pathways of self-love and self-recognition. You are ordained to embody all the divine qualities of Sophia, including Her ecstasy and bliss. The Sophia Code within you contains the original blueprint for pristine tantric communion. The nectar of life courses through your body when sexuality is consecrated as a personal practice for spiritual awakening and attunement.

The Horus guides you as an initiate to discover that the tantric path of worshiping The Beloved is a communion calling you to merge with the light of Sophia within you and another. Sacred sexuality attunes you to a direct path of accelerated spiritual awakening. Therefore, it is essential to reclaim and consecrate your sexuality as a holy vehicle for discovering your divinity.

Claim Your Sovereign Divinity

Let's fly together as you awaken the vast illuminating life force within your precious human body. As the wings upon my back spread wide to soar with your own, the Divine Feminine strength and power that I embody is yours to know within yourself. My Keycode 1 is a teaching transmission for confidently claiming the freedom of your sovereign divinity.

Just as I put Osiris's body back together piece by piece through the rites of resurrection, so too will I initiate your consciousness to recognize the divinity and royalty within your own body, heart, and mind. I offer you the light mantles of my Oversoul to be wrapped as sacred ritual cloths around your awareness so that any hidden belief denying your divinity may dissolve in peace.

It is safe to receive my initiations rebirthing your self-confidence: in these rites I honor your courage with anointing oils and bless you with the ceremonial grounds of stardust, dragon pearls, and lapis. I am always here for you, available within the inner pyramids that you can enter through meditation and prayer.

Within these inner sanctuaries, I facilitate healing ceremonies for your awareness to receive the Higher Self initiations that knit together places within you that do not feel whole. My loving presence activates you to claim your innate wholeness and bravely ascend the throne of your own *I Am Presence*. Uplifted in my wings, your divinity is witnessed, proclaimed, and honored.

When you step into my perspective for your life, you experience how I focus an infinite number of all-seeing eyes that access helpful information about your divine purpose from every dimensional reality within the one *Eye of Ra*. I uplift your spirit in the empowerment of my wings, guiding you in how to integrate your many gifts and talents into a unified offering of joyful service. My Presence accelerates and activates your personal and global mission for this lifetime. Receive my ever-present support for embodying your Higher Self and it is so.

Although the original context of my ancient Egyptian rituals is no longer understood as it once was, my Keycode 1 transmission resurrects those rites of alchemical magick stored within your DNA. It is from within the hallowed halls of your crystalline chromosomes that you will activate the gene for alchemical magick as a holy quality of your divine inheritance.

As you journey through my following Keycode initiation, you may experience remnants of these Egyptian rites arising as unexpected tactile memories, thoughts, and sensations within your inner sight or emotional body. For example, you may experience the distant scent of lotus oil or feel the simple luxury of my fine linen dress brush against your skin. It is safe to physically experience my presence supporting your empowerment. Together we will open stargates of magick for miracles to pour into your life.

I am here to guide you throughout the many chapters of initiation ahead. Together we will unlock the power of your ancient spiritual memories and training. Although unconscious resistances may arise, you are safe to remember and reclaim the sovereign power of magick within you that was mastered as an art in Egypt. You are ready to align with that same alchemical magick through the guiding wisdom of your Higher Self as The Horus.

As you open to the Keycode initiations of this codex, envision my wings around you, with my eyes beholding The Beloved within your own. I am guiding you in how to resurrect the power of these Divine Feminine Christ lineages within your own DNA that will awaken the wholeness of your true divine self in human form.

Your understanding is not required to mentor with me as a guide. Only your faith is needed to let go and receive my initiations, mystery teachings, miracles, divine interventions, and masterful support for The Way ahead. I invite you to fly with me into the vista of your own sovereign divinity.

My presence creates an authentic supportive space to explore and embody your freedom as a sovereign creator. In the journey of our mentor relationship, you will often experience laughing with me during an ah-ha moment of personal revelation and whispering back to me "of course" with a cellular-soul remembrance of your true self.

Celebrating your divinity and supporting your empowerment is the delight of my heart. The divine love that we share across all your lifetimes is now washing upon the shores of your heart. What was never lost is now returning to you in this moment.

I am Isis.
I have been seen.
I lift my eyes to the starry night sky of Nut and I declare that it is good.

KEYCODE 1
THE ISIS INITIATION

Accepting the Sovereign Divinity of Your Humanity

I now prepare a ceremonial space within and around me for transformation. I call forth concentric circles of amethyst violet light and diamond white light to surround me now. Centered within these encoded circles of light, I am now seated upon a blue lotus throne.

I am now in ceremony – free from the constructs of space and time – where instantaneous healing and divine knowing exist.

Before me flows a great river of starlight. It is the Milky Way and the Nile River merged as one river of light. Above me shines a crescent new moon. Along the riverbed a warm night breeze gently ripples with papyrus reeds. The scent of lotus and myrrh fills me with a sweet awareness of my true self.

I feel the blood within my body softly humming as I peer into the great river of starlight before me. I recognize that the river is flowing with the same holy essence humming within my own blood.

Above me, I witness the ivory white crescent moon mirroring the smile of my lips. Beneath me, I am supported by the lush petals of my blue lotus throne. The petals embrace my legs with grace. My awareness is permeated by the Earth's delight that I deeply feel at home in this present moment.

I now relax into this gentle, present moment of self-recognized oneness. I now relax into this cellular awareness that my human body is humming with the same starlight and holy water that fills everything I see. In this present moment, I feel safe in my connection to All That Is.

In this present moment, it feels easy to be one with All That Is. In this present moment, it feels pleasurable to be humming with the same starlight and holy water that flows within this river of light

I breathe in the Breath of Life.
I breathe out the Breath of Life.

The mighty river of starlight is breathing with me, matching the rise and fall of my breath. I feel relieved that what is breathing the Breath of Life within me is the same Holy Spirit breathing within all.

In the beauty of this present moment, I recognize my pure, original intention to live as starlight and holy water breathing within a human form. I now take confidence in the holy breath of my humanity, which is the same Holy Spirit animating all of life.

I now invoke the full presence of my Higher Self to fill my human body and these concentric circles of light with my own Holy Spirit.

I now invite the Divine Feminine Ascended Master Isis to join me for this ceremonial invocation.

In the distance, I see a woman walking towards me along the river's shoreline. Her sheer white linen dress ripples lightly in the breeze. The rustling of feathers follows her every step. Her outline is tall and framed by mighty wings that curve along her back. Her great presence deftly moves with the musculature of one who is always in communion with her environment. The warm night breeze preludes her arrival with the scent of lotus, frankincense, and myrrh emanating from her skin. Uplifting my senses higher and higher, I breathe in the revelations of the woman walking towards me.

Rising up from Isis' forehead is a golden horned crown that cradles a radiant sun disk, illuminating her path ahead. Against the dark night sky, I watch light-encoded hieroglyphs shimmering along Isis' elegant arms and legs. A celestial symphony of Hathor's many voices mysteriously sings from Isis' Sacred Heart. I am captivated by their perfect geometries of harmonic sounds. Each angelic note aligns my awareness to now receive the full presence of Isis.

Isis now stands before me. Her strong and beautiful face smiles with satisfaction that this moment together is finally happening. Illuminated by the sunlight of her crown above, Isis' warm, dark eyes glitter with mirth, confidence, and unconditional love. Outstretching her arms and iridescent black wings, Isis guides my awareness to now fully focus myself within her all-loving gaze.

ISIS SPEAKS:

"Thank you for welcoming me as a mentor, guide, and friend for your heroic human journey. My Divine Feminine embodiment of sovereign creative power provides a clear mirror for you to recognize this same divine power within you.

"Today is ordained by your Higher Self to dissolve your unconscious commitments to fearing the sovereign power within you. I am Isis, and in the sanctuary of my wings you are safe to unfurl your own. This is your lifetime to fly free in the vista of your personal sovereignty.

"I come to you as a loving witness, mentoring your awareness to accept the royal divinity of your soul. You are now ready to receive your Higher Self activating the full potential of your divine genome and human body.

"Allow the words of my Sacred Heart to guide your awareness in the acceptance that this is your lifetime to shine. Your true nature is holy. Your true nature is joy. Your true nature is peace. Your true nature is the same creative power that birthed the stars above.

"When your personal power is guided by the pure motives of your Sacred Heart, you are singing a new reality into form, protected by your own invincible nature. I assure you: it is safe to be seen. It is safe to lead.

"You are here to contribute your Legacy of Love – your heart's vision for Heaven on Earth – for the dawning of this next golden age. To fulfill your great purpose for being here, you must relinquish small ideas about yourself and believe in your divine, sovereign power to create a new world.

"My presence is with you now, guiding and blessing this ordained opening to our mentor relationship. You are safe to access my sovereign power guiding you to embrace your own: for you are ready to be guided by your own divinity now. Wait no longer for the divine inheritance that is already yours. Your destiny calls. Your Higher Self is ready to activate you now."

A translucent pyramid of gold and platinum light rises up from the earth beneath me. The pyramid's foundation anchors upon my concentric circles of amethyst and diamond light. The peak of this pyramid rises 33 feet directly above my crown chakra, instantaneously aligning all my energy bodies in preparation to release what no longer serves my awareness. As I breathe in, I feel the high frequency shift in the molecules of air around me.

As I breathe out, I resume eye contact with Isis. In her steadfast gaze I deepen into my breath, circulating the pyramid's high frequency energy within me. Isis sparkles as she smiles back at me. The feathers of her wings now transform in color from vulture black to pearlescent white. Isis raises her angelic wings high above my head, opening a stargate of pure, unconditional divine love to now pour through my crown chakra.

My crown chakra spins open as the mouth of a chalice. Unconditional divine love now pours through my crown chakra, flowing down the center of my head, baptizing my heart, and filling every cell of my body, all the way to my feet. Wave after wave of loving reassurance invites me to deepen into this present moment.

Isis guides my awareness to become fluid and flow with these currents of divine love through the rise and fall of my breath. I hear the voice of my Higher Self focusing all of my attention upon my heart, inviting me to intimately explore the sovereign power of my divinity within my body. I take courage and open to receive a greater awareness of my true self now.

I now clear what does not serve me, in preparation to accept the sovereign divinity of my humanity, with the following declaration.

As a sovereign creator of the One Sophia Source, by the power of my I Am Presence, I now declare this invocation heard and answered by the unified field of my whole self:

I command that every Akashic Record of all my physical incarnations now be opened. In the safety of this present moment, I step forward to witness the architecture of all my physical lifetimes that I am simultaneously living now to re-write their belief systems, as directed by my Higher Self.

I ask my Higher Self to bless me with the courage and will power to authentically love myself as I explore what is ready to be transformed within me, and in all my parallel lifetimes, through the power of my own Holy Spirit.

As I face the collective beliefs of humanity within my carbon-based DNA, I liberate all beings from their need to suffer any longer for these beliefs.

I allow my Higher Self to now guide my awareness to recognize and release the following unconscious beliefs in which I have disowned my sovereign power and true self in any or all of my physical incarnations.

I do this first for myself, and as I do, I dedicate this transformation for the benefit of all beings. I now command this transformation through my divine rite of summoning.

By the power of my I Am Presence, I now clear the following soul contracts with all earthly and interstellar religions from my carbon-based DNA:

From within, I summon the shame that I was created to live in a fallen state of sin.

From within, I summon the strife that I am in a struggle with God for power.

From within, I summon the confusion that I have to save God through acts of service.

From within, I summon the painful vows of impoverished service to God.

From within, I summon the exhaustion of proving myself worthy to a God outside of myself for a spiritual reward after death.

From within, I summon the rage that I have to defend God to and from others.

From within, I summon the terror that there is a force stronger than God.

From within, I summon the arrogance that God created a hierarchy of religious beliefs to separate good humans from bad humans.

From within, I summon the despair that God only blesses certain people, places, or things.

From within, I summon the self-belittlement that others have a more direct connection to God than I do.

From within, I summon the terror that God has the power to punish me.

From within, I summon the despair that God could abandon me to a hellish realm.

From within, I summon the terror that salvation is bestowed from a power outside of myself.

From within, I summon the panic that I cannot save myself.

From within, I summon the anxiety that I am inherently separate from God.

From within, I summon the grief of never being good enough for God's love.

From within, I summon the self-mutilation of punishing myself to be good enough for God.

From within, I summon the despair of my actions that hurt others in the name of God.

From within, I summon the self-hatred of my humanity and the humanity of others to please God.

From within, I summon the anxiety that God controls my destiny.

From within, I summon the terror that an external God has the power to exact life changes that are out of my control.

From within, I summon the judgment that one gender is more connected to God than another.

From within, I now summon the belief that the Earth should be feared as a temptation and obstruction to my salvation and enlightenment.

From within, I summon the rancor of crucifying my true self for any religion.

From within, I summon the despair that I will never achieve enlightenment.

From within, I summon the belittling of my humanity for the "Glory of God."

From within, I summon the lethargy of abdicating the responsibility of my sovereign Godself to another.

From within, I now summon the Holy Spirit of my Higher Self to prepare my body, heart, and mind for the full clearing of these religious beliefs from my carbon-based DNA.

In addition, I now summon to clear the following soul contracts placed upon my personal sovereign power as stored in my carbon-based DNA:

From within, I summon the fear that stepping into my personal power will defy God.

From within, I summon the fear of being killed for embodying my personal power.

From within, I summon the suffocation of my voice for speaking in my personal power.

From within, I summon the dread of isolation for being seen in my personal power.

From within, I summon the self-rejection and self-shaming of my human body to resist my personal power.

From within, I summon the determined confusion to separate me from my personal power.

From within, I summon the refusal of my personal power to bless others and myself.

From within, I summon the fright that my personal power, which includes my sexuality, comes from an unholy source.

From within, I summon the terror that my personal power will harm myself or others.

From within, I summon the shaming that others have more right to my personal power than I do.

From within, I summon the debts of poverty from denying my personal power.

From within, I summon the blame of others to prevent me from accessing my personal power.

From within, I summon the refuge of victimhood to defend my limitations and deny my personal power.

From within, I summon the blinding of my own eyes to my personal power.

From within, I summon the self-agreed slavery to a power outside of myself.

From within, I summon the rejection of my divine consciousness within a human form.

From within, I summon the self-judgment that my soul does not belong to me.

From within, I summon the dread that the One Sophia Source, which created me, exists as a separate entity outside of myself.

From within, I now summon the Holy Spirit of my Higher Self to prepare my body, heart, and mind for the full clearing of these beliefs placed upon my personal sovereign power as stored within my carbon-based DNA.

I now peer back into the loving eyes of Isis before me. As my steadfast witness and guide for this empowerment, Isis assures me that I am safe and supported within our ceremonial space resonating with the frequency of unconditional self-acceptance. She thanks me for my courage to claim and speak aloud the unconsciously held beliefs, both within me, and in the collective field of humanity's carbon-based DNA.

I feel relief sweeping through my body from declaring these unconsciously held beliefs about spirituality, religion, and personal power. This relief flows through me in healing waves, catalyzing stagnant energies to release throughout my entire body now.

Isis is preparing me to receive more of my true sovereign self today, as directed by my Higher Self. She reminds me that remaining present to the rhythmic rise and fall of my breath keeps me in a fluid state of receptivity.

Opening her hands to the sky, a golden-white *Ankh of Life* now emerges from Isis' Sacred Heart. The ankh rises before my eyes to anchor and levitate above my crown chakra. Slowly, the ankh begins to rotate clockwise and gently expand in size. As its size and rotation expand, the ankh's radiance dances across the pyramid, flashing with rays of violet, gold, and diamond white light. The ankh's rays of healing light soothe my heart and inner eyes.

I feel safe in this moment. Isis invites me to spiral open my crown chakra as a doorway for the Ankh of Life to descend into my body. I feel my body instantaneously respond to Isis' request, opening as a receptive column of light, from my crown chakra to my feet.

I breathe in and the golden-white ankh begins its descent, spinning down through my crown chakra, my third eye, and my throat chakra. I breathe out and the ankh slows to now anchor and rotate at the center of my heart chakra. I breathe in and the rotation of the ankh begins to accelerate, creating a vortex for the Sophia Christ light of my Higher Self to now illuminate the stagnancy of these unconscious beliefs hidden within my carbon-based DNA.

I deeply exhale to receive this shining, healing light of my Higher Self filling every cell of my body with self-compassion, self-acceptance, and self-love. In the grace of this moment, I witness the sovereign one within me, who explored those unconscious beliefs and survived their devastating manifestations. I recognize the invincible nature of my true self.

I breathe in to consciously connect with this sovereign fabric of my true being. I breathe deeply into every cell of my body. I witness the invincibility of my sovereign divinity shining beneath every unconsciously held belief.

As my breath deepens, I feel the weariness of turning away from my true self in every lifetime washing out of my body with every exhale. This weariness dissolves within the ankh's violet ray of light. I breathe into the cloudy confusion and disempowering feelings about my past and future. I witness this internalized chaos lift from my mind and dissolve into the ankh's golden ray of light. I bless the darkness of previous self-defeating behaviors with the power of my breath. Rinsed clean by my own Holy Spirit, these patterns of self-sabotage dissolve into the ankh's diamond white ray of light.

I bear witness to how much pain and suffering I have experienced from believing that I was created less than the I Am Presence within me, which is my Higher Self. Within this present moment, I recognize the opportunity for quantum healing and empowerment across all my parallel lifetimes and I take courage to wholly forgive and accept myself now.

I accept that I hold the golden keys to my Heaven on Earth.
I accept that I create my reality, by the power of my word.
My word is good, my heart is pure.
By the loving power of my pure word, I call forth and invoke the full presence of forgiveness for myself now.

Through the power of my own forgiveness, I now set myself free from following unconscious beliefs about religion, spirituality, and God:

I forgive myself for believing that my humanity is a fallen state of sin.

I forgive myself for struggling against myself for a divine power that already exists within me.

I forgive myself for striving to save a God of omniscient power that is the eternal Source of unconditional divine love.

I forgive myself for the destitution created by vows of poverty that have kept me separated from the abundant, prosperous Godself within me.

I forgive myself for seeking approval outside of the worthiness of my true divine self.

I forgive myself for forgetting that heaven is always within me.

I forgive myself for defending an idea of an external God separate from others and myself.

I forgive myself for indulging in the terrifying illusion that there is a force stronger than the Godself within me that could end my life.

I forgive myself for participating in the arrogant hierarchy of religious beliefs that separate humanity from its absolute divinity.

I forgive myself for despairing over the absolute blessed nature of All That Is.

I forgive myself for belittling my direct connection to the Godself within me.

I forgive myself for perpetuating terror that an all-loving God would desire to punish me.

I forgive myself for believing in a hellish realm that my eternal soul could be imprisoned by.

I forgive myself for seeking salvation from a power outside of myself.

I forgive myself for the belief that my innocent true nature needed to be saved.

I forgive myself for the anxiety that I could ever be separated from the holy Godself within me.

I forgive myself for grieving that I am not good enough for the divine love within me.

I forgive myself for every act of self-punishment and self-mutilation that I committed to become the goodness that I already am and will always be.

I forgive myself for hurting others in the name of God because I despaired that I was not God.

I forgive myself for hurting myself with hatred for the qualities of humanness within others and myself.

I forgive myself for believing an external God could control my destiny.

I forgive myself for believing any external force could alter the course of my sovereign life choices.

I forgive myself for judging one gender as more divinely aligned with God than another.

I forgive myself for fearing the Earth as a temptation and obstruction to any spiritual goal.

I forgive myself for the rancor of crucifying my innate divinity for any religious or spiritual belief system.

I forgive myself for believing that I must achieve a state of enlightenment to be one with my Godself.

I forgive myself for belittling my humanity for the worship or glorification of an externalized God figure.

I forgive myself for the lethargy of abdicating the responsibility of my sovereign Godself onto another.

Through the power of my own forgiveness, I now set myself free from following unconscious beliefs and manifesting their devastating effects in my life, which causes me to fear my personal sovereign power:

I forgive myself for allowing the fear of an external God to separate me from my personal power.

I forgive myself for fearing that I will die for embodying my personal power.

I forgive myself for suffocating my own voice to prevent the full expression of my personal power.

I forgive myself for dreading an outcome of isolation for living in my personal power.

I forgive myself for the acts of self-rejection and shaming of my human body that I committed to blatantly resist embodying my personal power.

I forgive myself for the practice of self-determined confusion to separate me from the aligned actions of my personal power.

I forgive myself for relinquishing my personal power to bless others and myself.

I forgive myself for the frightening feelings caused by believing my personal power comes from an externalized place other than the Godself within me.

I forgive myself for the terror of believing that if I accessed my personal power I would hurt others and myself.

I forgive myself for the self-shaming belief that others have more right to my personal power than I do.

I forgive myself for incurring debts of poverty from denying my personal power.

I forgive myself for the practice of blaming others to distract me from accessing my personal power.

I forgive myself for taking refuge in victimhood to defend my limitations and deny my personal power.

I forgive myself for blinding my own eyes to the truth of my innate personal power.

I forgive myself for every belief and soul contract of self-agreed slavery to any power outside of myself.

I forgive myself for the self-rejection of the Holy Spirit within my human form.

I forgive myself for the self-judgment and doubt that my soul does not belong to me.

I forgive myself for the dreadful belief that the sovereign power which created me was outside of my true self.

By the power of my I Am Presence, the Godself within me, I now summon the Holy Spirit of my Higher Self to release and dissolve these unconscious beliefs, vows, oaths, and soul contracts from the matrix of my carbon-based DNA.

I call forth the Holy Spirit of my Higher Self to now fill every cell of my body with self-forgiveness and the Breath of Life.

I forgive myself.
I forgive myself.
I forgive myself.
By the power of 3, a perfect trinity: It is done.

I welcome the presence of Isis to support my Higher Self in the full-body integration of this cellular-soul clearing, throughout all four levels of my being now.

Isis raises her wings to bless me as I integrate the power of my own forgiveness. I feel my eighth chakra open as a gateway above my head. The full presence of my Higher Self begins to descend as a mighty waterfall of pearlescent white light through my eighth chakra, flowing down through my crown chakra and filling every cell of my body.

I witness my Higher Self anchoring and integrating the Sophia Christ light of my soul into all of this new, available space within me. I deeply breathe out to relax my body and welcome the radiant waves of my sovereign divinity downloading within me now.

Isis smiles. Reflected in her glittering dark eyes, I see myself smiling back at her. As a witness and friend, Isis' unconditionally supportive presence encourages me to bravely explore the full creative power of my own sovereign divinity. In the guiding light of her majestic embodiment it feels easy to clearly remember my full potential.

I witness the elegance and magick that Isis commands to create sacred space for my personal healing. In the grace of her support, I clearly recognize that it is my own Higher Self orchestrating this initiation as Isis masterfully supports me to remain steadfast in fulfilling my heart's desires.

Isis sweeps her wings in a series of infinity loops throughout my auric field. Every movement is a blessing and I feel her angelic feathers settling my awareness. I exhale with deep satisfaction and appreciation for this opportunity to peer into my true self.

She whispers to me: "You're ready now. It is safe to accept your sovereign divinity."

Within the quantum zero still-point of this present moment, Isis guides my awareness to witness all of my parallel lifetimes, across the space-time continuum, in which I am now releasing these same unconscious beliefs. Upon the holy electrons of my human body, I now send out this quantum healing of self-forgiveness across all realities to all of my simultaneous incarnations happening now, as directed by my Higher Self.

I hold eye contact with Isis and stare in wonder at this unlimited power within me that can heal every dimension of my soul. Isis gently reminds me to remain present to my breath, which connects me to every part of myself receiving this healing now. We breathe together in harmony.

In honor of my expanding awareness, Isis reveals an alabaster jar of blue lotus oil and asks to ceremonially anoint my body. I accept her invitation and Isis steps forward to anoint me with her blue lotus oil on my crown chakra, third eye, heart chakra, upper back, both hands, and feet.

The purity of this anointing oil awakens every sense of my soul within my body. I feel the blue lotus oil sinking deeper and deeper into my skin, relaxing my neurological pathways and stimulating every gland in my body to come into alignment with the divine will of my Higher Self. My breath becomes a vehicle of total empowerment. As I drink in the spirit of the blue lotus, I am carried in blissful waves to explore the beauty of my true nature.

Isis begins to sing over me in the celestial light language of Hathor, soothing my body and awareness to soften and open as a blue lotus. I feel myself accessing unconditional love for the true purpose of my humanity as a sovereign embodiment of divinity.

I realize that to embody my sovereignty requires a willingness to accept that my true nature is already perfect, pure, and divine. As I watch Isis blessing me, my heart whispers a simple prayer to now embody the same graceful, loving, sovereign power of Isis within me, every day of my life.

In immediate response to my silent prayer, Isis lifts her eyes to ask if I am ready to awaken the crystalline chromosome that carries the divine qualities of Keycode 1 of The Sophia Code within my DNA. I look into Isis' eyes, feeling safe and deeply inspired to continue forward in my empowerment with her. I breathe in ... and I breathe out. I respond to her gaze with an audible reply:

"Yes, I am ready to activate Keycode 1 of The Sophia Code within my DNA."

Isis gently places her left hand at the base of my spine and her right hand rests on the top of my head. I breathe into the comforting weight of her healing hands on my skin.

A warm liquid light begins to gently rise from the base of my spine, traveling up three serpentine pathways, which all meet within my heart chakra. I watch as blue flames of divine will bless the organ of my heart. My solar plexus chakra expands as a warm sun whose radiant arms reach throughout my body, which causes my heart chakra to spiral open even wider.

As I continue to relax and breathe, this warm liquid light expands far out from my spinal column, glowing throughout my entire body. I breathe into my lower abdomen. Isis moves her right hand to now make a mudra that touches my third eye. I feel a portion of the warm liquid light gather as a flame of diamond light within my pituitary gland, at the center of my head.

Breathing in.
Breathing out.

I hear the buzzing sound of bees and birds singing within me. I witness thousands of Hathor angels singing the innumerable names of Sophia from the temple of Isis' Sacred Heart. Isis has activated my inner vision. With eyes to see and ears to hear, I may now clearly commune with the Holy Spirit within me, when I so choose, regardless of all circumstances.

Isis now brings her left hand to rest lightly on my upper chest and I breathe into the weight of her bejeweled hand. I feel the ankh of violet, gold, and diamond white rays of light begin to rotate again at the center of my heart, radiating out a transmission of my sovereign power to create as Sophia creates.

Within every cell of my body, I feel the frequency of new vital energy awakening now. Illuminating my inner sight with a great flash of awareness, I am drawn inward to witness the crystalline chromosome that carries Keycode 1 of The Sophia Code within me.

Its radiant outlined shape of immaculate light instantaneously feels familiar to my soul. I hear thousands of angels singing and monks chanting a never-ending "OM" as I recognize the divine genome of my own soul. I peer closer to see golden spiraling ladders of divine helices that are encoded with all the immaculate qualities that Isis embodies, which also exist within me.

In appreciation, I breathe in.
In appreciation, I breathe out.

I am deeply moved that these same heavenly qualities, embodied by Isis, exist within the earth of my own body. With a deep breath in, I now accept Isis' invitation to activate Keycode 1 within my DNA. This initiation, as directed by my Higher Self and overseen by Isis, aligns my awareness to consciously express and embody these divine qualities in my human life now.

In honor of the Breath of Life within me, I breathe into this resurrection.
In honor of my body as the living Ankh of Life, I breathe out.

I welcome Isis into my life as a loving mentor for embodying these divine qualities of Sophia, as revealed by her Keycode 1 transmission. I take

courage and now open to receive more of my true self today by invoking the
following empowerment:

I accept that I hold the golden keys to my Heaven on Earth.
I accept that I create my reality, by the power of my word.
My word is good, my heart is pure.
**By the loving power of my pure word, I now activate Keycode 1 of
The Sophia Code within me.**

**By the loving power of my pure word, I now download perfect acceptance
for the sovereign divinity of my humanity from my Higher Self.**

*In the presence of Isis, I declare these revelations now arising from my surrender
to grace:*

In my *delight* to accept the sovereign divinity of my humanity,
I am aware of my innocence.

In my *transcendence* to accept the sovereign divinity of my humanity,
I am aware of my eternal power.

In my *commitment* to accept the sovereign divinity of my humanity,
I am aware of my true creative potential.

In my *peace* to accept the sovereign divinity of my humanity,
I am aware of my true worth.

In my *willingness* to accept the sovereign divinity of my humanity,
I am aware of my omniscient Source.

**I now speak with the voice of my Higher Self speaking as a transmission
from within the halls of my divine genome, Keycode 1 of The Sophia Code
within me.**

**I now speak with the breath of my own Holy Spirit, my Higher Self, with
whose power I now activate The Tree of Life within me.**

83

1.

As I am the Tree of Life, I honor the Sephira of Malkuth, the "Kingdom" breathing within me:

I summon the elemental power of earth within me:

I am a holy human being created to live an abundant, prosperous life on Earth. I now accept the divine will for my life to prosper in every way. I seek first the Kingdom of loving my true self, and all earthly blessings follow.

I summon the elemental power of water within me:

I am a holy human being created as a living chalice for the overflowing waters of my divinity nourishing all of life on Earth. I now accept these ever-flowing blessings returning to me a thousand-fold.

I summon the elemental power of fire within me:

I am a holy human being created to tend the sacred flames of Heaven on Earth that always exist within me. With the power of these sacred flames, I bless my life as a sanctuary for all to take refuge in their divinity as well.

I summon the elemental power of air within me:

I am a holy human being created to breathe the Breath of Life with appreciation for my true worth. I now accept the breath of my own Holy Spirit as the infinite wealth of my divine inheritance.

I summon the Holy Spirit within me:

I am a holy human being created as a stargate for my Higher Self to flow forward and abundantly bless all of life, especially myself. I now accept my innate holiness and allow myself to be at peace with my divinity.

I affirm this truth independent of any passing understanding:

I AM THE HOLY HUMAN CHALICE FOR BIRTHING HEAVEN ON EARTH, I AM THAT.

2.

As I am the Tree of Life, I honor the Sephira of Yesod, the "Foundation" breathing within me:

As a holy human being, I stand on the foundation of my true self and declare that it is safe to express and enjoy the qualities of my whole, divine nature.

As a holy human being, I stand on the foundation of my true self and declare that it is my divine right to create new realities from the prosperous peace of my Sophia Christ consciousness.

As a holy human being, I stand on the foundation of my true self and declare that wherever my feet walk, the Earth is blessed.

As a holy human being, I stand on the foundation of my true self and declare that I am a safe steward for the creative Source of power within me to flow freely now, in my life and in the lives of others.

I affirm this truth independent of any passing understanding:

I AM THE HOLY HUMAN FOUNDATION FOR THE CREATIVE EXPRESSION OF MY SOVEREIGN POWER, I AM THAT.

3.

As I am the Tree of Life, I honor the Sephira of Hod, the "Splendor" breathing within me:

I open the wings of my soul to reveal the splendor of my invincible divine nature.

I open the wings of my heart to reveal the splendor of my unconditional love.

I open the wings of my throat to reveal the splendor of Sophia's languages of light.

I open the wings of my mind to reveal the available empty space within me for the glory of my divinity to shine.

I open the wings of my infinite being to reveal the unlimited splendor of Sophia within me, blessing this same Source within all, as joint heirs of the Most High.

I affirm this truth independent of any passing understanding:

I AM THE WINGED HOLY SPLENDOR OF MY HIGHER SELF'S CHOSEN HUMAN FORM, I AM THAT.

4.

As I am the Tree of Life, I honor the Sephira of Netzach, the "Victory" breathing within me:

As a holy human being, I take confidence in my divine right to perfectly commune with my Higher Self. My victory is absolute: I now clearly hear the voice of my own Holy Spirit.

As a holy human being, I take confidence in my divine right to rest in the sanctuary of my perfect divinity. My victory is absolute: I now deeply relax into the authenticity of my true self.

As a holy human being, I take confidence in my divine right to unconditionally love myself with passionate self-care. My victory is absolute: I now surrender to the regeneration of self-adoration.

As a holy human being, I take confidence in my divine right to experience the absolute freedom of my sovereignty within form. My victory is absolute: I now allow the Holy Spirit within me to manifest my reality.

As a holy human being, I take confidence in the victory of my awareness surrendering to the all-loving power of my Higher Self guiding my every step. My victory is absolute: I now trust that every step I take is leading to my happiness.

I affirm this truth independent of any passing understanding:

I AM A UNIFIED FIELD OF SOPHIA CONSCIOUSNESS EXPRESSING MY SOVEREIGN POWER IN THE VICTORY OF MY HUMAN FORM, I AM THAT.

5.

As I am the Tree of Life, I honor the Sephira of Tiphereth, the "Compassionate Beauty" breathing within me:

I am blessed: I am designed as a perfect hologram of Sophia.

I am blessed: I am basking in the generous radiance of my eternal innocence.

I am the blessing: I am speaking directly to the Holy Spirit within *all* others. Regardless of all outer circumstances, my clear compassion spontaneously arises from within me, without effort.

I am the blessing: I am the Holy Spirit honoring the beauty of humanity within myself and all others, regardless of all outer circumstances.

I am the blessing: I am the voice of the Holy Spirit speaking divine revelations for living in the embodied wisdom that honors all, regardless of all outer circumstances.

I affirm this truth independent of any passing understanding:

I AM THE RADIANT BEAUTY OF COMPASSION ILLUMINATING MY HOLY HUMAN FORM, I AM THAT.

6.

As I am the Tree of Life, I honor the Sephira of Geburah, the "Strength and Power" breathing within me:

I honor the divinity of my humanity by consecrating the strength and power of my body as a holy temple for the mighty presence of my Higher Self to live entirely within me.

I honor the divinity of my humanity by consecrating the strength and power of my mind to fulfill my Higher Self's destiny for this lifetime.

I honor the divinity of my humanity by consecrating the strength and power of my free will to fulfill the divine will of my Oversoul.

I honor the divinity of my humanity by consecrating the strength and power of my ability to command miracles to be in sovereign service for the highest good of all.

I affirm this truth independent of any passing understanding:

I AM THE PERFECT HUMAN VESSEL FOR THE STRENGTH OF MY SOVEREIGN POWER TO CONSECRATE A NEW GOLDEN AGE, I AM THAT.

7.

As I am the Tree of Life, I honor the Sephira of Chesed, the "Mercy and Glory" breathing within me:

I am the holiness of mercy in human form. Within me, this pure force of mercy overcomes all inner and outer obstacles to unconditionally love my divinity.

Within me, this pure force of mercy keeps my feet upon the path of righteousness. By the power of mercy within me, I now reconcile all my lifetimes for the glory of Sophia within me.

I now welcome and integrate every aspect of myself – both the light and the dark within me – into the glory of my unified self. I am the embodied glory of a whole human being creating in a world of form.

Within me, this pure force of glory sanctifies my every action. Within me, this pure force of glory acts as a divine, loving, and generous ally to the Earth.

I now dedicate all my actions for the glory of Sophia within me and Sophia within all beings. I now align with the sacred waters of unstoppable success flowing within me. I allow the glorious illumination of the Holy Spirit within me to radically shift my self-perception in every present moment.

I affirm this truth independent of any passing understanding:

I AM THE MERCY OF SOPHIA GUIDING ME TO THE GLORY OF MY BRILLIANT HUMAN POTENTIAL, I AM THAT.

8.

As I am the Tree of Life, I honor both the Sephira and the Void of Da'ath, the "Spirit of Holiness" breathing within me:

I am a holy human being speaking with the tongue of my own Holy Spirit.

I am a holy human being awakening to my body as the Ark of the Covenant.

I am a holy human being embodying the Divine Feminine and Divine Masculine Christ light as a unified field within the temple of my body.

I am a holy human being prophesying direct revelations that spontaneously arise from the light of Sophia within me.

I am a holy human being prophesying spiritual blueprints for this next Golden Age of Miracles and peace on Earth.

I affirm this truth independent of any passing understanding:

I AM THE PERFECT SOPHIA CHRIST LIGHT FROM WHICH MY BODY ARISES AS AN ANSWERED PROPHECY, I AM THAT.

9.

As I am the Tree of Life, I honor the Sephira of Binah, the "Throne" breathing within me:

As I have been made in the exact image and likeness of Sophia, I now claim The Sophia Code as my rightful divine inheritance.

As I have been made in the exact image and likeness of Sophia, I now consecrate my body as the temple of my I Am Presence.

As I have been made in the exact image and likeness of Sophia, I now take up the mantle of my divinity and present precious offerings to the altar of my own I Am Presence.

As I have been made in the exact image and likeness of Sophia, I now ascend to the throne of my I Am Presence.

I allow my silent awe to worship in thanksgiving for the ineffable mystery of my divinity, that I now behold within me.

I baptize and sanctify my human awareness as the throne of consciousness that invites me to an understanding free of all thought.

I affirm this truth independent of any passing understanding:

I AM BOTH THE THRONE AND THE ONE ASCENDING THE THRONE TO WORSHIP THE DIVINITY OF MY HUMAN EXPERIENCE, I AM THAT.

10.
As I am the Tree of Life, I honor the Sephira of Chokmah, the "Wisdom" breathing within me:

I am the sacred space of a holy human being that allows both Divine Feminine and Divine Masculine Christ wisdom to arise within me as needed.

I am the sacred space of a holy human being expressing a perfect measure of Sophia consciousness within my choice of gender.

I am the sacred space of a holy human being that contains both the black womb of no-thing and the light of life.

I am the sacred space of a holy human being taking responsibility for these divine wisdom revelations that travel at the speed of light from the Source of my soul to the gateway of my tongue.

I affirm this truth independent of any passing understanding:

I AM THE MULTIDIMENSIONAL SOVEREIGN SPACE THAT REVELATIONS OF DIVINE WISDOM ARISE FROM WITHIN MY HUMAN FORM, I AM THAT.

11.
As I am the Tree of Life, I honor the Sephira of Kether, the "Crown" breathing within me:

I dissolve into the Holy of Holies within me. I let go.

I allow the ineffable mystery of this divinity within me to be both the silence and all-consuming voice that I seek and take refuge in.

As I continually allow all limited understanding about the divinity that I am to pass by unobstructed, I create a clear space within me for whatever revelation is arising next, to spontaneously download the pure divine love that I am.

I allow myself to know nothing: therefore I am always reborn anew.

I allow for everything to exist within me, therefore I experience an unlimited thanksgiving of praise for the great mysteries and miracles of Sophia within me.

Beyond all wisdom and understanding, I now consciously accept this unknowable holiness as the Source of me.

I exist as a sovereign expression of this Source and my human body is a vehicle for discovering this mystery.

As such, my human body is the Ark of the Covenant containing these

91

mysteries, and is worthy of my absolute love, adoration, worship, and self-care.

I affirm this truth independent of any passing understanding:

I AM THE ARK OF THE COVENANT WORTHY OF THE HIGHEST DEVOTIONAL LOVE, I AM THAT.

12.

Within the Breath of Life, I am one with the Ain Soph Aur, Sophia's "Limitless Light" that created my soul in sovereignty:

I now consciously commit to activating and integrating the limitless light of my crystalline divine genome.

I now consciously commit to embodying the limitless light of my divinity.

I now consciously commit to blessing myself and others with the limitless light of my Christed Self.

I now consciously commit to living in the limitless light of my personal power as the safest, and only, way to unconditionally love myself and others.

I now consciously accept that I am worthy of my personal power and that *all* others are worthy of their personal power as well, which is equally given to all in the limitless light of our shared divinity.

I affirm this truth independent of any passing understanding:

I AM THE LIMITLESS LIGHT OF SOPHIA EMBODIED IN A HOLY HUMAN FORM, I AM THAT.

13.

Within the Breath of Life, I am one with the Kavod Penimi, the "Inner Glory" that illuminates all the universes of Sophia:

I keep my eyes focused upon the inner glory of Sophia illuminating the Universe. My eyes shine with the light of Christ, for Her reflection is all I see.

I proclaim that the inner glory of my Sophia Christ consciousness is the heavenly reality that I am manifesting on Earth.

I have come to reveal this inner glory of heaven within me, hand-in-hand and heart-to-heart with a new generation of humanity on Earth.

This Golden Age of Miracles is my soul's opportunity to reveal and praise Sophia as the inner glory of creation in entirely new ways.

I affirm this truth independent of any passing understanding:

I AM A CHRISTED EMBODIMENT FOR REVEALING THE INNER GLORY OF SOPHIA THAT ILLUMINATES ALL UNIVERSES, I AM THAT.

With the following declaration I now seal these thirteen empowerments of The Shekinah in the light and fire of my own Holy Spirit, activating my Christed embodiment for this next Golden Age of Miracles.

I accept that I hold the golden keys to my Heaven on Earth.
I accept that I create my reality, by the power of my word.
My word is good, my heart is pure.
By the loving power of my pure word, I wholly accept the sovereign divinity of my humanity now.

By the loving power of my pure word, I now command my Higher Self to activate all the crystalline divine qualities of Keycode 1 of The Sophia Code within me as the new operating system for my carbon-based DNA.

I now integrate this initiation throughout my entire body, on all four levels of my Be-ing, with grace and ease.

I have received more of myself today.

It is done.

It is done.

It is done.

By the power of 3, a perfect trinity: It is done.

I hear Isis' voice chanting a closing prayer over my body as she places her right hand in a mudra of anointed blessing upon the center of my heart. With her healing touch the ankh of violet, gold, and diamond white light spinning within me dissolves into holy water. Filled with the light of each ray, every drop of the ankh's holy water rapidly flows into every cell of my body, nourishing the Keycode 1 chromosome now awakening within my DNA. I feel my body deeply drink in this blessing.

I feel an appreciative wonder as I witness the activation of my sovereign divine genome. I see the limitless light of the Universe within my crystalline chromosomes coming into perfect alignment with my carbon-based DNA, to override all viral codes.

My soul is filled with thanksgiving as I reclaim this personal power to increasingly access more and more of my true self by activating The Sophia Code of my soul. I smile with relief into the beautiful face of Isis and she warmly smiles back at me. We have immensely enjoyed creating this space of ceremony together.

Isis then places her left hand as a mudra of blessing upon the center of my third eye. She transmits an indigo ray of light that enhances my inner vision. I am shown those places in my life that will now benefit from this initiation. Isis affirms that she is always available as an ever-present mentor, friend, and support for successfully navigating the journey of resulting transformations ahead.

As she continues to transmit her indigo *Eye of Ra* blessing over me, Isis reveals to my inner sight how activating Keycode 1 awakens an acute focus and pristine commitment within me for aligning with my Higher Self's divine will to fully embody my sovereign divine power in this lifetime.

Isis wraps her wings around me in a final blessing, sealing her indigo transmission with a closing prayer. Within her embrace, I can feel how easy it is to access Isis' great presence in any moment. I welcome her as a mentor for embodying the divine qualities of Keycode 1 within all my daily choices. I am assured of our continued friendship and accept Isis' overlighting support to mentor my highest potential every day.

I now close this ceremony with appreciation and thanksgiving in my heart. I thank you Isis for the blessings of your pyramid, your wings, your rays of resurrection, and your Ankh of Life. Thank you for your steadfast support as my loving witness, guide, and friend throughout this initiation.

This empowerment to activate Keycode 1 within my DNA is now accomplished. I now close this ceremony with appreciation, thanksgiving, and reverence in my heart for all that I have received, both known and unknown to my awareness. I thank the power of my Higher Self and the love of All That Is supporting my eternal success.

Amen.

KEYCODE 2
"SHE OF A THOUSAND VOICES"

True intimacy leads to joy. In the covenant of The Sophia Code, joy is an essential quality of your divine inheritance. I am here to guide you in how your body is the ultimate vehicle for communing in electro-ecstatic bliss with your multidimensional self.

Hathor's Legacy of Love on Earth

THE HATHOR STAR NATION SPEAKS:

WE ARE THE HATHOR Star Nation, a collective voice of initiates that ascended with Hathor during a legendary golden age in Egypt. It is our great honor to introduce Hathor as "She of a Thousand Voices," a Divine Feminine Christ teacher for activating your voice to speak in the many tongues of Sophia's Holy Spirit. We amplify Hathor's transmission as an accompanying congregation of angelic beings that sing in harmonic frequency with her teaching embodiment.

In our human ascension with Hathor we activated the full expression of our angelic DNA. When you receive Hathor's initiations, you may hear our voices singing within thousands of rustling wings and eyes that tone as tongues within spinning wheels of light: for we ascended to become ophanim angels of the highest order in service to the Shekinah light of Sophia. We represent Hathor's ability to initiate the prophet within you for the fulfillment of a great commission, just as we did for Ezekiel. ^(Ezek 1-3:3)

Our collective presence as The Hathor Star Nation activates your own tongue to sing as an angel on Earth so that we may joyfully co-create this next golden age together. For within Hathor's guiding light transmission, you will discover the unlimited power of your voice to act as an omniscient creator of new quantum realities.

Hathor's Keycode 2 transmission is a unique genetic sequence of The Sophia Code that also initiates your awareness to access and integrate the unlimited, multidimensional power of your body. The fully integrated activation of Keycode 2 liberates your body from the laws of the space-time continuum while still maintaining your form, so that you may express the creative genius of your unlimited divinity on Earth.

During an important golden age in ancient Kemet, Hathor revealed these divine qualities of Keycode 2 within her revolutionary spiritual leadership. In this legendary lifetime, Hathor created a Legacy of Love that would go on to support ascension initiates for thousands of years into the future.

For ages far beyond her time on Earth, Hathor continues to peer into the eyes of humanity from her unforgettable images carved in the temples of Egypt. We can assure you that these relics are but a shadow of her radiance. The deification of Hathor spanned for thousands of years, originating before your current recorded history. As a result of her legacy, the human worship of Hathor as a goddess was practiced for ages to cultivate the qualities of fertility, immaculate birthing, abundance, creative genius, empowered beauty, and radiant divine love within the devotee.

However, before her rise as a worshiped goddess, Hathor was an extraordinary human woman living in extraordinary times. It was a golden age that was a precursor to Lemuria, in which a large majority of humanity lived in an awakened collective awareness of its innate divinity and vast multidimensional sovereign power.

Every child was educated in self-mastery practices that served to recognize and nurture their own unique Keycode. The sacred arts and sciences of this golden age provided an ideal, enlightened environment for Hathor to blossom as a child, and eventually fully activate The Sophia Code within her.

Living in a community that nurtured latent human abilities supported Hathor's passionate commitment to expand upon the leading edge beliefs of what was deemed physically possible during her lifetime. As such, Hathor and we, her devoted initiates, accessed and embodied the genetic ability to bilocate and time travel for the purpose of affecting future outcomes.

In our community, Hathor was a master teacher for how to consciously participate and coexist within simultaneous lifetimes. She mastered and taught these techniques by weaving accumulated wisdom gathered from her quantum travel between two consciously embodied parallel lifetimes.

Unlocking the full potential of her body, Hathor became an oracular stargate priestess, communicating an interstellar exchange of ascension information being passed between two parallel worlds through her heart chakra. She used the quantum access points within her body to regularly bilocate between her life in the Sirius star system and her life here on Earth.

In both of these parallel lifetimes Hathor taught her communities through her radical living embodiment, becoming a renowned facilitator, spiritual teacher, and master ceremonialist. Hathor's oracular ability to articulate and embody her discoveries, within a congregational witness of interstellar communities, placed her at the forefront of this golden age as a Divine Feminine Christ leader of unlimited Sophia consciousness.

As a master of ceremony, Hathor utilized her understanding of universal laws, quantum physics, sacred geometry, and the science of sound to orchestrate a multidimensional container in which her oracular voice would open physical stargates. This facilitated a safe space for her communities to practice interstellar travel and fulfill prophetic timelines for future chapters of humanity's ascension journey. These ceremonies also reflected Hathor's creative genius and love for beauty by administering her rites of initiation through sacred dance, music, and singing.

Countless individuals were able to consciously experience their own ability to time travel, bilocate, and receive direct revelations from Sophia as they would step into the stargates opened by Hathor's confident abilities. She patiently devoted herself to training others in how to open these stargates for themselves so that the teachings to do so would remain on Earth for as long as possible. As an engaging mentor and facilitator of quantum learning experiences, Hathor's courageous embodiment inspired innumerable initiates to follow her in walking The Way of this sacred magick.

Eventually the word of Hathor's leadership spread as a holy fire of radiant new consciousness to several corners of the Earth. Mystery schools were organized to offer the teachings of Hathor to as many future generations as possible. Temples were constructed for large populations of initiates to explore the ceremonial arts of divine magick and receive Hathor's oracular rites of initiation for embodying creative genius.

Hathor's mystery schools were also instrumental in translating and recording light languages that became foundational for written communication between dimensional realities and for speaking with those from other star systems. An interstellar spiritual movement swept Hathor's known world and for a time, large populations of humanity were participating in a conscious diplomatic dialogue with other Star Nations.

Over the arc of her human lifetime, Hathor's interstellar ambassadorship included guiding large groups of initiates to travel through her stargates to visit and learn from the Sirian High Councils. To balance the scales of cosmic evolution, Hathor also facilitated Sirian elders coming to Earth as visiting teachers of their ancient wisdom. During these hyperspace learning immersives, initiates received training in how to focus their thoughts upon the electrons of a desired physical outcome or location.

Hathor's conscious ability to simultaneously navigate within multiple incarnations allowed her physical features to shapeshift at will. Depending on the need of her teaching embodiment, Hathor could choose to exhibit the atomic arrangement of her Sirian or human attributes in either location. As such, Hathor's renowned ability to shapeshift into her Sirian form gave rise to her image being immortalized in ancient Egypt with features of the sky cow. One of her prodigy initiates would successfully carry forth this legacy of shapeshifting, when Isis revealed her winged embodiment while still in human form.

In her authentic and radiant Divine Feminine Christ embodiment, Hathor lived as a beloved global ambassador for Sophia consciousness. Everywhere Hathor walked, humanity's heart was blessed by her spiritual vision and creative genius. Her global offering was a testimony to the power of living in ecstatic alignment with the divine will of Sophia to prosper all.

At the completion of her human life, Hathor chose to open a stargate to depart the physical plane of Earth and redirect her focused awareness more fully within the Sirian star system. Many highly trained adepts of Hathor's teachings chose to ascend by walking with her through this stargate to Sirius.

We are these highly advanced beings who departed for Sirius with Hathor that have become the collective consciousness known as The Hathor Star Nation. We lived for centuries on Earth serving side-by-side with Hathor as she initiated a prolific golden age cycle for humanity. We have returned with Hathor to support you in this next Divine Feminine Christ awakening that is sweeping your planet now. Our tools for ascension are available to you once again.

Your Voice as an Omniscient Creator of Quantum Reality

MOTHER MARY SPEAKS:

In my human lifetime I was an ordained Oracle and High Priestess of Hathor's lineage. As an honored council member of the Hathor Star Nation, it is a great joy for me to share in Hathor's teaching transmission, which reveals how to use your voice as an omniscient creator of quantum reality by activating your throat chakra as an alchemical technology of sound vibration.

Hathor has invited me to share with you several interrelated topics that highlight the sovereign creative power of your throat chakra for affecting manifestation. As in all mystery school teachings, the full embodiment of a teaching's empowerment may only be actualized through divine love. May the union of your vision and voice be blessed and consecrated for the highest good of all, as you create a new reality through the power of your word.

The Power of Every Syllable Defines a Manifestation

My spiritual training included mastering the high art of manifestation from Egyptian, Kabbalist, and Yogic mystical lineages. Communication is a paramount skill in the art of manifestation and our physical expression of communication is experienced through the interface of language.

The languages of these mystical lineages were developed during golden ages of humanity's clear connection to the Source. This inherently allowed for the creation of highly complex scripts that reflected a more accurate vocabulary of our multidimensional quantum universe. As a High Priestess, I excelled in the scholarship of golden age languages with an eloquent mastery that accurately conveyed and empowered my divine transmission.

Student mastery could require days of practical memorization and meditation on the intonation and origin of a single alphabetical character, called a glyph, before moving on to a combination of several characters grouped together to form a syllable sound. Such mystery school traditions rigorously trained an adept to become conscious of the power seeded within every spoken word to invoke a desired thought into form by working with universal laws of magnetism.

The power of the spoken word to manifest desires into form was taught with meticulous care in our mystery schools. Before uttering a single sound of incantation, students were trained to identify the meaning of every root syllable within each word of their intentionally written statement to appropriately 'spell out' the elements of a desired manifestation.

Eventually, an adept would be invited to test the solidity of their carefully spelled out incantation by ritually speaking aloud their conscious intention. This invitation was extended when a student had successfully demonstrated parallel progress in navigating their inner world with emotional intelligence, maintaining a high level of focus through meditation, and had consecrated their throat chakra to be a vehicle for their Higher Self to speak through.

I share the history of our mystery school training as an allegory for the modern seeker to remember the full power of his or her words. Independent of whether consciously spoken or not, your every word continues to manifest the life you are living now. Impressed upon the quantum fabric of physical reality, the spoken words of your root belief systems can either create chains of lack or cornucopias of prosperity in every area of your life.

Within every present moment, you have the power to speak those words that project your Heaven on Earth reality into form. Allowing your Higher Self to guide your speech incrementally aligns you with prosperity consciousness. The voice of your Higher Self will only speak words which generate a continuous flow of abundance, supporting you to live in your full authentic expression.

Tell the story every day – word for word – about your successful Legacy of Love. I invite you to witness how *all of creation* will then imprint itself upon each syllable of your heart's desire.

The Anatomy of Your Throat Chakra

Spinning at the front and back of your neck, the throat chakra rotates as two wheels of light that connect in a funneled point at the center of your larynx. As a subtle organ structured from your Higher Self's light, the metaphysical properties of this chakra interface with the anatomy of your throat, which governs speech. The throat chakra is responsible for the physical health of your tongue, mouth, jaw, and larynx, as well as the spiritual health of your communication, authentic expression, and creative will power.

The wavelength of light emitted from the throat chakra vibrates as royal blue. Spiritually, the Royal Blue Ray represents the divine will for creative expression, clear communication, aligned leadership, self-mastery, revealing truth, and freedom of speech.

While resting, the throat chakra will appear as a sphere of royal blue light. In the act of an authentic expression, the subtle energies of the throat chakra expand far beyond the physical throat, surrounding your body in a field of high frequency light waves vibrating as every hue of blue.

In yogic anatomy, the architecture of the throat chakra's subtle energy is illustrated as a lotus flower of 16 petals that interfaces with your body. Each petal is called a vrittri and governs an aspect of communication, creativity, and manifestation. Place your finger upon the suprasternal notch at the base of your throat, just above the collarbone, and begin to tone. Feel the remarkable waves of light and sound that vibrate against the press of your fingertip.

This tiny cavern in the landscape of your throat is considered the temple gateway for the alchemical vrittri of manifestation. When focused intentions pass through this acoustic doorway as defined sound waves of your spoken desire, they then intersect with the quantum fabric of physical reality according to their encoded direction, generating new form and experience.

As you consciously activate your throat chakra, you become increasingly aware of your sovereign power to create any reality through the power of your word by witnessing what you attract and manifest. Harnessing the magick of your word requires a personal practice for becoming present to the creative power of your speech.

Consider your words before they launch your intentions into a Universe that must magnetize and arrange your reality according to how you've spelled it out to be, word for word. The first step in creating this personal practice for empowering your speech is to invite your Higher Self to always guide you in contemplation before you speak.

When you invoke your Higher Self, your tongue is increasingly drawn to express the language of your heart, which always speaks with well-chosen words that honor you, the divinity in others, and all of life. Your Higher Self loves to use language that activates and integrates The Sophia Code within you, choosing words that invoke your highest potential and draw forth the outer manifestations of your innate divine inheritance.

This inspiration to honor all of life through the power of your voice may eventually inspire you to sing your intentions. Singing can be used in your personal practice to connect the authentic expression of your heart with the power of your throat chakra. Listening to and singing along with music that includes high frequency tones, invocations, positive affirmations, and loving intentions accelerates the magick of your manifesting power.

Electro-Ecstatic Union with Your Multidimensional Self

HATHOR SPEAKS:

I am Hathor, a Divine Feminine Ascended Master devoted to awakening the highest multidimensional potential of your human experience. My Keycode 2 transmission activates your awareness to explore and expand into the quantum fabric of your miraculous human body, which is a living chalice for your unlimited Oversoul to participate in universes of form.

The infinite ever-changing variables of quantum reality provide a helpful contrast for highlighting your invincible and unchanging divine nature. To know *who you really are* within every possible circumstance is to know your true self with unshakable faith and intimacy. Incarnation is a creative vehicle that stimulates your cellular-soul growth as you discover your limitless nature through the seeming limitations of form. Therefore, your Oversoul has chosen to become human, as a vehicle for quantum self-discovery.

Your Oversoul also has the omniscient ability to orchestrate and simultaneously exist within multiple lifetimes at once. Know that as you read this codex, you are going about your purpose within other bodies as well, living out your Oversoul's divine will for creating within multiple parallel lifetimes. My Keycode 2 transmission awakens your ability to consciously engage with all your lifetimes happening now.

In addition to being human on Earth, your Oversoul has chosen to simultaneously explore incarnating within a multitude of species and forms that are vehicles for self-realization in parallel realities. All of your Oversoul's physical embodiments share a common denominator: *the electron*, which magnetizes and organizes the quantum particles that create your many forms. Every incarnation requires trillions upon trillions of electrons to assemble the hologram of your embodiment into a physical reality.

Electrons are the first vehicle of embodiment for your Oversoul's descending light manifesting as a physical experience. Every one of your bodies can be thought of as a supercomputer for your Oversoul, which provides a wealth of invaluable information carried upon your electrons. Your electrons stream a live broadcast of neurological biofeedback from your many bodies back into the light of your Oversoul. This streaming feedback loop of physical, emotional, and mental stimulation is absolutely exquisite to your Oversoul.

In my lifetime as Hathor, I consciously experienced this neurological biofeedback as ecstatic states of union with the light of my Oversoul, reveling in both the harmonious and challenging circumstances that my physical reality provided as stimulation. It was my deep curiosity about this biofeedfack that led me to a daily meditation practice for exploring my soul's consciousness carried within the electrons of my body. Every time my awareness reached out through the vehicle of my body's electrons I began to increasingly identify and experience more of my other selves in physical reality.

With every additional incarnation that I met of myself, I experienced an expanding, conscious intimacy with the unified field of my whole being. Therein, I discovered that transcendent states of bliss arose from the electro-ecstatic communion with all my selves in reality. As I tracked the breadth of this electro-ecstatic communion, it was revealed that all of my physical incarnations were intimately connected with one another's emotional, mental, and spiritual development.

With every embodiment that I became consciously awakened within, I reclaimed my full access to the electrons creating that form. I would bask in each additional body that became a part of my conscious identity. Eventually, I discovered that it was possible to dissolve and reassemble any of my bodies into another location at will or reabsorb the electrons of that embodiment back into my earthly form for cellular-soul cultivation purposes. This fluidity of form was orgasmic biofeedback for my Oversoul.

Fully activating and unifying my conscious awareness within all of my incarnations eventually dissolved every illusion of separation from myself and others, while also immersing myself in the sovereignty of my own soul. I discovered my body's electrons were an *Ark of the Covenant* vehicle to worship the divinity of my Oversoul as a sovereign hologram of Sophia.

Further, I identified that my many bodies experiencing this electro-ecstatic union within the unified field of my whole self created a multidimensional temple for learning that my Oversoul is a holographic fractal reflecting the countless souls incarnating as the one body of Sophia Christ. In this journey of remembering the powerful purpose and reality of my multidimensional self, I experienced a quantum leap awakening to the totality of my own sovereignty within Sophia.

When you access all of you – and all of you exists everywhere through your electrons – your awareness expands to finally accept and celebrate your true divine nature. Omnipresent awareness is the foundational ground for authentic intimacy. Accepting your divinity is essential for truly loving yourself. Authentic love for yourself opens the stargate of your heart, which opens the door to any world that you wish to travel to or create within.

As your awareness discovers its ability to engage with your unlimited nature through the many incarnations of your Oversoul, you realize the radical truth of *who you really are* in a multidimensional universe. Loving yourself becomes natural. Self-discovery becomes joyful. Limitations invoke your laughter and divinely inspired creativity. The world of form becomes your cosmic playground.

My Keycode 2 transmission awakens your curiosity to explore the quantum fabric of your body so that you may experience this personal freedom. To discover how to play in the quantum reality of your outer world, you must have a foundational understanding of the quantum world within you.

Witnessing the quantum universe of encoded light and energy within you opens your awareness to engage with these same particles existing within all of your incarnations and also within everything you see. That simple awareness alone is a strong foundation for you to explore your true creative power as a divine being having an intimately human experience.

True intimacy leads to joy. In the covenant of The Sophia Code, joy is an essential quality of your divine inheritance. I am here to guide you in how your body is the ultimate vehicle for communing in electro-ecstatic bliss with your sovereign multidimensional self.

The Electron Is the First Vehicle of Your Embodiment

Quantum awareness begins within the atom, and it is here you can now direct your awareness to the electron. An elementary quantum particle traveling at the speed of light, a single electron acts as a wave function of infinitely complex energy fields capable of existing in every direction and dimension simultaneously. The electron's spin of angular momentum magnetizes the majority of an atom's mass in protons and neutrons. Inside the atomic universe, it is the electron that animates the mass of your human body.

As directed by your Higher Self, it is also this same electron that is intimately involved in constructing and maintaining your many forms in parallel realities. Therefore, the electron can be understood as the access point for your awareness to directly interact with all your simultaneous lifetimes.

Traveling at the speed of light, the electron is also an access point to every probable future and instantaneously maps these innumerable outcomes. It is aware of both the infinite routes and outcomes resulting from every option that your awareness may choose to live as an experience or created reality – because it exists within all these probabilities.

These quantum characteristics of the electrons in your body are both a pure reflection and frontline manifestation revealing your divinity within form. As your omniscient Oversoul emerges from the black womb of no-thing to encode its Self into the Light Realms, an astronomical number of electrons participate in making this transfer of empty space into form possible.

As a carrier vehicle for your Oversoul, these electrons are charged with the magnetism of your Higher Self consciousness descending into a desired physical matrix. The quantum particles of potential mass and future probabilities that orchestrate the parameters of your incarnation are attracted to these magnetized electrons. These electrons create your body while simultaneously existing everywhere in the space-time continuum.

Let's explore the universe of a single human cell together. A single cell is a highly complex world of organized structures performing a miraculous variety of functions that sustain the projected hologram of your body within physical reality. At the center of this cell is a nucleus which, from our current subatomic perspective, can be experienced as an enormous temple complex for the living library of your carbon-based chromosomes. Step inside the nucleus of this single cell, as you would enter a temple.

Choose to engage with one of the 23 chromosomes before you, and walk towards it. As you approach this chromosome, readjust your vision to witness the billions upon billions of DNA strands that are perfectly woven together within the body of this chromosome. Reach out your perception and allow it to be drawn into these infinite sequences of encoded light that record and animate the functions of your human body.

Most of your DNA is made up of the same four nucleobases that endlessly spiral as a double helix staircase of sequenced information. Stepping lightly onto a rung of this ladder, you see how the mass of a single nucleobase is made of chemical elements woven together by their magnetic attraction to one another. The orbit and wave function of every electron within every atom of every chemical element weaves this magnetic attraction through the bonding act of sharing atomic orbitals with other electrons.

Now I invite you to explore how every electron is pulsing with the light and presence of your Higher Self consciousness in a unified field of radiating energy. Witness how the light of your Higher Self is anchored within every electron of your DNA, and is intimately engaged with replicating the vital details of your human body within this single cell.

As this one cell represents the inner workings of *every* cell in your human body, I invite your perception to be baptized by the radiance of your Higher Self as it animates every atom of your physiology.

To prepare for my Keycode 2 Initiation, let us review the foundational principles regarding the electron as your first vehicle for embodiment:

- The electron acts as both a physical vehicle and frontline interface for your Oversoul to descend as your Higher Self into a chosen physical matrix within the space-time continuum.

- As a vehicle for your Higher Self consciousness, the electrons in your body magnetize all that is needed to create and sustain your human physiology.

- The electron is a quantum particle traveling at the speed of light, which also acts as a wave function of infinite complex fields, and therefore exists in every direction and dimension of reality simultaneously.

- Directing your human awareness inside an electron is an access point for you to track the infinite probable future outcomes of your every decision.

- You can engage with and speak directly to all of your parallel incarnations by traveling through the electrons of your human body to where they simultaneously exist within your other selves.

KEYCODE 2
THE HATHOR INITIATION

Your Voice as an Omniscient Creator of Quantum Reality

I now prepare a ceremonial space within and around me for transformation. I call forth concentric circles of light to surround me now: an inner circle of iridescent gold light and an outer circle of royal blue light. I am now centered within these circles of light, seated upon a golden lotus throne.

I am now in ceremony – free from the constructs of space and time – where instantaneous healing and divine knowing exist.

I invoke my Higher Self to fill my body and this circle of light as the presence of my own Holy Spirit. I feel my Higher Self now descending through my crown chakra as the dove of peace that surpasses all understanding. My cells are humming in response: for invoking the Holy Spirit of my Higher Self accelerates the velocity of every electron orbiting within my body.

A radiant sun appears above my head. Encircling the sun above me are thousands of angelic wings with eyes that sing: "I Am."

In surrender, I take a deep breath in. The Holy Spirit within me rejoices with the angels. For this day is ordained by my Oversoul to liberate my awareness from the illusions of physical limitation and separation. By the grace of Sophia, I declare that this is so.

In relief, I now exhale and release all past striving for the divinity that I already am. I breathe in and the radiant sun surrounded by the rustling wings of holy eyes begins to descend through my crown chakra.

The radiant sun passes through my pineal gland.
Thousands of angel wings descend from the sun to clear a path of pure white light from my head to my heart.
I now accept the gift of *divine knowing* as my birthright for remembering The Sophia Code within me.

The radiant sun passes through my pituitary gland.
Thousands of angelic eyes singing *"Holy! Holy! Holy! I Am!"* activate the diamond light temple of my third eye.
I now accept the gift of *divine seeing* as my birthright for revealing The Sophia Code within me.

The radiant sun passes through my throat chakra.
Tongues of holy fire emerge from the eyes, speaking their blessings of light language over my voice.
I now accept the gift of *divine speech* as my birthright for activating The Sophia Code within me.

The radiant sun now anchors at the center of my heart chakra.
Brilliant wheels within wheels spin open the stargate of my heart to reveal a universe of light within me.
I now accept the gift of *divine communion* as my birthright for embodying The Sophia Code within me.

The radiant sun now expands to fill my entire body with the manna of my own Holy Spirit. I feel the resonant tone of my Higher Self speak from within me: "I Am."

I am filled with a great peace. I am now aware of my Higher Self directly communicating to my human awareness. The voice of my Higher Self speaks through my heart and resonates within every cell of my body.

I recognize that it is the presence of my Higher Self who instantly responds to my every invocation. I now invoke my Higher Self to direct the wave functions of my electrons to expand their orbit of communion and to be filled with an ever-increasing measure of my own Holy Spirit.

I am fully present now.
It is safe for my body to relax into the radiant light that I am.
Everything that I seek is orbiting within me.
There is nowhere to go but to the universe of light within me.

Embodying the omniscient presence of my Higher Self, I now declare that I am a unified field of my whole self. The Holy Spirit that I am is orbiting within me, circling above me, descending within me, arising as the holy seraphim within, and anchoring at my heart to expand and surround me in sanctuary.

My human body silently purrs in the perfect orchestration of my physiology as the final manifestation of my Higher Self's light manifesting into form. In this moment, I am somatically aware of my physiology moving at the speed of light within every electron of my DNA. In the zero still-point that I am in every present moment, I witness the universe within me.

I now invite Hathor, "She of a Thousand Voices," to join me in this ceremony as a multidimensional mentor who went ahead of me to reveal The Way before me.

Hathor, I welcome your presence to initiate me and activate Keycode 2 of The Sophia Code within my DNA now.

Hathor now appears before me as a radiant embodiment of golden light. Within the silence of her smile Hathor speaks a thousand blessings upon me, baptizing my awareness with her joyful clarity. I peer into her soft dark eyes glittering with the starlight of Sirius; Hathor's gaze activates divine love to radiate out from my core, filling every cell of my body with warmth.

Her graceful musculature is defined by a long sheer white linen dress with vibrant gold jewelry that breathes and sings as a part of her body. Upon Hathor's head lightly rests a crown of gold that rises up with the two long horns of a sky cow. Hathor's night black hair tumbles down her back and rests between her iridescent gold wings, which trail behind her. As Hathor approaches me, her every movement broadcasts the elegance of embodied joy. Her presence dances with the ease of vitality.

Hathor's smile is contagious, lifting my spirit to explore the frequency of joy from the perspective of her blissful embodiment. Framing Hathor's outline is The Hathor Star Nation: angelic beings who sing in resonate frequencies with her transmission. Their many eyes and rustling wings whirl in wheels of adoration behind her.

I feel the electrons within every cell of my body accelerating their velocity of orbit. My Higher Self responds to Hathor's presence by spontaneously speaking in a celestial tongue of golden sound waves. My inner ears are purified by these harmonic tones flowing through me.

I now prepare my heart to receive the word of Hathor initiating my consciousness. I simultaneously feel lighter and more whole. Hathor opens her arms to me. Wheels within wheels of light spiral open her heart chakra, creating a stargate of heavenly communion to flow between us.

HATHOR SPEAKS:

"I am here as your loving witness, in reflection of your worthiness to receive every blessing of your unlimited divine consciousness. You are worthy of the Holy Spirit's creative power within you to manifest heavenly realities on Earth. Just as I once walked the Earth birthing a golden age movement, you have also chosen this lifetime to participate as a leader in humanity's next Golden Age of Miracles.

"The true joy of this human lifetime is to discover how unlimited you are in your ability to heal, empower, and create any outcome that you desire, for the sheer pleasure of your self-realization. Your awareness is seeking to consciously experience and gather the momentum of your multidimensional self through an electro-ecstatic communion with all of your incarnations. Guided by your own Holy Spirit, this electro-ecstatic communion is the vehicle for creating the peace that you – and all of humanity – are seeking.

"You are here to heal and empower all of your parallel lifetimes through the initiations and activations of this single lifetime. The electrons in your body are the Ark of the Covenant vehicle for your awareness to unify all of your Oversoul's sovereign power in this lifetime. As a leader in this next Golden Age of Miracles, your authentic embodiment of this holy communion will activate others to access this same potential within themselves.

"As your guiding mentor, I declare to your consciousness that all knowledge about the quantum universe exists within your own DNA. I now invite you to directly access this encoded information, by journeying with me to the inner temples of your sub-atomic universe.

"It's safe to be curious about *who you really are*. Discovering that your body is actually a hologram of perception held in place by electrons does not devalue its worth. Rather, this discovery returns you to the elegant equation of your own divinity manifesting your many bodies through electrons. Your human form is a manifested miracle that is worthy of your highest respect. Exploring the Holy of Holies communion available to you within every electron of your body sets your consciousness free from the limitations of form.

"The Sophia Code within you can be activated for living in electro-ecstatic communion with all the manifestations of your selves giving birth to new realities. My Keycode 2 transmission mentors your awareness to access and explore your multidimensional abilities for navigating within and beyond the quantum space-time continuum. As you are destined to learn in this next golden age cycle, accessing your multidimensional gifts will be essential for leading humanity through its next evolutionary leap. I am here to mentor you as a wayshower of unlimited access to divine potential."

Hathor steps towards me. As she does, the ophanim wheels and wings of light rustle in resonance with her every movement. Raising her iridescent golden wings high above her crown, Hathor lifts a golden Ankh of Life to my lips. I immediately hear the sound of bees buzzing in my ears and the smell of frankincense fills my senses. The voice of my Higher Self instructs me to open my mouth. The Ankh of Life passes over my lips and dissolves down my tongue as sweet nectar.

Placing one hand over my heart and one hand on my crown chakra, Hathor begins to sing The Songs of Sophia over me. Her voice carries me through the light of her stargate and into the center of my own being.

I now open to receive this empowerment to activate Keycode 2 within my DNA, with the following declaration.

As a sovereign creator of the One Sophia Source, by the power of my I Am Presence, I now declare this invocation heard and answered by the unified field of my whole self:

I accept that I hold the golden keys to my Heaven on Earth.
I accept that I create my reality, by the power of my word.
My word is good, my heart is pure.
By the loving power of my pure word, I now recognize and accept my electrons as the quantum access point and vehicle for expressing the sovereign power of my unlimited divinity in human form.

At the center of my being, I locate the original blueprint zygote cell from which all the cells of my body have been replicated. I see it glowing within my heart, surrounded by an emerald green light.

I journey at the speed of light through the plasma membrane of this cell. I walk on water across an ocean of humming organelles. I pass through the great labyrinth of endoplasmic reticulum and arrive at the temple gate of my cell's nucleus. My awareness is welcomed and invited into the holy halls of my chromatin.

I adjust my eyes to the brilliant light that floods my awareness. Billions upon billions of electrons now come into focus; my awareness is illuminated by the infinite living libraries of DNA before me.

Hathor appears beside me. She guides me to focus upon the infinitely looping strand of DNA that creates chromosome 3. From this cellular perspective, chromosome 3 is enormous, and I marvel at its perfect library of information that continually regenerates parts of me. Hathor now invites me to step upon the spiral helix of my DNA's ladder. The ladder is both form and formless, a chemically bonded configured sequence whose architecture is highly activated by my presence upon it.

Hathor directs my awareness to peer closer at the DNA helix whose rungs are made up of conjoining nucleotides.

HATHOR SPEAKS:

"Reclaim your sovereign power today by blessing and affirming that these electrons are your unconditional divine inheritance from Sophia to create your DNA. As you stare into the light of these electrons, feel how the presence of your Higher Self is carried within every one of them. The totality of your whole self can be experienced within this quantum particle wave function. Reach out and bless this vehicle as a chariot for your divinity."

I step onto the nucleobase for *Adenine*. Its molecular formula is $C_5H_5N_5$.

I declare the following activation for every Adenine nucleotide of my carbon-based DNA to now be operated by the crystalline chromosomes of The Sophia Code within me.

By the power of my I Am Presence:
I now affirm, bless, and consecrate the animating light of my *Adenine* nucleotide as the Ark of the Covenant vehicle for my Higher Self's divine will.

I activate the 30 electrons orbiting as Carbon.
I activate the 5 electrons orbiting as Hydrogen.
I activate the 35 electrons orbiting as Nitrogen.

From this quantum access point I now broadcast this activation and declare the consecration of the 70 electrons within my Adenine nucleotide to every Adenine nucleotide within my human body.

From this quantum access point I now broadcast this activation and declare the consecration of the 70 electrons within my Adenine nucleotide to every Adenine nucleotide animating all my parallel incarnations across all dimensional realities.

I am filled with the presence of my Higher Self's creative power expanding and reaching through my Adenine activation into every incarnation of my multidimensional self. I take courage in this cellular-soul biofeedback, as I witness my electrons emitting a natural joy from my Higher Self traveling upon them into every direction simultaneously. Blessing the momentum of this DNA activation, I follow Hathor's lead to keep going.

I step to the right on my ladder of DNA and stand upon my nucleobase for *Thymine*. Its molecular formula is $C_5H_6N_2O_2$.

I declare the following activation for every Thymine nucleotide of my carbon-based DNA to now be operated by the crystalline chromosomes of The Sophia Code within me.

By the power of my I Am Presence:
I now affirm, bless, and consecrate the animating light of my *Thymine* nucleotide as the Ark of the Covenant vehicle for my Higher Self's divine will.

I activate the 30 electrons orbiting as Carbon.
I activate the 6 electrons orbiting as Hydrogen.
I activate the 14 electrons orbiting as Nitrogen.
I activate the 16 electrons orbiting as Oxygen.

From this quantum access point I now broadcast this activation and declare the consecration of the 66 electrons within my Thymine nucleotide to every Thymine nucleotide within my human body.

From this quantum access point I now broadcast this activation and declare the consecration of the 66 electrons within my Thymine nucleotide to every Thymine nucleotide animating all my parallel incarnations happening now across all dimensional realities.

I step up one rung on my ladder of DNA and stand upon the next nucleobase for *Guanine*. Its molecular formula is $C_5H_5N_5O$.

I declare the following activation for every Guanine nucleotide of my carbon-based DNA to now be operated by the crystalline chromosomes of The Sophia Code within me.

By the power of my I Am Presence:
I now affirm, bless, and consecrate the animating light of my *Guanine* nucleotide as the Ark of the Covenant vehicle for my Higher Self's divine will.

I activate the 30 electrons orbiting as Carbon.
I activate the 5 electrons orbiting as Hydrogen.

I activate the 35 electrons orbiting as Nitrogen.
I activate the 8 electrons orbiting as Oxygen.

From this quantum access point I now broadcast this activation and declare the consecration of the 78 electrons within my Guanine nucleotide to every Guanine nucleotide within my human body.

From this quantum access point I now broadcast this activation and declare the consecration of the 78 electrons within my Guanine nucleotide to every Guanine nucleotide animating all my parallel incarnations across all dimensional realities.

Hathor directs me to step to the left to declare the following activation upon my nucleobase of *Cytosine* within every strand of my DNA. Its molecular formula is $C_4H_5N_3O$.

I declare the following activation for every Cytosine nucleotide of my carbon-based DNA to now be operated by the crystalline chromosomes of The Sophia Code within me.

By the power of my I Am Presence:
I now affirm, bless, and consecrate the animating light of my *Cytosine* nucleotide as the Ark of the Covenant vehicle for my Higher Self's divine will.

I activate the 24 electrons orbiting as Carbon.
I activate the 5 electrons orbiting as Hydrogen.
I activate the 21 electrons orbiting as Nitrogen.
I activate the 8 electrons orbiting as Oxygen.

From this quantum access point I now broadcast this activation and declare the consecration of the 58 electrons within my Cytosine nucleotide to every Cytosine nucleotide within my human body.

From this quantum access point I now broadcast this activation and declare the consecration of the 58 electrons within my Cytosine nucleotide to every Cytosine nucleotide animating all my parallel incarnations across all dimensional realities.

I accept that I hold the golden keys to my Heaven on Earth.
I accept that I create my reality, by the power of my word.
My word is good, my heart is pure.
By the loving power of my pure word, I wholly accept that I am an omniscient creator of quantum reality as revealed by my divine inheritance of electrons.

By the loving power of my pure word, I now command my Higher Self to activate all the crystalline divine qualities of Keycode 2 of The Sophia Code within me as the new operating system for my carbon-based DNA.

I now integrate this initiation throughout my entire body, on all four levels of my Be-ing, with grace and ease. I have received more of myself today.

It is done.
It is done.
It is done.
By the power of 3, a perfect trinity: It is done.

Hathor raises her hands to me in a Golden Ray Blessing for embodying Divine Feminine Christ wisdom. She sings a closing prayer over me. I feel my Higher Self sealing these activations of The Sophia Code in the light and fire of my own Holy Spirit, across all dimensions and parallel realities.

As the electrons of my body whirl into alignment, I witness their orbital pattern as the ophanim wheels within wheels of light that exist within me, singing the praises of my own divinity. Hathor smiles at me as I recognize my own angelic nature taking flight within my human embodiment.

She places two platinum ankhs, bejeweled with sapphire eyes, into my hands. As I balance their weight and beauty upon my palms, I feel the currents of my body deeply ground into a renewed connection with the Earth. Hathor anoints my second chakra, throat chakra, third eye, and heart chakra with frankincense. I breathe in the sacred oil, and its glorious scent immediately shifts my awareness into this present moment of completion.

I look into Hathor's kind and beautiful face smiling in bliss before me. Countless Hathor angels surround her in a whirling golden radiance, embracing me in their unified field of unlimited divine love. I now accept the opportunity to mentor with Hathor as an exceptional Divine Feminine Ascended Master teacher for embodying my Higher Self's full quantum potential in human form.

With an overflowing heart, I thank you, Hathor, for blessing me with your golden Ankh of Life and awakening me to my angelic human potential. Thank you for your joyful support as my mentor, guide, and friend throughout this empowerment.

This initiation to activate Keycode 2 of The Sophia Code within me is accomplished. I now close this ceremony with appreciation, thanksgiving, and reverence in my heart for all that I have received, both known and unknown to my awareness. I thank the power of my Higher Self and the love of All That Is supporting my eternal success.

And so it is.

KEYCODE 3
"SHE OF A THOUSAND STARS"

I am *The Star* within *The Tree of Life* revealing the cosmic serpent of Sophia's light. I release all judgments and understanding about the nature of reality so that my innocence may guide me to the womb of no-thing. It is here that I increase my embodiment of living wisdom by allowing what is arising to inform my ever-present now, for the liberation of all beings.

Green Tara's Ascension
in the Sirius Star Nation

GREEN TARA SPEAKS:

I WELCOME YOU TO the sanctuary of my Keycode 3 transmission. I am the *Radiant One* and Divine Feminine Christ teacher: Green Tara. My Sophia embodiment title is "She of a Thousand Stars" in reflection of my interstellar diplomacy, for which I am renowned throughout the cosmos.

In Tibetan Buddhism, my embodiment as Green Tara is honored as the first manifestation of Sophia's light. Yet, my journey to you as an Ascended Master mentor began in a human form in the Sirius star system on a planet called Karnak. To my people *Karnak* means "Secret Chambers of the Heart."

For many lifetimes I walked on the planet Karnak, just as you now walk the Earth. I endured lifetimes of suffering to become an embodied vehicle of transcendent compassion. I share the story of my ascension in Sirius so that you may know that I understand the human experiences of your own journey through form.

For eons of spiritual evolution on Karnak, we waged a bitter war upon ourselves, exploring the alchemical synthesis for the dark and light dualities of our collective free will power. We dissected our vulnerability by examining how our hearts would emotionally evolve and generate compassion through the testing ground of escalating planet-wide atrocities.

In essence, we were a people torn over how to evolve as a compassionate race of beings. We tortured ourselves for our own mastery. We created the demons of our greatest fears to stare us in the face. As free will creators, we discovered what the sovereign power of our divine inheritance truly meant. Just as humanity now struggles to ascend beyond war consciousness, we as a people struggled for eons to transcend our needless harm and destruction of form in order to gain knowledge and wisdom.

I lived on Karnak for every defining juncture along this evolutionary timeline. I suffered in an astounding amount of incarnations, exploring my ability to remain in communion with the Holy Spirit within me regardless of all outer circumstances. Lifetime after lifetime, I took *bodhisattva* vows, committing myself to become an awakened, embodied solution for transmuting the collective suffering of an entire population and planet. It was my people that birthed the spiritual concept of being a bodhisattva on Karnak and delivered that practice to Earth.

The grace of Sophia descended at the height of our collective suffering when She appointed council members from The Sophia Dragon Tribe to incarnate in generational waves upon Karnak. With a tipping-point ratio of Golden Dragon teachers incarnating as awakened masters, the many free will experiments causing an epidemic of war finally gave way to a shift in collective common sense.

The Way home to embodying planetary-wide peace began as the first golden age cycle on our planet. It would take the rise and fall of many additional golden age cycles for our people to fully heal the "Secret Chambers of the Heart" of Karnak. From this evolutionary journey arose the Sirian alchemical resurrection teachings that Isis and Osiris are known for on your planet.

Just as I had incarnated through eons of suffering, I then committed to incarnational cycles as an embodied master of Sophia consciousness for the benefit of my people, my planet, and all beings. In my final embodiment on Karnak, I lived as a celebrated Divine Feminine Christ teacher in a golden age cycle called *Shambhallah.*

The Golden Age of Shambhallah on Karnak created such an extraordinary blueprint for embodying divine love, through a balanced feminine and masculine heart intelligence, that our planet ascended in its sovereignty beyond the gravitational limitations of orbiting the star, Sirius C. In the collective rapture of divine love, we merged into the sun of our solar system.

We as a people and a planet continued to live a physical existence at a much higher dimensional reality of light, joy, and purpose. Our ascended civilization became revered as The Sirian Star Nation and was initiated into the interstellar Family of Light with the honor of becoming a contributing diplomatic High Council.

Our Sirian civilization provides a system for tracking the evolutionary timelines of incarnating souls across quantum reality. As a result of my steadfast commitment to embodying sovereignty and compassion in all of my lifetimes, the history of my many incarnations on Karnak became legendary. The contributions that the Holy Spirit of my Higher Self made as a Divine Feminine Christ embodiment were recognized as an essential contribution to the ascension of Karnak.

As such, at the height of Shambhallah's glory, my service in Sirius was complete. I received my final rites of initiation and became an Ascended Master. Within the ecstatic bliss of my ascension, I was called by the voice of Sophia into this High Council and was invited to become an evolutionary Keycode embodiment for The Sophia Dragon Tribe.

Sophia spoke to me of a twin planet to Karnak called Sophia Gaia, also known as your Mother Earth. In honor of those who went before me preparing The Way for Karnak's ascension, I chose to be initiated as a Golden Dragon teacher for the ascension of humanity and Sophia Gaia.

My most well-known lineage on Earth is currently Tibetan Buddhism, which was originally seeded in India. However, signs of my involvement within other cultures can be found around the world, including emanations such as Celtic Tara of Ireland and as *Star Woman* to the Cheyenne people of North America.

Descending through my light body into northern India, I appeared to a small community of Shivite masters, whose purified hearts and inner eyes were open to receive my Sacred Heart blueprints for living Sophia Christ consciousness in form. I provided direct revelations on the interwoven principles of universal laws, quantum reality, magnetic prosperity, regenerative immortal health, spiritual alignment with the one universal Source, and the bhakti of unconditional divine love. My Sirian teachings transmitted to these Shivite masters became the foundation for Vedic practices that arose in the Indus Valley Civilization.

Eventually the heart of my teachings would be swept into the momentum of Buddhism and carried to the openhearted indigenous people of Tibet and Nepal. There I seated my consciousness upon the throne of the Himalayas, transmitting The Way of Shambhallah to a listening civilization. I am most known on Earth through this Tibetan Buddhist lineage that honors me as *The Mother of All Buddhas* and as *The Swift Saviouress* of liberation and compassion. There are many practices in this lineage that originate from my Sirian civilization, including the tracking of incarnational cycles for recognizing exemplary spiritual leadership.

When you feel drawn to me as a mentor, this indicates that you are directly connected to an evolutionary arc of secret Sophia lineages that originated from Sirius and beyond. Your many incarnations reflect our shared journey in seeding Sirian ascension teachings on Sophia Gaia, to prepare humanity for this next Golden Age of Miracles. It is also an indication that your Higher Self is ready to shine the ascending starlight of your divinity in the vehicle of your human body. Just as I have walked The Way ahead of you – *you* are preparing to become an Ascended Master as well.

My presence awakens your own direct connection and involvement with the many interstellar diplomatic councils working together for your planet's peace. Your Mother Earth is an essential Keycode for the ascending universal body of Sophia Christ. My Keycode 3 transmission helps you navigate the deluge of challenging feelings that arise on such a heroic human journey to reconcile your species as stewards of peace. It is safe for you to reveal and embody the cosmic code of Sophia's covenant for the liberation of humanity through the remembrance of your own sovereignty.

Your Eco-Ascension Studies within Sophia Gaia

The divine qualities of Keycode 3 are connected with anchoring the descent of heavenly realities into form. As a Divine Feminine Christ embodiment for this planet, my overlighting transmission encodes the crystalline ascension teachings from multiple star systems into the Akashic Record library of your Mother Earth.

I am an active ambassador for Sophia Gaia, amplifying and broadcasting the Divine Feminine wisdom that arises from the perfect intelligence of her ecosystems. I guide humanity in its role as both a steward and student of her grace. Those souls drawn to my teaching embodiment are part of an ancient lineage of angelic guardians for Sophia Gaia, who have participated in this planet's ascension for millennia.

Let us be clear: the original Shambhallah teachings that I brought to this planet do not devalue the powerful choice to incarnate into form. Rather, my transmission reveals that your body and your planet are holy vehicles for awakening your awareness to the holiness of *all form;* for form is the one body of Christ within Sophia's consciousness. I represent the Divine Feminine Christ light of Sophia's descent as the *Shekinah* into form: the Holy Spirit that manifests your body, and this planet, to reveal Her divine nature within all things.

Those magnetized to my Green Tara practices have a relationship with nature as a living intelligence that informs their consciousness. My initiates know that animals speak and teach through telepathy. Those embodying my teachings are drawn to indigenous practices that honor the elemental devas and guardian spirits tending to the natural balance of Sophia Gaia's countless ecosystems. Honoring this bridge of eco-communion naturally arises within the hearts of my initiates. Therefore, those drawn to mentor with me often have a strong inclination to shamanic practices that include ritual, ceremony, divination, offerings, altars, and consecrations.

Your planet is a highly sought after academy for environmental ascension studies. Lightworkers from across the universe apply for the great honor to study planetary eco-ascension templates within the body of Sophia Gaia. Mother Earth's vast curriculum for eco-ascension studies includes tracking the spiritual evolution of millions of species, both seen and unseen at higher dimensional frequencies; a multitude of complex ecosystem relationships; as well as the etheric astral planes and Inner Earth civilizations that interface with Sophia Gaia's body.

Sophia Gaia is an Oversoul completely dedicated to her divine service of creating space and form for initiates to experience and remember their sovereign Christ light. As a goddess of overflowing abundance and generosity, she creates unlimited space for billions of species to explore their free will and limitless divine nature by incarnating within her body.

Your planet was birthed within the heart womb of a Sophia Dragon. As such, Mother Earth is a holographic matrix of seraphim DNA perpetually giving birth to environments that likewise provide space and time for you to explore your own ability to birth the divine will of Sophia into form. Therefore, incarnating within Sophia Gaia's consciousness mentors you as an immaculate birther of reality.

When you feel magnetically drawn to my Keycode 3 transmission, you are consciously awakening to your divine inheritance for creating Heaven on Earth containers that birth new paradigm realities into form. My presence activates your awareness to recognize the many ways that Sophia Gaia's eco-ascension curriculum is directly informing your personal journey of ascension.

While you are here in human form, you are simultaneously participating in her ascension. As you live in daily appreciation for this miraculous opportunity, your spiritual journey matures to embody Sophia Christ consciousness for the benefit of your entire planet and all beings learning alongside you.

In your mentor relationship with Mother Earth, you are ultimately participating in an *interstellar* ascension story for the reconciliation of the one body of Sophia Christ that inhabits all form. Although your ascension is a personal journey, it is also connected to evolving a much larger unified field of the One Self. Your Mother Earth is an extraordinary Divine Feminine Christ teacher for learning how to gracefully and generously embody this same spiritual commitment to serve others as yourself, just as she does.

My Keycode 3 transmission supports your awareness to make the quantum leap discovery that the more you consecrate your personal life to the happiness of your whole cosmic Self — which is to say for the happiness all beings within the one ascending body of Sophia Christ — the more your human journey of ascension will become deeply fulfilling for you.

A Vajrayana Vehicle for Embodying Your Holy Spirit

As Green Tara, my Vajrayana Dakini Guru embodiment serves as the highest office of the primordial mother's *Secret Dakini* lineage: to reveal the totality of Sophia's ineffable mysteries as the unlimited space of no-thing within the container of form. I mentor your awareness through direct revelations of Sophia that are whole and complete visions. My presence instantaneously dissolves your obstacles of inner resistances and activates your will power to embody the truth of your divinity.

When you are drawn to mentor with me as an Ascended Master, your Higher Self is guiding you to the Vajrayana pathways for awakening your consciousness through the *innocence* of your Higher Self. Your innocent nature knows the omniscient totality of your divinity, beyond all reasoning and qualification for it. My transmission awakens the qualities of Keycode 3 that support your awareness to move beyond all limitations of understanding and embody your sovereignty through downloads of divine knowing.

Initiating you beyond the insatiable need for understanding, the *Dakinis* are my supporting angelic order that transmits complete Rays of Wisdom for instantaneously activating Keycode 3 within you. They broadcast the totality of Sophia's unconditional love for you as mighty guardian angels of your innocence, appearing to you on the inner and outer planes.

Dakinis act as the lightning bolts for self-realization: they appear in both wrathful and heavenly embodiments of important divine qualities for awakening you to your sovereignty. In the glory of her Holy Spirit's fire, a wrathful Dakini activates a will power within you to overcome your unconscious attachments to suffering and self-hatred. Adorned in mantles of naked beauty, a heavenly Dakini assists your human awareness *to become vulnerable* and surrender to the light and sovereign creative power of your unlimited Higher Self.

My Green Tara embodiment is the complete blueprint of all Dakini Light Rays arising from my one consciousness as the manifested Sophia. My emerald skin represents the prosperous and powerful lifeforce of Sophia's transcendent wisdom taking action as the Holy Spirit. I offer a complete Vajrayana blueprint for awakening your own embodiment of Sophia's totality within you. Everything associated with me – the Dakini angels, my body, my name, and my mantras – acts as a unified field that broadcasts complete revelations to access the two-fold path for embodying your own Holy Spirit.

The Sanskrit root of my name Tara is *'Tar'*, which is a seed syllable that activates your awareness to seek me as a mentor for surrendering to and integrating spontaneous self-realization beyond understanding. *Tar* is also a root syllable in the Sanskrit words for *tree, to cross over,* and *star.* My name Tara is a vehicle that unifies this trinity of meaning into a single word mantra that reveals a two-fold path of Vajrayana awakening.

DESCENDING PATH OF THE HOLY SPIRIT

The first neurological pathway of Tara illuminates the descending Holy Spirit into form and is called *The Star that Crosses Over and Becomes a Tree of Life.* This pathway reveals how to receive, ground, manifest, embody, and act upon cosmic light rays of Sophia's wisdom descending into a physical reality.

In this first path *The Star* represents the following: the Holy Spirit of your Higher Self descending into form, wisdom teachings from the Ascended Masters and Star Nations coming to Earth, and the sovereign Sophia Christ light that arises from the limitless space of no-thing to create and exist within all form. *The Tree of Life* points to this descending energy creating the holy vehicle of your human body and that of your planet Earth and, ultimately, the holiness of all universal form that can only exist within Sophia.

ASCENDING PATH OF THE HOLY SPIRIT

My Keycode 3 transmission simultaneously activates a second neurological pathway of the ascending Holy Spirit called *The Tree of Life that Connects Every Star.* This second pathway is a tantric vehicle for your awareness to commune with the ascending Holy Spirit within your body and within All That Is.

The ascending pathway of the Holy Spirit is forever climbing up The Tree of Life to worship its own divinity as a sovereign creator of divine will within the very forms it is creating new realities through. Your human body contains a microcosmic blueprint of this ascending pathway, as revealed by the three major neurological channels designed for the Holy Spirit to rise up within you as the kundalini lifeforce.

Therefore, the second pathway resonating within my name Tara is the journey of your ascension in form: which is to become ever-increasingly conscious of your communion with the Holy Spirit of your Higher Self rising up within your human body and animating all form. Although ascent is likened to an upward flow, when carried on the vehicle of your electrons, ascending energy radiates into all directions simultaneously. Therefore, as the kundalini lifeforce of your Holy Spirit ascends, it activates your consciousness to simultaneously expand further and further *within you* to commune with the light of your own Holy Spirit.

Expanding into the universe within you is paralleled with your consciousness expanding far into the cosmos of form. The second pathway of ascension in form activates your awareness to stretch out your arms as The Tree of Life to receive a Universe of direct knowledge, wisdom, and divine love. In the ascent of your awareness, the Holy Spirit connects you to The Star within the Earth and The Star of all ascended civilizations within every star system of this universe. To know your legacy of participation in the ascension of form is to know your home in the universal family as the one body of Sophia Christ.

The two-fold tantric pathway of my Vajrayana transmission mentors you in completing all guided actions to fulfill the divine will of the Holy Spirit within you. Activating the divine qualities of Keycode 3 fulfills the Holy Spirit's descending requests for heavenly visions to manifest on Earth through your human life. Keycode 3 also activates your ascending awareness to consecrate your relationship with form as a holy communion with and in joyful service to the Holy Spirit within your planet, your cosmic family, and the universes of Sophia.

131

The Liberating Power of OM TARE TUTTARE TURE SOHA

A Sanskrit mantra is a tantric vehicle for commanding transformation in your awareness through the power of your voice. Your Higher Self guides you to use the power of mantras for self-actualizing peace. Mantras gather your divided consciousness back into a unified field of light that focuses you solely upon the divinity within you.

Every quantum leap in your spiritual evolution requires a next-level relinquishment of your attachments to suffering. You cannot experience the heaven within you when you are gripping onto the hell of suffering. When you suffer, speaking a mantra softens that grip. Its sound waves set forth a guiding intention for your awareness to focus upon the light of Sophia within you as your salvation. It is only in Her Presence of unconditional divine love that the root of all your attachments to suffering may be reconciled by Her undivided holy nature.

In the Tibetan Buddhist cosmology, I represent the first embodiment of Sophia's Emerald Ray of Abundant Life arising from the primordial space of no-thing. From the unified field of my Green Tara embodiment there are an additional *21 Emanations of Tara* that are revealed as a motherboard of Sophia's divine qualities and rays of wisdom. Each of my Tara emanations are an embodiment of liberation from your every attachment to suffering, harmonizing your awareness with the light of divinity within you.

Although there are many sanskrit mantras for each of my 21 Emanations, they all arise from the one pearl of my Green Tara mantra: OM TARE TUTTARE TURE SOHA. I invite you to explore how the vehicle of this mantra opens the door to our mentor relationship. When you speak these words aloud, you join the momentum of other Lightworkers on this planet and others, who are activating their own divinity, even amidst great suffering.

It may feel difficult to accept, but the solution to your suffering is far simpler than your wounds would have you believe. My foundational mantra is a pathway for healing beyond the obstacles of understanding. It is seeded with a multi-ray transmission of Sophia's light for liberating your greatest fears and taking up the mantle of Sophia Christ consciousness.

As you speak my mantra, I stand in solidarity with you. When you invoke me for help, I bless you with my omniscient support and divinely intervene with miracles for every area of your life. Let's step inside the vehicle of my mantra together, to feel how I am holding you within every seed syllable of OM TARE TUTTARE TURE SOHA.

<u>OM</u> TARE TUTTARE TURE SOHA

Toning OM invokes my presence as a guide through your suffering and as a mentor for your happiness.

OM is the sound wave that appears as Sophia's heart womb gives birth to the light. It is also the sound of Sophia's omniscient voice sustaining the quantum fabric of Her universes. Toning the sound of OM clears your mind of negative projections designed to keep your awareness from these ineffable mysteries of Sophia that are foundational for your peace.

When you speak OM in my Green Tara mantra, you invite me as a guide for returning to Sophia's light and unconditional love as your only resolution to all suffering. In the Tibetan Buddhist cosmology, I am invoked as *The Saviouress* who carries you across an ocean of suffering to the shores of enlightenment. Notice that the defining syllable of enlightenment is the *'light.'* You can visualize me as both a Saviouress blueprint within you and as an Ascended Master mentor for guiding you to the shores of Sophia's light in any moment of suffering.

The first syllable, OM, opens the space within you to admit that you need help for reconciling your attachments to suffering. Admittance is the first step for overcoming the painful resistances that keep you from your own vulnerability. However painful it may feel, admittance welcomes the wisdom of your vulnerability that is always guiding you to seek the relief of support. In your vulnerability, you recognize that transforming your relationship with suffering requires the assistance of a divine power that is *greater* than your attachment to that suffering.

Asking for the help of that divine power is a clear prayer that allows immediate support to flood your awareness. If all you can utter is "Help!" in a moment of despair, know that I instantly respond by guiding your awareness to that pathway of divine power within you. My presence softens your defenses to receive unconditional divine love. I help you welcome the presence of your Higher Self and *all* your spiritual guides deeply supporting your journey back to the inner light of self-reconciliation.

I know The Way ahead as a guide to your happiness that exists beyond all suffering. When you invoke my support through the tone of OM, my right foot instantly steps forward and I am by your side. My presence activates the divine qualities of Keycode 3 within your crystalline chromosomes, to awaken *The Swift Saviouress* within your heart, who is ever in communion with the light of Sophia.

OM **TARE** TUTTARE TURE SOHA

The seed syllable TARE declares that you are laying down your attachments to suffering in exchange for non-circumstantial happiness and reconciliation with your divinity.

You are a sovereign being with a free will to choose any belief system according to your desire. However, the root of all suffering arises from the belief that divinity is imperfect and has failed you. You can visualize this root belief system planted in the words *"divinity is fundamentally flawed."* From this root belief springs forth branches of viral belief systems that construct entire worlds of suffering for you to explore in your mind the illusion that life is unsafe.

Entertaining any viral belief in the flawed nature of divinity and life creates instantaneous suffering in your mind. Suffering is a shocking experience for the innocence of your human heart, which fundamentally knows itself as the throne of your Higher Self's divinity.

When your free will embraces contradictory belief systems about divinity, your human awareness agonizes over how to negotiate and organize these illusions within the limited constructs of dualistic understanding. Left unchecked, the agony that is felt when attempting to resolve unresolvable illusions eventually becomes unbearable to your ego, which then launches a thousand ships of accusations upon the perfection of divinity.

These projections resist and punish divinity as a failure responsible for the root cause of your suffering. Therefore, the root of all suffering is a *divided Self:* your limited understanding at war with the truth of your perfect divinity and the perfection of life revealing that divinity to you.

TARE invokes my miraculous intervention to help you *let go* of controlling your suffering through the ego's demands of limited understanding and to reestablish trust in your Higher Self, who is always guiding you back to an omniscient knowledge of your divinity. TARE also invokes personal willingness and the courage to reestablish trust in the divinity of life that is perfectly orchestrating your greatest relief from suffering in all ways, always, regardless of all personally held illusionary beliefs and outer physical appearances of samsara.

A direct knowing of your divinity dissolves the excruciating attachments and chains of confusion created by viral belief systems that cause you to suffer needlessly for who you are. TARE is a bridge for walking away from disbelief, hate, and resentment – and crossing over – back into the light of your true nature. On the other side of this bridge is the happiness that exists beyond all suffering: the home of your own self-realized divinity.

OM TARE **TUTTARE** TURE SOHA

TUTTARE is a seeded sound wave of self-love that liberates your awareness from the eight great fears by taking refuge in your own divinity.

Your experience of suffering is quite real and sacred – and is in no way minimized by the illusion of form's physicality. Your holographic reality is perfectly designed to stimulate every physical, emotional, and mental aspect of your human body. This includes your free will ability to suffer the agony of your mind through the neurological biofeedback of form. You may choose to experience suffering for your evolution and for the evolution of other souls on their ascension journey; your soul chooses this suffering to discover the unlimited reign of its free will.

When you choose to experience viral belief systems in physical reality, you experience life as a holographic living hell. When an entire collective consciousness of a species chooses to participate in these viral belief systems together, there is an amplified momentum for collective agony, which can manifest as war, rape, and annihilation consciousness on a planet.

Humanity's next quantum leap in releasing its attachment to suffering is to remember that what it thinks it is experiencing as physical reality is actually a holographic illusion. How can you cut the pure space of emptiness that is the true nature of all form? How can you divide light rays of a single electron that exists everywhere simultaneously?

Yes, hellish deeds, realities, and realms exist upon the Earth – but look through your inner eyes to witness that they are a physical illusion nonetheless. However, this in no way diminishes humanity's experience of suffering within the collective mind creating this simulacrum of form.

Attachments to suffering are conceived when your ego feels betrayed by the emotions that naturally arise from the experience of pain. There is nothing wrong with feeling your emotions as a natural indicator of suffering; but when the ego decides that these feelings are *attacking you* it responds with fear to keep you from feeling any further, blacking out your common sense with defensive behavior.

As your awareness is blacked out by the powerful defenses of your unconscious ego, you temporarily forget that it was always your sovereign free will to choose the experience of suffering for your evolution. An attachment to suffering becomes deeply rooted with every attempt to use the limited power of your localized human understanding to reconcile the pain of your suffering in this contracted state of denial and defensiveness.

In the shock of suffering there are the *eight great fears* that can take root in your mind as harmful addictions to pain. These eight great fears are designed to separate you from your happiness and the truth of your sovereign divinity and are as follows: ignorance, attachment, hatred, arrogance, jealousy, miserliness, doubt, and projections.

TUTTARE invokes my presence guiding your awareness beyond the eight great fears that keep you as a prisoner wrestling with understanding. I walk you back to faith and the direct knowing that it is your divine inheritance to live in a happiness beyond suffering. TUTTARE is a free will command that when spoken aloud allows me to intercede on your behalf.

When toning TUTTARE I can assist your awareness and corresponding neurological pathways to make quantum leaps for dissolving your attachments to the eight great fears. In my Tibetan Buddhist lineage, this is called taking refuge in my overlighting presence. However, know that when you take refuge with me through TUTTARE, I am actually guiding your awareness in how to take refuge in the divinity of your own Higher Self.

Embodying my Keycode 3 calls forth the self-compassion, courage, and assertion to embrace the demons that arise within the body of your mind. Awakening the divine qualities of my Keycode 3 liberates your awareness from these eight great fears by activating their corresponding virtues of direct knowing, unconditional self-love, self-forgiveness, self-knowing, self-communion, prosperity, faith, and omniscient awareness.

Regardless of all circumstantial fears, the heavenly reality of *emptiness and bliss* exists in unlimited measure within the universe of your body, heart, mind, and soul. I tell you the truth: *there is so much heaven to focus upon within you,* yet, humanity is addicted to the hellish creations of its collective mind. In this lifetime, your Higher Self is guiding you to embody a great happiness that is also for the liberation of all beings.

OM TARE TUTTARE **TURE** SOHA

TURE declares your oneness with all beings as the root of your happiness that is sovereign from all attachments to suffering.

Humanity's addiction to using dualistic polarities for transformational alchemy creates a collective need to scapegoat an *'other'* into the role of an enemy or perpetrator. As you loosen your own grip upon duality, you will witness the miracle of demonic energies within humanity's collective ego instantaneously transmute back into a state of all-consuming love.

Your greatest happiness arises from releasing all judgments about anything or anyone as 'other' than yourself. Only the unconditional love of Sophia Christ consciousness, also known as Buddha consciousness, initiates your awareness to the true happiness that exists when worshiping the One Self, beyond all justification or conditional circumstances. Divine service that is inspired from this self-knowing leads to an invincible joy. It is possible to serve the light of humanity with happiness and compassion, without suffering for it.

Oneness with all beings is a Sophia Christ consciousness that anchors in your mind through successive initiations of embodying your Higher Self. Every time you speak TURE you are anchoring more of your Higher Self's light within your human body and awareness. There is no need to force or rush the development of your Buddha mind, for the light of Sophia that already exists within you *is* this consciousness.

TURE invokes your free will to lay down all understanding of how to do anything, which releases the need for controlling yourself with the eight great fears. Surrendering to the light of Sophia within you creates the space for your Higher Self to guide you in experiencing both your sovereignty and oneness with all beings through successive stages of deepening maturity and integrative self-acceptance.

The ego only releases its grip on attacking or judging an 'other' outside of you when your Higher Self is given permission to be your guiding light. TURE grounds the heavenly reality of your Higher Self's mind into your human awareness so that you may experience the safety, grace, and prosperity of living in oneness with all beings, beyond the poverty of judgment.

OM TARE TUTTARE TURE **SOHA**

SOHA commands the blueprint of this mantra to activate your DNA and consecrate your Sacred Heart to live in happiness, for the liberation of all beings.

SOHA plants the seeds of my mantra in your heart. From these seed syllables grow a garden of new belief systems that flower as sovereign creations in your life. Living a peaceful and prosperous embodiment, free from attachments to suffering, is the greatest compassion and divine service you can offer humanity.

SOHA consecrates *all* your emotions as vehicles of your divine consciousness arising with important information for your awareness. This seed syllable relieves the agony that causes your ego to attack the emotions that naturally arise throughout cycles of self-revelation birthing you beyond duality. The self-compassion of your Sophia Christ consciousness is your divine inheritance, and SOHA commands that compassion to download and take root within you.

As you speak the sound of SOHA, may you feel the winds of my abundant blessings sweeping through your awareness, awakening you to the light of Sophia that is already *enlightening* you from within. This final seed syllable seals the momentum of goodness that arises from speaking my mantra within your heart.

SOHA illuminates the pathway of divine power within you so that you may always remember to take refuge in the radiance of your own Higher Self. When you release your attachments to suffering, you create space in your heart and mind to be guided by the power of your holy innocence, which is a divine quality of your Higher Self.

Your Innocence Is the Guide and Guardian

The innocence of your heart is a precious jewel that shines as your greatest gift to the world. Nothing can compare in wealth, wisdom, or knowledge to the innocence of your pure heart. A pure heart has nothing to prove, as it abides in a continuous state of wonder at the world. Questions arise from the stillness of your innocence without forethought and ego. Questions arise for the very delight of marveling at All That Is.

There is a spontaneous exchange of truth for those who relate to one another through innocence. Your innocence is a *Holy of Holies* curiosity that invites miracles. Jesus spoke of inviting your innocence to step forward as the master within you when he said: 'Bring the little children unto me, for theirs is the Kingdom of God.' (Mk10:13-6)

Truth is not feared by those who take refuge within their innocence; for truth is all they seek to see within all things, as the essential nature of divine love. Those who embody the innocence of their heart often wonder why others turn away from their gaze, curled over in the fears of yesterday. For those who embody their innocence can see this same innocence within others, regardless of all circumstances and beyond how others judge themselves.

The paradoxical pearl of innocence is that its absolute vulnerability is invincible: for the guardian of innocence is its own holy, *indivisible* nature. Innocence cannot be bought or manipulated or torn apart. I invite those who have suffered in body and mind from the imbalances and violations of others to take courage – for your innocence can never be stolen from you. Your innocence remains steadfast within you, waiting for the storms to recede, safely hidden within *The Rose* of your heart.

As the Breath of Life, your innocence remains pure throughout every incarnation. Innocence always awaits its rightful recognition from you. It can never change or leave you, and can only be temporarily forgotten. It is safe for you to take up the mantle of your invincible innocence and be baptized by your own vulnerability.

Reconciling with your innocence requires forgiving others – *and yourself.* The act of forgiveness does not mean you are condoning harmful behavior. Forgiveness is the willingness to free yourself from the past controlling your life in the present moment. Your willingness to release the past through forgiveness invites you into a clear space of surrender. In this space of surrender arises a creative hunger to know your true self beyond definitions of your previous suffering. Forgiveness allows you to seek out new experiences that accurately reflect your original innocence, free of the past.

I invite you to commit to an essential practice of self-forgiveness for reclaiming the sovereign power of your innocence. It is impossible to receive the fullness of your divine inheritance when you judge yourself for past suffering. Bless the teachings that came to you through suffering, be generous and forgive yourself, taking refuge in your divinity – which was never lost.

Likewise, forgiving others is essential for your freedom. Carrying the trespasses of others upon your back denies your own freedom in this lifetime and into the next. Lifetime after lifetime, many souls choose to repeat incarnations of sorrow for millennia because they believe their innocence was stolen forever and that to withhold forgiveness will somehow make what was *wrong* right again.

In truth, *nothing can make a wrong right,* for there is nothing right or reasonable in attacking the innocence of pure consciousness. A wrong can only be understood and dismissed as the insanity of those who suffer and therefore forgiveness sets you free from being entangled with this insanity. This is why Jesus prayed: "... forgive them Father, for they know not what they do." (Lk 23:34a)

When you believe that your innocence is damaged or even lost forever, your awareness temporarily slips into this dark insanity of suffering, and blindly lashes out on others. Yet even in this great suffering, the light of your Higher Self is within you, ever ready to respond to your vulnerable requests for help in remembering your innocence. In fact, making this humble request for help to your Higher Self is the first turning back to the truth of your invincible innocence. As your awareness reaches out into the vulnerable unknown for help, it is your own innocence that always responds with solutions rooted in unconditional divine love.

Claiming your sovereignty reinstates your innocence as a gift and guide for creating a new paradigm in this world. Embodying your innocence guides others who are grappling to free themselves from their grip upon samsara. It is your divine right to invoke your sovereign power and create heavenly realities on Earth that are a sanctuary for innocence to flourish.

Your human awareness does not need to have all the answers and understand everything to be perfect. Your innocence is your perfection and also your perfect guide to all divine solutions. For it is your natural curiosity, appreciation, and wonder about the miracle of life that frees your awareness to download these divine solutions without effort.

Your innocence knows its own beauty through its wonder. That wonder is the medicine for your relationship with life. You are meant to feel wildly alive, every day, in every moment. Your original design is that of an astounding capacity to feel joy, bliss, yes – even ecstasy, every day. But, most important is the *peace* that deeply satisfies you by honoring your innocent nature.

The delight of your heart is the exhale of Sophia. You complete Her breath when your innocence delights in the gift of your life. You were designed by Sophia to appreciate the gift of life as a dialogue with your own Holy Spirit. This ongoing dialogue continually honors, humbles, and empowers those who abide in their innocent nature. Innocence always chooses the spiral path of unconditional divine love, which honors your own heart in ever-increasing measure, within all circumstance.

The only real dialogue we can have with one another begins with knowing nothing but the wonder before a single thought may arise. It is safe for you to dialogue with life through the openness of your heart. In that vulnerable space, your innocence can only magnetize to you the wondrous blessings of your divine inheritance and those who are here to co-create Heaven on Earth with you in this lifetime.

KEYCODE 3
THE GREEN TARA INITIATION

It Is Safe to Create Your Heaven on Earth

I now prepare a ceremonial space within and around me for transformation. I call forth concentric circles around me: an inner circle of iridescent white light and an outer circle of emerald green light surround me now. I am now centered within these concentric circles of light, seated upon a white lotus throne. My white lotus throne floats upon a still ocean of gold and white light.

I am now in ceremony – free from the constructs of space and time – where instantaneous healing and divine knowing exist.

Beyond space and time, I see the warm black womb of Sophia breathing in that same stillness. I remember that I am always here in this present moment of both form and formless. I remember that I am always here in this present moment of stillness and motion.

I feel the quiet and pleasant sensation of curiosity that is my innocent nature witnessing and exploring this present moment. I remember how familiar this present moment feels and I exhale. The sweet scents of jasmine, lotus, and rose permeate the air around me.

I am now aware of a warm golden light emanating from a star at the center of my heart. I breathe in and expand the star's light to fill my entire body with its glow. I am now filled with a golden energy that expands my feeling body in abundant waves of radiance.

I hear the sound of HUM emanating from my heart in continuous rounds of inner toning. In this present moment, I remember this voice and its familiar timbre. The sound of this voice toning HUM fills me with a profound love for myself.

I now easily recognize the voice chanting HUM within my heart as my Higher Self. My awareness opens with this recognition and the sound of HUM becomes even clearer and broadens within me.

HUM is the sound wave of my invincible, unified field of divine love as spoken into form by my Higher Self. I am indivisible divine love and I am loved entirely by the Holy Spirit within me. My innocent nature easily responds to this love and eagerly invites more love to flow in now.

I invite the full presence of my Higher Self, vibrating within my heart, to now merge with my awareness. My Higher Self immediately responds to this invitation and fills my ceremonial space with the full presence of the Holy Spirit *within me.* I am now aware of every electron in my body, and in the air all around me, pulsing with the frequency of my Higher Self.

In the unified field of my awareness, I now invite Green Tara to assist me in this ceremonial activation.

My attention is directed to notice that in the far distance, within the warm black womb of Sophia, a shooting star slowly rises from the no-thing. In harmony with the sound of HUM toning within me, I hear the voice of the shooting star softly whisper to my consciousness.

GREEN TARA SPEAKS:

"Listen to my voice guiding you from within this distant shooting star as you witness it arising from the no-thing. This star is my radiant heart – the first vehicle from which I speak to your awareness. In our communion you will feel and know more of your true self. It is safe for your innocent nature to play with me.

"As your eyes focus upon the star's trail of light, you may also feel the presence of a great tree surrounding your body now. I am speaking directly to your awareness within this tree as well, embracing you in divine love. Invite the long roots of my *Tree of Life* to descend past your lotus throne and deeply anchor into the ocean of gold and white light upon which you float.

"Keep your eyes focused within my star as you continue to feel my Tree of Life rapidly grow around you. Your body can relax and be held within this tree. Ring after ring of golden light rises up from your roots, forming a solid trunk of my heavenly awareness around you.

"My shooting star is drawing closer to your sight. Hold the vision of my star steady within the center of your eyes while we grow this Tree of Life together. The tree trunk rises into the night sky above you, unfolding hundreds of branches that now easily expand and grow out from your crown chakra. I invite your awareness to reach out within their long arms.

"Look! My star is almost before you. Continue to steady your gaze upon its brilliance. As it approaches, notice how my star flashes with a pearlescent white radiance that sparkles with gold, sky-blue, emerald, and rose pink light. At the core of my star is a warm black womb of no-thing, from which the source of my starlight arises.

"With your gaze fixed upon my approaching star, stretch out your awareness within the branches of my tree, merging with the consciousness of your body. Allow your awareness to travel along these branches at the speed of light, far into the cosmos. Notice how each branch intentionally connects you to stars in your galaxy and beyond as a blueprint of specific interstellar coordinates for your soul."

In such close proximity, the shooting star completely illuminates my vision. My eyes are flooded by the star's radiance and flashing colors. I become one with the star and merge with its mighty, all-consuming light.

I follow Green Tara's voice and allow my consciousness to become one with the superhighway of tree branches rising out of my crown chakra that connect me with important star coordinates for my soul. Within Green Tara's Tree of Life, I now download the omniscient intelligence of these specific star coordinates to expand my human awareness.

This present moment feels familiar.

My awareness opens to welcome the intelligence of these star coordinates flowing their blessed consciousness to specific neurological points and pathways within my body. I recognize that my body is designed as a map of their universal intelligence, lit up with the corresponding nodes of their interstellar coordinates.

My innocent nature is delighted that my human body is a blueprint of the Universe. I feel relieved in this self-realization. Within Green Tara's Tree of

Life, I am rooted in the stillness of my sovereignty while connected to the constant movement and radiance of the stars expanding my awareness.

I sink deeper into my body.

I sink deeper into my expanded awareness.

I anchor my awareness of this universal map for Star Nation consciousness, reflected in the holy architecture of my human body, within my rooted being now.

At the center of my third eye chakra, I witness a ray of emerald green light gently gather before me. From its pristine, verdant energy lithely steps out the form of Green Tara. Her face is youthful and her large dark eyes brightly sparkle above a riveting smile, inspiring me to easily smile back at her.

Framing her face are large hoops of gold, embedded with tiny orbs of starlight that twinkle from her ears. Upon her head is a crown of living stars illuminating her high cheekbones and soft, vibrant green skin. Beauty dances from every movement of Green Tara's taunt musculature as she gracefully steps towards me with open arms. She wears a sash upon her bare breast and her stride is clad in the outline of sheer leggings. In her left hand, Green Tara holds a blue lotus, shimmering with dew. Her right hand extends to me a mudra of her warmest blessing, welcoming my smile to widen even further in reflection of her own.

GREEN TARA SPEAKS:

"I am Green Tara. I come to you as a reflection of your pure and innocent nature. My Keycode 3 transmission liberates your awareness to authentically enjoy your sovereignty and free will to create Heaven on Earth. I initiate and mentor your awareness through the many teaching manifestations of my one consciousness, which are known as the *21 Emanations of Tara*. Some of these aspects reflect the righteous wrath required to love yourself beyond self-inflicted hatred.

"Activating Keycode 3 of The Sophia Code within your DNA awakens your willingness to enjoy your success, overcoming any viral programming that would have you ignore your own power to prosper. Further, the divine qualities of Keycode 3 activate a full-body remembrance of your innocent nature. Your innocence is the perfect joyous guide within you, leading your awareness through the step-by-step manifestations for all of your highest aspirations to come true.

"The fully integrated activation of Keycode 3 returns you to the true essence of enlightenment. I invite you to consider enlightenment as simply recognizing the light within you and deciding to never look away from that light again. You may also explore the idea of enlightenment as no-thing, for that is the true empty nature of your mind. I speak of *enlightenment* lightly, for too much has been made about a pure state that has never left you. Can you hear my laughter? I hold the weight of the Universe within a single atom – how much lighter shall we hold a concept such as enlightenment? I come in reflection of the master that already exists within you on Earth.

"With the power of your own voice, allow my mantra of OM TARE TUTTARE TURE SOHA to activate Keycode 3 within you. Let us step into the quantum universe of your DNA to activate your highest potential together. I am a loving guide to the 'happiness that knows no suffering,' and my Divine Feminine Christ embodiment offers you a clear reflection that it is safe to create and embody your inner reality of Heaven on Earth."

As a Sovereign Creator of the One Sophia Source, by the power of my I Am Presence, I now activate Keycode 3 within the unified field of my whole self.

I accept that I hold the golden keys to my Heaven on Earth.
I accept that I create my reality, by the power of my word.
My word is good, my heart is pure.
By the loving power of my pure word, I now awaken Keycode 3 within me through the holy vehicle of Green Tara's mantra: OM TARE TUTTARE TURE SOHA activating my DNA.

OM TARE TUTTARE TURE SOHA
OM TARE TUTTARE TURE SOHA
OM TARE TUTTARE TURE SOHA

I am the pure sound wave of OM.
I am the pure sound wave of OM activating my DNA now.

I am the pure sound wave of OM manifesting as the holy architecture for *all life.*

I am the pure sound wave of OM manifesting as the holy empty space of my mind.

I am the pure sound wave of OM manifesting as my holy human voice.

I am the pure sound wave of OM manifesting as my holy human body.

I am the pure sound wave of OM manifesting as my holy communion with life on Earth.

I am the pure sound wave of OM, I Am That.

OM TARE TUTTARE TURE SOHA
OM TARE TUTTARE TURE SOHA
OM TARE TUTTARE TURE SOHA

I am the radiant sound wave of TARE.
I am the radiant sound wave of TARE activating my DNA now.

I am the radiant sound wave of TARE resonating as the peaceful form of no-thing.

I am the radiant sound wave of TARE resonating as my eternally free nature.

I am the radiant sound wave of TARE resonating as my innocent nature.

I am the radiant sound wave of TARE resonating as my joyful sovereignty.

I am the radiant sound wave of TARE resonating as my omniscient clarity.

I am the radiant sound wave of TARE resonating as the Holy Spirit within *all form.*

I am the radiant sound wave of TARE, I Am That.

> OM TARE TUTTARE TURE SOHA
> OM TARE TUTTARE TURE SOHA
> OM TARE TUTTARE TURE SOHA

I am the piercing sound wave of TUTTARE.
I am the piercing sound wave of TUTTARE activating my DNA now.
I am the piercing sound wave of TUTTARE that dissolves the 8 great fears.

1.
I am the piercing sound wave of TUTTARE that acts as the wisdom of elephants removing all obstacles from my path. My essential nature is direct knowing, which transcends the ignorance of my suffering.

2.
I am the piercing sound wave of TUTTARE that floods my life with divine love. My essential nature is unconditional self-love, which transcends my attachments to suffering.

3.
I am the piercing sound wave of TUTTARE that stokes the fire of my transfiguration. My essential nature is self-forgiveness, which transcends the hatred that feeds my suffering.

4.
I am the piercing sound wave of TUTTARE that causes the lion to lay down with the lamb. My essential nature is self-knowing, which transcends the arrogance of my suffering.

5.
I am the piercing sound wave of TUTTARE that awakens the serpents of

kundalini to rise within me. My essential nature is self-communion, which transcends the jealousy of my suffering.

6.

I am the piercing sound wave of TUTTARE that is the freedom from all bondage. My essential nature is prosperity, which transcends the miserliness of my suffering.

7.

I am the piercing sound wave of TUTTARE that my angelic nature is singing now. My essential nature is faith, which transcends the demons of my suffering.

8.

I am the piercing sound wave of TUTTARE resonating thieves and bandits into the remembrance of their divine inheritance. My essential nature is omniscient awareness, which transcends the judgments and projections of my suffering.

I am the piercing sound wave of TUTTARE, I Am That.

OM TARE TUTTARE TURE SOHA
OM TARE TUTTARE TURE SOHA
OM TARE TUTTARE TURE SOHA

I am the ever-present sound wave of TURE.
I am the ever-present sound wave of TURE activating my DNA now.

I am the ever-present sound wave of TURE originating from the One Source.

I am the ever-present sound wave of TURE abiding in the One Source.

I am the ever-present sound wave of TURE spoken from the One Voice.

I am the ever-present sound wave of TURE speaking as the One Voice.

I am the ever-present sound wave of TURE bridging my awareness to the One Voice.

I am the ever-present sound wave of TURE that is a living bridge for others to remember the One Voice *within them.*

I am the ever-present sound wave of TURE that is a living bridge for heavenly paradigms to manifest on Earth.

I am the ever-present sound wave of TURE, I Am That.

OM TARE TUTTARE TURE SOHA
OM TARE TUTTARE TURE SOHA
OM TARE TUTTARE TURE SOHA

I am the clear sound wave of SOHA.
I am the clear sound wave of SOHA activating my DNA now.

I am the clear sound wave of SOHA creating the space of every present moment.

I am the clear sound wave of SOHA breathing the first and last breath of every present moment.

I am the clear sound wave of SOHA joyfully laughing in my innocent nature.

I am the clear sound wave of SOHA hailing my true nature within a human form.

I am the clear sound wave of SOHA celebrating my holy human divinity.

I am the clear sound wave of SOHA expanding my awareness for humanity's ascension.

I am the clear sound wave of SOHA activating my sovereign power to create Heaven on Earth.

I am the clear sound wave of SOHA activating Keycode 3 within me now.

I am the clear sound wave of SOHA, I Am That.

> OM TARE TUTTARE TURE SOHA
> OM TARE TUTTARE TURE SOHA
> OM TARE TUTTARE TURE SOHA
> OM TARE TUTTARE TURE SOHA
> OM TARE TUTTARE TURE SOHA
> OM TARE TUTTARE TURE SOHA
> OM TARE TUTTARE TURE SOHA

By the power of 7, self-realized heaven: It is done.
I now multiply the power of 7, self-realized heaven, by the power of 3, a perfect trinity, to reveal the 21 aspects of Green Tara *within me.*

I accept that I hold the golden keys to my Heaven on Earth.
I accept that I create my reality, by the power of my word.
My word is good, my heart is pure.
By the loving power of my pure word, I now activate the 21 aspects of Green Tara's Keycode 3 transmission within me.

> OM TARE TUTTARE TURE SOHA

I now recognize and activate the 1st aspect of Keycode 3 within me:
I am The Swift One of Heroic Glory.

I am the waves of self-realization that swiftly arise from my innocent nature. I am the heroic guide to the salvation of my innocence. My eyes flash with the lightning of wise counsel. I rejoice in the glory of Sophia's light as the covenant of Heaven on Earth within me, for the liberation of all beings.

> OM TARE TUTTARE TURE SOHA

I now recognize and activate the 2nd aspect of Keycode 3 within me:
I am The One of Supreme Peace.

Pure as autumn moonlight and bright as a thousand constellations, my innocent nature reflects the supreme peace of my divinity's light. As a wayshower for all, I walk upon the rays of my guiding light innocence to live in authentic peace with myself. Abiding in the supreme peace that arises from following my heart, I am a living foundation for building Heaven on Earth realities, for the liberation of all beings.

OM TARE TUTTARE TURE SOHA

I now recognize and activate the 3rd aspect of Keycode 3 within me:
I am The One of the Golden Life.

I am perfectly designed to enjoy and increase life in all ways. In honor of the gift of life that I am given, I choose to live a golden life. I unconditionally bless life, embodying the Golden Ray of wisdom, receptivity, generosity, and prosperity. I choose to enjoy my golden life by increasing the reality of Heaven on Earth, for the liberation of all beings.

OM TARE TUTTARE TURE SOHA

I now recognize and activate the 4th aspect of Keycode 3 within me:
I am The One of Complete Victory.

Homage! I crown the sovereign Holy One within me. I sit in honor upon a yellow lotus throne embodying the virtues of my highest potential in this lifetime. I am the pure positive focus of my innocence aligning the victories of divinely guided action. I consecrate all my creations arising from the actualization of Heaven on Earth as a complete victory, for the liberation of all beings.

OM TARE TUTTARE TURE SOHA

I now recognize and activate the 5th aspect of Keycode 3 within me:
I am The One Who Proclaims the Sound of HUM.

In this proclamation of my sovereign divinity, the eight great fears bow before me. I embody the commitment of TUTTARE and consecrate myself to the eight great virtues of self-love. Through the power of my voice, I summon the Holy Spirit within every realm of space and form to co-create my reality of Heaven on Earth, according to the divine will of Sophia for me to prosper in all ways. I bless myself with mudras of golden wisdom aligning the right use of my sovereign power to summon this new reality, for the liberation of all beings.

OM TARE TUTTARE TURE SOHA

I now recognize and activate the 6th aspect of Keycode 3 within me:
I am The One Who Is Completely Victorious Over the Three Worlds.

No person, place, or thing has power over my direct connection to the Source. I see through the holographic illusion of the Three Worlds and take refuge within Sophia's light. The laws of form have no hold over me as I abide in my Golden Dragon Light Body. In the Christ light of my divinity, paradigms of darkness must bow to the heaven within me. Demons bow at the throne of my sovereignty, dissolving into the light that I am. I activate the crystalline chromosomes of The Sophia Code within me to embody my sovereignty over the Three Worlds, for the liberation of all beings.

OM TARE TUTTARE TURE SOHA

I now recognize and activate the 7th aspect of Keycode 3 within me:
I am The One Who Conquers All Viral Beliefs.

The Sophia Christ light within me is impervious to collective viral belief systems. Made as a sovereign creator, I am also a sovereign *destroyer* of that which does not serve me. Drawing my right leg in, I extend my left leg out and set ablaze all inherited viral belief systems within the righteous fire of my central sun. I summon the Christed power of my divinity to clear the black magick controlling humanity, for the liberation of all beings.

OM TARE TUTTARE TURE SOHA

I now recognize and activate the 8th aspect of Keycode 3 within me:
I am The One Who Conquers All Fears.

I am the ever-present sound wave of TURE dispelling all dissonant thoughts of imbalance and separation from my true self. My reality of Heaven on Earth is protected by the omniscient sound of TURE conquering all fears about my imminent success. Every atom of my body hums in a perfect symphony of divinely orchestrated peace between space and form, for the liberation of all beings.

OM TARE TUTTARE TURE SOHA

I now recognize and activate the 9th aspect of Keycode 3 within me:
I am The One Who Protects from All Fears.

It is within my sovereign power to abstain from terrorizing my awareness with fear. I unify my awareness with the unconditional divine love of my Higher Self consciousness, as a whirling mass of light in which no darkness may abide. This light shines in every direction so that my thoughts always know which way to return home to the peace within me. I bless my heart with mudras that dispel the eight great fears, for the liberation of all beings.

OM TARE TUTTARE TURE SOHA

I now recognize and activate the 10th aspect of Keycode 3 within me:
I am The Radiant One Who Liberates Illusions with the Laughter of TUTTARE.

A garland of a thousand stars adorns my crown chakra and my eyes shine with an ocean of unconditional divine love that subjugates all demons of fear. There is no dark paradigm that can withstand the sovereign peace of my joyful divinity. My heart rings the bells of sovereignty for All That Is. I laugh in the ease of my reign over all fears and dance in the wrathful joy of TUTTARE, for the liberation of all beings.

OM TARE TUTTARE TURE SOHA

I now recognize and activate the 11th aspect of Keycode 3 within me: *I am The One Who Creates Abundant Prosperity & Freedom.*

I stand as a living bridge between the formless and the world of form. My wealth consciousness is a formless inheritance that I now manifest as physical prosperity supporting my reality of Heaven on Earth. I lay down all attachments and vows to physically suffer in a poverty of spirit. I live in a quantum universe that is designed to fulfill my every heart's desire, as spoken by the power of my word. I self-actualize the freedom of my wealth consciousness, for the liberation of all beings.

OM TARE TUTTARE TURE SOHA

I now recognize and activate the 12th aspect of Keycode 3 within me: *I am The One Who Grants All That is Auspicious.*

I embody the good fortune of living in alignment with divine will. My alignment magnetizes every auspicious blessing for my Heaven on Earth reality to manifest into form. Therefore, I am empowered to abundantly bless others as directed by my Higher Self. I consecrate my reality of Heaven on Earth to act as a white flask of good fortune, pouring forth auspicious blessings, for the liberation of all beings.

OM TARE TUTTARE TURE SOHA

I now recognize and activate the 13th aspect of Keycode 3 within me: *I am The Holy One Who Blazes Like Fire.*

I am the blazing fire purifying every earthly obstacle. Homage to the Holy Spirit within me! I accept a victory wreath of sacred flames crowning the sun of my being and I surround my human awareness in its protective rays now. I accept and embody this liberating fire of the Holy Spirit as my Higher Self, for the benefit of all beings.

OM TARE TUTTARE TURE SOHA

I now recognize and activate the 14th aspect of Keycode 3 within me:
I am The One Who Destroys the Demons of the Past.

My unconditional divine love for the one body of Sophia Christ guides me in all ways; therefore, I am willing to embody all wrathful aspects of my divinity. Karmic ages have no hold over me: I walk the Earth in alignment with a divine will that prospers me in all ways. I confidently destroy all attachments to the past that keep me from living Heaven on Earth. With the fierce sound wave of HUM I proclaim the good news of my sovereignty across space and time. I am rooted in the present moment and consecrate the lightning realizations of my Higher Self, for the liberation of all beings.

OM TARE TUTTARE TURE SOHA

I now recognize and activate the 15th aspect of Keycode 3 within me:
I am The One of Supreme Peacefulness.

I consecrate my awareness to readily forgive the suffering of my human experience, taking up the mantle of my Sophia Christ consciousness now. Wherever there is the darkness of suffering, I am the steadfast light of nirvana. The stillness of my true nature baptizes my thoughts as vehicles for manifesting solutions that create peace on Earth. I embody the calm clarity of my supreme peace as a living bridge to Heaven on Earth, regardless of all circumstances, for the liberation of all beings.

OM TARE TUTTARE TURE SOHA

I now recognize and activate the 16th aspect of Keycode 3 within me:
I am The One Who Arises from the Intrinsic Awareness of HUM.

I open my heart to the sound of HUM clearing out the projections of others upon me. I open my mind to the sound of HUM revealing the empty nature of my reality. I open my soul to the sound of HUM consecrating the pilgrimage of my body through form. I release all judgments and understanding about the nature of reality so that my innocence may guide me to the womb of no-thing. It is here that I increase my embodiment of living wisdom by allowing what is arising to inform my ever-present now, for the liberation of all beings.

OM TARE TUTTARE TURE SOHA

I now recognize and activate the 17th aspect of Keycode 3 within me:
I am The One Who Causes All Obstacles to Tremble, Shake, and Dissolve.

As a Golden Dragon embodiment, my feet joyfully stomp upon the Earth, causing all obscurations projected upon humanity's divinity to shake, uproot, and dissolve. My Sophia Christ light commands all obstacles to humanity's ascension to instantaneously tremble and flee. In the unified field of my multidimensional being, I stand in *every* realm as the radiance of Sophia, dissolving all viruses that separate humanity from its divinity. My tongue speaks as the lightning of HUM, and *all* is reconciled by the sovereign power of my word, for the liberation of all beings.

OM TARE TUTTARE TURE SOHA

I now recognize and accept the 18th aspect of Keycode 3 within me:
I am The One Who Embodies the Serpentine Power of My Kundalini Life Force.

My kundalini life force is the ascending Holy Spirit of Sophia, transfiguring my awareness to radiate as the Christ light within human form. This omniscient intelligence continually consecrates and seals immortal health within the 28 major chakras downloading my human body into form. My Golden Dragon embodiment alchemizes all poisonous belief systems and correlating diseases into the medicine that activates self-realization for all. I consecrate the power of my kundalini life force to manifest sanctuaries of Heaven on Earth for the reconciliation of humanity's relationship with its divinity. I am *The Star* within *The Tree of Life* revealing the cosmic serpent of Sophia's light, for the liberation of all beings.

OM TARE TUTTARE TURE SOHA

I now recognize and activate the 19th aspect of Keycode 3 within me: *I am The One Who Alleviates All Suffering.*

I release humanity's attachments to suffer in conflict by embodying *The Peace that Passeth All Understanding.* From the empty space within me arises every radical solution for awakening humanity from its nightmare of dualistic belief systems. As the dove of Shekinah's grace, I have descended to Earth to prophesy the golden key of our collective sovereignty. I embody the seed of happiness that is free from all suffering, as a leader in this Divine Feminine Christ movement, for the liberation of all beings.

OM TARE TUTTARE TURE SOHA

I now recognize and activate the 20th aspect of Keycode 3 within me: *I am The One Whose Radiance Removes Viral Epidemics.*

I am the radiance of a thousand full moons summoning an ocean of TUTTARE to baptize humanity from its addiction to the eight great fears. With wrathful frowns and thunderous laughter, I dispel the epidemic of disasters designed to separate humanity from knowing its divinity. My eyes blaze with the rising sun of Shambhallah as I show The Way to our next Golden Age of Miracles. I terminate the rampant viruses that imprison our planet in suffering by activating The Sophia Code within me and embodying my Sophia Christ light returning to Earth now. I consecrate my life to the power of the Holy Spirit proclaiming this covenant of sovereignty now, for the liberation of all beings.

OM TARE TUTTARE TURE SOHA

I now recognize and activate the 21st aspect of Keycode 3 within me:
I am The One Who Perfects All Enlightened Activities.

My body is a green flask for Sophia's unconditional divine love to pour forth, baptizing humanity's awareness to accept its birthright of enlightenment. Walking The Way ahead, I embody the master who is guiding me from within to lead by example. TARE: I step forward with my right leg and raise my left hand to bless this generation birthing a new Golden Age of Miracles.

I consecrate my sovereign power to serve all of creation with grace, humility, and unconditional divine love for all beings. As a living star on Earth, I broadcast the multi-ray transmission of Sophia's light for The Tree of Life to flourish in the heart of humanity now. As a living master in service to the goodness of life, it is safe for me to command the supreme magick for manifesting the reality of Heaven on Earth, for the liberation of all beings.

OM TARE TUTTARE TURE SOHA

I accept that I hold the golden keys to my Heaven on Earth.
I accept that I create my reality, by the power of my word.
My word is good, my heart is pure.
By the loving power of my pure word, I wholly accept that it is safe for me to create my reality of Heaven on Earth.

By the loving power of my pure word, I now command my Higher Self to activate all the crystalline divine qualities of Keycode 3 of The Sophia Code within me as the new operating system for my carbon-based DNA.

I now integrate this initiation throughout my entire body, on all four levels of my Be-ing, with grace and ease.

I have received more of myself today.

It is done.

It is done.

It is done.

By the power of 3, a perfect trinity: It is done.

Green Tara stands before me on the back of a pearlescent white Sophia Dragon; she blesses me with her mudras for success, happiness, and peace. From her Emerald Ray arises the 21 Emanations of Tara. Flashing smiles of red, gold, yellow, white, and black, they each transmit their auspicious blessings to my heart from an array of lotus thrones. Above me, fiery Dakini angels dance across the sky, showering me with garlands of Sophia's light. With profound appreciation, wonder, and delight I bow in Namasté for these great blessings bestowed upon me.

Green Tara's laughter rings within every cell of my body, carrying my awareness beyond thought into the black no-thing of Sophia's womb. Within this zero still-point I now accept the blissful opportunity to mentor with Green Tara as a Divine Feminine Ascended Master mentor for revealing the ineffable mysteries of Sophia as the true foundation for creating my reality of Heaven on Earth. I thank you Green Tara for your overflowing generosity as an accessible guide, mentor, and friend overlighting my journey to embody the fullness of my own soul's radiance.

This empowerment to activate Keycode 3 within my DNA is accomplished. I now close this ceremony with appreciation, thanksgiving, and reverence in my heart for all that I have received, both known and unknown to my awareness. I thank the power of my Higher Self and the love of All That Is supporting my eternal success.

And so it is.

KEYCODE 4
"SHE OF A THOUSAND ROSES"

As a mentor for fulfilling prophecy, I guide your awareness to access every opportunity and resource that is available for you to live out your destiny as an important wayshower for your generation. I am here to support your courageous mission: to speak the new prophecies of ancient wisdom, which will initiate this next Golden Age of Miracles.

Mother Mary Is a Mentor
for Fulfilling Your Prophecy

MOTHER MARY SPEAKS:

I AM THE DIVINE Feminine Ascended Master teacher known as Mother Mary, and it is with great pleasure and anticipation that I now reveal myself as Keycode 4 in The Sophia Code cosmology. Within the High Council, I am honored as "She of a Thousand Roses," for my transmission broadcasts *The Teachings of the Rose* for walking the spiral path to open your Sacred Heart.

When my individual voice arose in an asking to be born within the still no-thing of Sophia's womb, it was heard by the angelic witness as the ecstasy of a rose opening to morning sunlight, baptized by the dew of a new dawn. Since the conception of my soul's light, my prayer remains the same: to nurture and grow the children of Sophia's creation. As such, I am called upon as the *Mother of Mothers*.

Guided by my soul's prayer throughout eons of divine service, I have lived many lifetimes in loving support of humanity's evolution. In my most recent and final lifetime on Earth, I came as a highly advanced soul incarnating as a Hebrew woman, named Mary, into a spiritual community called the Essenes.

I was born into an important messianic prophecy. Before I was even conceived, the ancient texts declared me as a mother of salvation for humanity. My birth and the birth of my son, Jesus, were foretold by the prophets of my people hundreds of years prior to our arrival.[Isa 7:14]

Many angelic signs and messages were sent to my mother, Anna, during her pregnancy with me. These messages announced the importance of both my destiny and that I receive extensive training for fulfilling my divine life purpose. With my birth, I stepped into an age of great suffering that was praying for courageous leaders to fulfill the prophecies of the past and create a sovereign future for generations to come.

Both the prophetic circumstances that I was born into and my soul's natural passion to serve humanity created a highly focused lifetime. I was born with clear memories of my spiritual training from other lifetimes that prepared me to fulfill this destiny. From early childhood, I knew in my heart that I had returned to help many, many people. My mother Anna was a gifted oracle, priestess, and a devoted mother; she arranged for my mystery school training to begin at the age of four, when I began asking to be initiated.

My early life was peaceful, yet rigorous, as I devoted myself to the spiritual education of my Essene community. The initiations I received eventually revealed that I was a reincarnated oracular High Priestess of Isis-Hathor, with the extraordinary potential to immaculately conceive and birth a high frequency being through my body. Immaculate conception was an ancient oracular practice of genetic soul-to-soul light weaving that was highly revered in Egypt during Hathor's golden age. In essence, I was perfectly designed to fulfill the prophecies of my people and birth my son, Jesus, as was foretold. My name, Mary, is a title of ordination that points to this training, for *Mery-Isis* means 'Beloved of Isis.'

At the crossroads of humanity's destiny, your generation is also born into a prophecy of similar proportion. For several hundred years there has been an increasing momentum of prophecies spoken throughout the world that foretell of the *ancient ones* returning in the form of little children at the dawning of this next golden age.[1] These returning souls would carry a clear remembrance of their unique purpose within their spiritual DNA. From the knowledge of all their lifetimes, they would effortlessly recall how to administer the ancient rites of initiation for humanity to awaken as peaceful stewards of the Earth. For these ancient ones, it is prophesied that their greatest initiation would be opening humanity's heart to remember its divine origin.

Yes, much has been spoken of about *you*. You are here to immaculately birth the return and reconciliation of the Divine Feminine Christ with the Divine Masculine Christ energies for the heart of humanity. As you read this codex, know that I see you as an ancient soul who has returned to fulfill the prophecies of your ancestors; I intimately understand the depth and passion of your personal calling.

Also know that you are meant to fulfill the prophecies of this next golden age with the innumerable masters that are incarnating alongside you. At this time, your world is filled with the light of many stars walking upon the Earth. You are here to shine together as an invincible light that transforms all darkness, just as the prophecies said you would. This age is for the one body of Sophia Christ to be revealed by each of you, working together as one, seamlessly supporting one another with your extraordinary talents and unique gifts.

Just as I intuited from early childhood, you have also felt a deep calling to serve humanity from a young age, knowing that a treasure map of destiny lay within your Sacred Heart. And so, my friends, in our great willingness to love humanity and serve the Earth, we are the same. As children of prophecy, we have come from the One Source to walk as the light of Sophia within and for the one body of Christ in form.

I offer you my support as an Ascended Master mentor who lived in human form, carrying important ancient wisdom within me, just as you are now.

---

1 Several prophecies that connect upon this theme include *The Whirling Rainbow* Hopi prophecy, *The Return of White Buffalo Woman* Sioux prophecy, Mayan 5th World prophecies, as well as many New Age prophecies announcing the Indigo, Crystal, and Starseed generations.

Stepping into an age for fulfilling prophecy brings a heightened awareness of your life purpose and spiritual destiny that may often feel daunting to your daily human life. I am here to help you navigate The Way ahead as an accessible teacher, friend, and guide for birthing the new prophecies of ancient wisdom carried within your own heart.

You can call upon me at any time, for I simultaneously serve a multitude of hearts on Earth. My omnipresent awareness allows for everyone to directly access my unconditional divine love and guidance through our communion of intentional dialogue, invocation, prayer, and meditation.

My deepest desire is for humanity to know itself as the divinity that it seeks. The disconnection between humanity and divinity has gone on for far too long. You are poised at a time of great planetary awakening: where humanity has unprecedented access to a global network of spiritual insight and support from countless masters, both seen and unseen. This quantum leap points to the readiness of humanity's heart to remember its direct connection to Sophia and its true worthiness as a species.

Just as I revealed The Way to many, you also came to be a wayshower of humanity's divine worth by believing in yourself and embodying your highest potential. As a mentor for fulfilling prophecy, I guide your awareness to access every opportunity and resource that is available for you to live out your destiny as an important wayshower for your generation. I am here to support your courageous mission: to speak the new prophecies of ancient wisdom, which will initiate this next Golden Age of Miracles.

The Teachings of the Rose

At the unknown center of Sophia's omniscient presence, exists the *Holy of Holies* womb, from which shimmering rose petals of quantum energy appear out of the no-thing. These petals spiral open as *The Rose* of infinite sacred geometries, light matrices, and Divine Feminine wisdom that are foundational elements for birthing all life. In my oracular training, The Rose is interchangeably referred to as the Sacred Heart of Sophia from which *The Teachings of the Rose* arise as direct revelations for experiencing the one Divine Mother within you.

As a living fractal of Sophia's Sacred Heart, your own heart chakra is also *The Rose:* a perfect and whole blueprint of divinity that calls you into a daily communion with Sophia. Communing within The Rose, you may learn directly from Sophia on how to access your personal power for birthing new creations and realities, as well as how to use your sovereign power with divine love, for the greatest wellbeing of all. Anointed by the sweet scent of direct knowing, stepping into your personal power becomes an irresistible invitation from The Rose.

As "She of a Thousand Roses," I initiate your awareness to discover that your heart chakra is The Rose blooming within the one Sacred Heart of Sophia, and so too are all hearts. The Teachings of the Rose provide a spiral path for awakening your awareness to your sovereign yet *interdependent* relationship with the hearts of all beings within the one body of Sophia Christ.

Daily communion within The Rose of your own heart creates a clear pathway for hearing the loving voice of Sophia, your Higher Self, and your Inner Child adoring you. It is here that you will receive every divine confirmation about your soul's unique beauty and meaningful purpose as a rose spiraling open within a cosmos of roses. If you doubt that you are worthy or loved, it is within your own heart that you will hear the voice of divinity worshiping you as an embodiment of Sophia.

When you listen to the voice of Sophia speaking through The Rose of your heart, your soul is quenched with the milk and honey of Her unconditional love for you. She crowns your sovereignty with a thousand transcendent pearls of applicable wisdom and outright adoration. This unconditional love is always available to you through your communion with Sophia. It is freely given to you – you cannot earn it, for it was always yours.

Within The Rose, your awareness acclimates to the beauty and sovereign power of your own divinity being embraced by the Source of all divinity. As one sniff of a rose shifts your emotional frequency, abiding in the petals of your own heart elevates your self-perception to accept the truth of your absolute worthiness to be loved.

The Teachings of the Rose provide a vehicle for bliss consciousness to directly honor and engage with the innocence of your heart, bypassing linear thinking, qualifiers, and judgments about why you should or shouldn't receive love. My Keycode 4 transmission spirals open The Rose of your heart to feel safe in experiencing bliss by receiving more unconditional divine love than you ever thought possible. I mentor your awareness in how to open your heart to love by unfolding one precious petal at a time, so that you may acclimate to and integrate how to live in ever-increasing states of bliss consciousness. In this way, The Rose teaches you that the beauty of bliss transcends your ego's irrational demands to earn the unconditional divine love that was always yours, blooming within your own heart.

The Teachings of the Rose offer an inclusive pathway of reconciliation and self-honor for all aspects that perfectly contribute to your embodiment of Sophia Christ consciousness. The soft beauty of a rose is incomplete without the silent ferocity of its thorns, and every teaching arising from The Rose is a reflection of this seeming paradox. As such, The Teachings of The Rose drip with pearls of wisdom alchemized from the positive creative tension that exists between two seemingly opposing polarities, which generate a transcendent third energy of wholeness.

As such, The Rose provides a pathway of reconciliation that frees you from choosing between dualistic polarities and shifts your focus to meditate upon the wholeness that is being created by two seemingly opposing forces. For example, you do not have to banish the thorns of your humanity to behold your divinity. Your human awareness and the ego structures that come with your physical body provide a necessary creative tension for seeking out your divinity and consciously embodying that divinity. Unconditional love and acceptance for the totality of you, especially your humanity, is the reconciliation that allows for your awareness and ego to fully integrate into the omniscient light and sovereign divinity of your Higher Self.

Your own unconditional love for the seemingly opposite polarities of your humanity and divinity is what spirals open The Rose, unifying your whole self to walk in peace with *who you really are* along the transcendent pathway of Sophia Christ consciousness. Your body is the vehicle, with both its beauty and thorns, and your Higher Self is the inner guide to embody the bliss of your divinity on Earth. Self-love continually blooms within The Rose of your heart with the honoring of all these essential parts of your whole self, working together as one.

It is my honor to guide your pilgrimage along every petal of this spiraling pathway to open your heart and receive the power of unconditional love for yourself arising from The Rose within you. As a Divine Feminine mentor, my gentle presence supports you through the grace of bliss, initiating your 'eyes to see and ears to hear' how worthy you are of divine love through The Teachings of the Rose. (Prv 20:12)

My Keycode 4 transmission facilitates an emotionally safe, supportive space for your Higher Self to unify the totality of your consciousness – both your shadow and light – through beauty and beyond duality. For The Rose welcomes every part of your consciousness as essential for your whole body ascension. I teach you how to walk with your arms wide open to the goodness of life, firmly setting your feet upon a middle path of self-mastery called *The Teachings of The Way*, or simply put, *The Way*.

Walking The Way

The Way is a daily spiritual practice for those initiated in The Teachings of The Rose who live in accordance with the guiding voice of their heart. For The Rose reveals that there is no higher guidance than following The Way of your own heart, which is the throne of your Higher Self. Therefore, an initiate of The Way chooses to actively embody the pearls of spiritual paradox offered by The Rose, to liberate their awareness from projections and judgments preventing them from following their heart.

Walking The Way of this creative tension is not a casual affair for the human ego, nor is it for the faint of heart. It's a spiritual path that requires a daily relinquishing of all attachments to suffering and a complete surrender to the voice of your Higher Self guiding you from your heart. Many question and even condemn those who follow their heart along The Way of personal awakening. It requires significant courage to trust your innocence guiding you to have faith and follow the path of your greatest potential. With that said, The Way is the simplest road and most direct route for living a joyfully aligned life and fulfilling your destiny.

Defined by both the path and your unique soul decisions as you journey upon it, The Way is a human life lived as the hero's journey. The quest is to intuitively follow the guidance spiraling open from The Rose of your heart so that you may live your highest destiny, regardless of all outer circumstances or influence.

I courageously walked The Way as my daily practice, remaining steadfast along its spiraling pathway of rigorous initiations, throughout every vulnerable moment of my human experience. My early self-mastery in The Teachings of the Rose prepared my young heart to become a chalice for the Holy Spirit to overflow with Sophia's light and direct revelations. It was my life commitment to walking The Way that guided me in the fulfillment of my destiny as a birther of a new paradigm for Sophia Christ consciousness, embodying Keycode 4 of The Sophia Code for this planet.

Humanity deified my Keycode embodiment of Sophia because my daily commitment to walk The Way, in every moment of my life, created an unforgettable Legacy of Love. In my sovereign free will, I chose to live in my highest potential *every day*, which created a legacy for the miraculous empowerment of many future generations to come – and so here we are now – connecting over 2,000 years after my ascension.

Simply put: I chose to show up and be fully present to the purpose of my human life. 'Even greater acts are possible than this' for your own *Legacy of Love* if you believe and follow The Way of your own heart in the extraordinary opportunity of this lifetime. [Jn 14:12]

Mentoring with Mother Mary

My Divine Feminine Christ embodiment transcends the boundaries of religion, indigenous traditions, and modern spirituality. Across the Earth, I am a recognizable and trusted central figure for seemingly different spiritual pathways that all lead to the one Source. As an Ascended Master teacher, I am mentoring humanity in how these many spiritual pathways intersect, beyond all seeming differences, within the one Sacred Heart of Sophia consciousness.

I appear as a prominent spiritual guide when you are ready to walk The Way back home to your heart and consecrate your life to the divine will of your Higher Self. It is a great joy for me to support the blossoming of your own self-mastery.

I highly value the human experience as an important vehicle for ascension, and how I interact with my initiates reflects this passion. I often move beyond the laws of form to reach those I work with by frequently appearing in dreams, visions, and through physical signs to those mentoring with me. I revel in the everyday details of your life that are all contributing to your journey of ascension. You can call on me for help with anything at all, for every moment of your life is precious to me.

My divine love is practical, tender, sweet, and tough enough to reflect the authentic support that you need in every present moment. For those of you who need a mother or a best friend that you've never had, I am here to joyfully embody those roles for you and help you heal unresolved wounds. I also awaken the *Inner Mother* and best friend within you, supporting the emotional growth of these important relationships with yourself.

In our mentor relationship, it is vitally important for you to remember that I am never judging your learning experiences – I support you to reach beyond religious ideas of self-shaming guilt. I believe that every step of your human journey is an essential part of your spiritual awakening, including your relationship with suffering. Know that I am here to walk with you as an unconditionally loving ally through every vulnerable, challenging step of releasing any and all addictions to complacency and victimhood.

My guiding light presence shifts your perspective from being a powerless bystander in life – or even a victim of life – to that of a sovereign co-creator with your Higher Self and Sophia. As a mentor, I know that this shift will occur for you in successive stages of integrative understanding. I work with your own pace, while always encouraging you to be persistent with your progress. I protect, ground, and guide you throughout your spiritual awakening from victimhood and walk with you every step of The Way to embody your full sovereign creative power.

Ascension is a heroic human journey, best traveled with good friends who know The Way ahead. I honor all of your vulnerable, often uncomfortable, human feelings about the journey along The Way. I come to you as an

Ascended Master mentor and friend who intimately knows the pressures and passions of living your full potential on Earth. My heavenly support is offered from the real-life perspective of all my human incarnations.

Your Higher Self intimately knows every facet of your being and is always speaking to you as the voice of your heart. When I incarnated as the mother of Jesus, I spent my lifetime in prayerful co-creation with the voice of my own Higher Self guiding me through every initiation of my soul. As your spiritual ally, I will only ever guide you to focus on the voice of your own Higher Self and your direct communion with the Source as your true salvation and birthright, never on another to save you or be placed above you.

It is important to understand that my Keycode 4 transmission mentors your awareness to step forth and *be seen* in the full embodiment of your Higher Self. When you choose to mentor with me, my presence accelerates your personal evolution to live in absolute alignment with your Higher Self's divine will for this lifetime, including as a leader, teacher, and advocate. I activate your awareness to persevere beyond every hidden resistance and personal challenge – so that you may fulfill the promise of your destiny.

My transmission for activating Divine Feminine Christ consciousness is a heart womb medicine that honors and soothes the growing pains of your own ascension journey – which is continually rebirthing your relationship with yourself and all of life. Allowing my unconditional love to shower upon you makes The Way ahead easier for you, as you lead a new generation in this next Golden of Age of Miracles. My arms are wide open to nurture and embrace your awareness awakening to the importance of your destiny.

Come sit with me often in the garden of my innumerable roses. The fragrance of my thousand roses anoints you with an instantaneous recognition of your true beauty as a divine being having a human experience. As a mentor, I continually shower you with rose petals of celebration and bless your awareness with life-changing revelations for the fulfillment of your destiny. Just as one sniff of a rose transposes a troubled moment into bliss, so too will my overlighting presence continually shift your perception to access the freedom of The Sophia Code aligning you now with your highest destiny.

Your Oversoul Is the Architect of Your Destiny

The subject of destiny is misunderstood by many as a mystical, unfathomable power outside of yourself that executes gifts of fortune or punishment upon you, herding you to a desired outcome that may or may not have anything to do with your own personal happiness. I can assure you that your destiny is not defined or controlled by any power outside of you. The *only* architect of your destiny is your own sovereign Oversoul.

For an understanding of destiny, we must review the architecture of your whole self. Long before you were born, your evolutionary intentions for this lifetime were carefully considered and mapped out by your Oversoul as a blueprint for the destiny you are living now. The whole of you exists as both your non-physical Oversoul and as your Higher Self descending into multiple physical realities and embodiments. Thus the term *Oversoul* indicates 'a choreographer of many incarnations' for it orchestrates and oversees your innumerable parallel lifetimes.

Your Higher Self is the intermediary voice between all your embodiments and your Oversoul's omniscient intelligence, which guides you. Your Higher Self is also known as your own Holy Spirit: it is both the messenger and fulfillment of your Oversoul's presence, which can be anchored within your heart and embodied as your Christed Self.

Each of your many embodiments are interwoven and imbued with a destiny that evolves your Oversoul's awareness of itself as a sovereign creator expanding consciousness across the cosmos. Therefore, for every lifetime that you have chosen to live there is a destiny to fulfill that was designed-in-detail, authored, and agreed upon by you – for the Oversoul is *you*.

Focusing upon and fulfilling the destiny you designed for this lifetime is an important mission for your Higher Self. Your Oversoul invests an incalculable amount of energy and intention to be creating through your human body. Fulfilling the destiny that you designed for this lifetime is an opportunity to accelerate your soul's evolution with joyful self-discovery, personal success, and by making a lasting contribution to the ascension of humanity and the wholeness of All That Is.

Further, lifetimes during golden ages are prized opportunities for accelerated soul growth. Following through on completing your destiny becomes a heightened experience, and may even carry a tone of underlying urgency, depending upon the breadth of commitments that you agreed to fulfill in this lifetime for the evolution of your Oversoul.

In accelerated lifetimes your personal destiny includes mastering one or several subjects of interest that deeply satisfy your heart. From a higher perspective, there is no hierarchy for the value of your interests. It is the joy generated by your love of exploring what is important to you that ultimately fulfills your destiny. For your heart, meaningful pursuits include any contribution of leadership and service in any field of interest that inspires you to birth new paradigms of creativity, support or wellbeing for individuals, families, and communities.

Viral social conditioning is designed to confuse your mind, deterring your awareness from listening to your heart's call to explore and master your true interests. You may battle personal fears of poverty, rejection, or condemnation on the journey to fulfill your destiny by embodying your true self.

All of these internal and outer resistances are eventually resolved when you take steps to follow through on your heart's guidance. Your highest destiny is to experience Sophia's divine will for you to prosper in every area of your life. You were never meant to be a martyr suffering for your personal power, feeling subjected to an unlucky destiny, or living in lack.

I assure you that a committed investigation into your heart will urgently remind you that these social conditionings must and can be released for you to access and fulfill your destiny. The peace of your heart and life depend upon this decision. Although it may require heroic internal effort to release yourself from old identifications of destiny and self-worth, you absolutely can do it and experience the wonderful life that your destiny is calling you to.

If you don't know how to begin or realign with the journey of fulfilling your destiny, remember that the treasure map of your destiny for this lifetime is within The Rose of your heart. Your natural interests will always indicate which subjects or life projects are essential for fulfilling your destiny. Destiny, as designed by your Oversoul, is living a life focused solely on creating the desires of your heart, with divinely orchestrated opportunities to collaborate with others in the areas of your most poignant interest.

Your destiny is designed to create a life for you that feels joyful, successful, connected, supported, loved, guided, and new – *every day*. Your destiny has many predetermined goals, for both your personal and planetary evolution, but remember that fulfilling your destiny is to be enjoyed as a spiral path, celebrating every unfolding petal along the way. Life, and fulfilling your destiny, is truly designed by your Oversoul to feel that good and rewarding.

When you choose to follow your heart's guidance you are rewarded with the treasures of your soul. It is up to you to access your inner resolve and commit to making this journey yourself, for it is impossible for anyone else to fulfill your destiny.

Every step that you take to honor your true interests allows your Higher Self to magnetize every collaborative component of support, synchronicity, miracles, and manifestations for the success of your unfolding destiny. Everything outside of you that is positively supporting your journey is a blessing or messenger of encouragement from your Higher Self.

Fulfilling your destiny is how to give and receive all the divine love you have ever wanted to experience in this lifetime. It is the story of you remembering how in love you are with yourself, as The Beloved. Fulfilling your destiny is also the story of discovering how much you love the gift of life and All of Creation. The adventure of your destiny provides the opportunity to discover that divine love in new ways, every day, for a lifetime. Your destiny was the best promise you ever made to yourself and you deserve to receive the gift of its fulfillment.

Following the Voice of Your Heart

The feeling nature of humanity has been demonized throughout centuries of patriarchal religious, governmental, and societal programming. As Mother Mary I once stood in a human body, just as you do now, with all of my tender, vulnerable feelings about living in a world rife with conflict and tyranny.

Although my destiny elevated me to the status of an internationally known figure, to the end of my life I was consistently challenged by the rampant repression of women. Everywhere I traveled for my ministry I faced the socially conditioned demands placed upon women to mute our feelings and relinquish our sovereign right to create reality.

My heart always guided me to act with courage, grace, and strength in response to these demands – to firmly stand in the truth of what was important for me to feel. Regardless of all outer circumstances, I met every temptation to shun my feelings with an inner resolve to follow the voice of my heart. As a result of this personal commitment to never turn against myself and deny my own feelings, I became a living sanctuary of emotional safety for my own heart. The integrity of emotional safety that I offered myself eventually became an important part of my Divine Feminine embodiment for others to witness and empower themselves by my example. Always remember that listening to and following your heart will always positively affect the evolution of humanity, far beyond your understanding.

You naturally begin to hear the voice of your heart once a practice is established for understanding the intelligence of your emotions. Exploring a dialogue with your heart often begins with a question to clarify what a feeling means. Certain emotions will stand out in their intensity, magnetizing your awareness to ask your heart questions, such as: "Is this decision right for me?" Your heart is always listening, waiting to engage with you and respond with the truth.

At first, the voice of your heart may feel curt or brief in its responses, simply replying with yes/no or short phrases. Do not give up. These brief answers will saturate your mind and body with startling truths that inspire your curiosity to engage further. By practicing the quieting of your mind and sincerely asking your heart questions, you will increasingly hear the voice of your heart speaking with greater regularity, ease, and detail. Your heart's voice grows in confidence as it is assured that you are actively listening for its responses. Further, your heart will reveal greater detail as you practice appreciating and giving thanks for every response that you receive. Your appreciation creates a sanctuary for this important self-dialogue to flourish.

Your heart does not want to move beyond that which your Oversoul is still learning through you and your heart also does not want to be left behind as your compass. A daily practice for listening to your heart's guidance initiates your awareness to live fully engaged within the present moment. For you can only access your highest potential in the *present moment;* it is from here that you move forward into every next step of your evolution. Your heart knows this and always remains true to its purpose by calling out to your awareness again and again, beckoning: "Follow Me."

Your mind is in an intimate relationship with the voice of your heart. All things, in all of creation, simply want to fulfill the purpose for which they were created, and the mind is no different. The mind was designed to be the empty space for the visions of your heart to be manifested through. The spiritual purpose of your mind is to interface with multiple dimensional realities that are involved with bringing that which did not exist before into physical form. The physical co-creation of your true desires, as orchestrated by a willing mind, reveals the power of your heart to fulfill your destiny.

When your awareness inquires into the heart's wisdom, there arises an immediate answer that intrigues your mind to become soft and open. As your daily practice develops for listening to the heart, your mind shifts its focus from that of dominating your awareness with the ego's demands, to a clear and well-equipped ally for following through on your heart's guidance. The mind may rest as the empty space it was originally designed to be, if it is assured that the heart is guiding your journey.

Religious texts recount the story of my son Jesus being tempted in the desert of his initiations, and I speak on behalf of my son and the entire council that the greatest temptation you repeatedly face is to turn away from your true self. Indeed, all temptations can be summarized as a turning away from your heart and abandoning the authentic, direct connection to your own divine guidance. Violence only arises when the voice of your heart is denied long enough to cause an outburst.

Every feeling counts in the navigation of fulfilling your destiny. Feeling your emotions and listening to their intuitive guidance is a revolutionary act for your Sophia Christ embodiment and the liberation of humanity. Only you can save your own heart and your salvation begins by feeling it.

Destiny Is a Promise You Made to Yourself

I now create a ceremonial space within and around me for personal transformation. I call forth concentric circles of shimmering pearlescent pink and sapphire blue light to surround me. I am now centered within these concentric circles of light, enthroned upon the blooming petals of a white rose.

I am now in ceremony – free from the constructs of space and time – where instantaneous healing and divine knowing exist.

From the sky above, a shower of soft pink rose petals gently floats down, caressing my soul with a blissful scent. A warm, safe sensation arises within my heart, filling my body with a golden energy of my innate goodness. The petals float steadily down, forming a lush pink path across my inner landscape.

Upon this path, the outline of a beautiful woman appears, walking towards me. My body deeply relaxes into the vision of Mother Mary as she approaches.

A warm breeze arises, softening my skin with its touch. Four golden-white *Angels of the Presence* appear, one at each cardinal direction of my concentric circles. Their mighty wings rustle open, creating a canopy of heavenly feathers above me as their eyes peacefully smile into my heart.

Mother Mary walks with confidence, her white and blue robes lightly dance across her silhouette. Her sandaled feet step in harmony with the rhythm of my heartbeat.

I feel the divine humanity of this woman walking towards me. Her Sacred Heart carries the Divine Feminine medicine of wisdom cultivated from many lifetimes of tears wept and embodied joy. Mother Mary's medicine calls to my heart: I feel the potency of her pearls of wisdom and how she desires to adorn me with every one of them.

I witness the camaraderie of her sovereign soul as she lovingly peers into my own. I feel the pure accessibility of her Divine Feminine Christ embodiment before me, with open arms of true understanding.

Mother Mary's crown chakra shines with a halo whose white energy is defined by a radiant sacred geometric pattern known as the *Flower of Life*. Little stars dance as nodes of light along its living lines, flickering as tiny angels within her hair.

With the permission of my beckoning arms and smile, Mother Mary steps under the arc of angelic wings and across the threshold of my concentric circles of blue and pink energy. I open to embrace Mother Mary and feel her confident arms hugging me in heavenly love and laughter. She is a cherished friend throughout the ages: an ever-present, perfect reflection of my true nature as a sovereign creator.

The white rose expands beneath us. Mother Mary and I now sit across from one another, comfortably enthroned in luxurious petals. My heart is hungry for her divine reflection, and for a moment we rest without speaking, enjoying the serene sacred mirror offered in each other's eyes.

MOTHER MARY SPEAKS:

"Thank you for meeting me, eye-to-eye, in this courageous moment of inner communion. My highest delight is when you recognize me as your equal and experience me as an essential ally, close friend, and divine reflection for your human journey. Thank you for opening your heart to know me anew in this lifetime. I have much more to offer you as an accessible friend than as an antiquated statue of worshiped stone!

"My Sacred Heart teachings are just as relevant as when I walked the Earth long ago, more so now than ever before. For you live at a time of global awakening, a time in which my teachings will now be needed in The Way they were originally intended, unobstructed by religious censoring.

"Thank you for opening to my presence and receiving my transmission:

As you receive my words, may you feel my accessibility as a mentor.

As you visualize my words, may they dissolve all your defensives to self-love.

179

As you hear my words, may you remember that your humanity is divine.

As you taste my words, may you savor that I too walked the Earth, just like you, and as such my assurance is trustworthy: whatever it is you desire, it can be done.

As you feel my words, may you understand that I am an ever-present friend.

As you integrate my words, may miracles abound in your life – miracles of your own sovereign creation that I will faithfully witness.

As you delight in my words, may you feel me walking by your side, without judgment, joyfully supporting your every step along The Way for creating Heaven on Earth.

As you live my words, may you rest in the sanctuary of our shared divinity."

I welcome the peace of Mother Mary's prayer for our communion. In the light of Sophia, I thank you Mother Mary, and I now affirm:

I receive your pearls of wisdom as guidance for my human journey.

I receive the message of your life and divine reflections as my sacred mirror.

I am clear that you come as a loving guide and steadfast friend, respectful of my pace, personal boundaries, and human feelings along the journey of my personal awakening.

I am present to my inner world, where we will meet in safe communion.

I receive your support to celebrate and activate my sovereignty.

I receive your help for embodying my true divinity.

I receive your Sacred Heart speaking clearly to my own.

I am aware that your presence activates The Sophia Code within me.

I receive this miracle of your friendship creating peace in my life now.

Mother Mary smiles back at me, her face lit with golden grace. From her robes emerges a crystalline bottle of anointing oil, over which she whispers a prayer. With her right fingertips, Mother Mary lightly touches the sacred rose oil to my crown, third eye, heart, hands, and the bottom of my feet.

As she anoints each part of my body, I feel her warm hands transmitting healing energy that awakens my awareness to the power of our communion. She whispers words of light language that my soul intuitively understands as blessings. I feel honored by her care and adoration of me.

Mother Mary steps back and motions to the presiding Angels of the Presence to bless me as well. Soft wings begin to sweep away the energetic debris of feelings and outdated beliefs that no longer serve my relationship with Mother Mary. Within my DNA, I feel the crystalline chromosomes recording this experience with Mother Mary as an essential moment for activating Keycode 4.

I feel relieved by the four angels, who help me relax into the depth of this personal transformation. They conclude their angelic blessing by arcing their wings in unison above my crown. Their golden wingtips connect at a single point from which a waterfall of divine love pours down, flooding my crown chakra with a pearlescent white light that flows into every cell of my body.

This angelic waterfall of Sophia light fills me with revelations of peace, and in response my crown chakra blossoms open as a thousand-petaled white rose. From the white rose arises a beautiful Flower of Life pattern, which glistens as a mirror reflection of Mother Mary's sacred geometric halo. Our eyes glint in recognition of one another as divine embodiments of Sophia, adorned in Her glorious geometries of light.

Mother Mary reaches towards me and we embrace in divine love. While held in her arms, royal blue and sapphire flames of peace surround us. I feel lifetimes of outdated religious vows and oaths dissolve. We laugh in celebration as I recognize that I can always begin anew in my relationship with Mother Mary; the past has no hold over our invincible love.

In our joy, sky-blue rose petals float down from above. Royal blue petals begin to spiral open from beneath our white rose throne. Sparkling with sapphire flashes of light, the royal blue petals create a spiral path that continues to widen and encircle us, far beyond my sight. I look out across the cosmos to witness an unending line of guardian angels appear along this spiraling path of divine will.

I watch souls arising as stars from the no-thing to descend and walk as pilgrims upon this spiral path of The Rose. The Angels of the Presence guide their every step with loving attention. Sky-blue rose petals fall fresh upon me, their sweet scent filling me with the bliss of direct knowing as I watch the pilgrims. I witness that it is divine love creating The Rose, it is divine love spiraling open the path for walking The Way, and it is divine love guiding every pilgrim along The Way with guardian angels of every form.

My gaze returns to Mother Mary's eyes. She stands before me now, adorned in radiant golden robes. Above her head shines a brilliant star from which a soft waterfall of luminescent gold energy flows, emanating as veils of light around her face. Her radiant beauty is an embodied transmission of *The Peace that Passeth All Understanding.*

She extends one of her open hands for me to hold and as I take Mary's hand I feel a great warmth fill my heart. For a moment I look back at the spiraling path of pilgrims and notice that certain rose petal coordinates along The Way are flashing for my recognition.

I hear the voice of my Higher Self speak from with my heart: "This present moment with Mother Mary is an important step along The Way for fulfilling your destiny."

MOTHER MARY SPEAKS:

"As your loving witness I reflect how worthy you are to live out the glorious fulfillment of your destiny. I offer you this golden energy to expand and fill your consciousness with the truth of how beautiful you are. Receive my guiding star's light to illuminate your inner vision: may you now clearly see and know yourself as both the architect and fulfillment of your destiny. As your loving mentor, I help you honor the promise you made to yourself that is worthy of your committed focus. It is safe to open your heart and allow this empowerment to support you in the fulfillment of this promise."

I now open to receive this empowerment to fully align with my soul's destiny, with the following declaration:

As a Sovereign Creator of the One Sophia Source, by the power of my I Am Presence, I now declare this invocation heard and answered by the unified field of my whole self.

I accept that I hold the golden keys to my Heaven on Earth.
I accept that I create my reality, by the power of my word.
My word is good, my heart is pure.
By the loving power of my pure word, I now recognize and accept my human experience as the embodiment of my non-physical Oversoul.

I look up through my eighth chakra, which is the gateway for my soul's eternal light, located about 18 inches above my crown.

I look up to explore the column of light that goes on forever as the countless temples of my Oversoul.

I feel the holy architecture of innumerable wings, which are my inner being's many angelic emanations, within the golden and white light halls of my great Oversoul.

I see the eternal forms of light within more Sophia light.

I see the warm black womb of no-thing from which my Sophia light arises.

I feel the vast orchestrations and aspects of my Oversoul, and how they are holy, and they are good. I am reminded of my goodness and I take confidence.

From my human perspective, I watch above as waves of Sophia light descend from an unknown place within my Oversoul.

Above me, these waves of light flow as a waterfall through the gateway of my eighth chakra. Written upon these light waves are my Oversoul's encoded intentions for a desired destiny, pouring forth into the quantum field of space that my body arises from.

My Oversoul's encoded intentions for this lifetime activate and sustain the physical creation of my body's 7 major chakra system, as overseen by my Higher Self consciousness.

These 7 major chakras create seven luminous fields of light, whose light energy moves at a rate of motion which manifests as the appearance of my physical body. $E = MC^2$

My physical body is passionately willed into physical reality through the power of my Oversoul's intention to create me as a human chalice for divine expression.

I Am The Word that Became Flesh:

The intention of my Oversoul's word is carried out by my Higher Self consciousness. My Higher Self opens the eighth chakra and maintains this gateway for my non-physical essence to continuously pour forth into this chosen physical matrix, manifesting as a human form. My Higher Self maintains this opening for the duration of my lifetime.

My physical body is a holy vessel, created for the purpose of knowing myself as a sovereign creator, made in the image and likeness of Sophia, who gave birth to my whole consciousness.

My Oversoul designed every detail of my destiny to accelerate my spiritual evolution and embody my highest potential. I am here to know myself as a sovereign creator, within every circumstance of life.

I am the Holy Spirit, with the power to simultaneously exist in flesh.
I am the Oversoul. Pi: π 3.14159...
I am the Higher Self traveling beyond the speed of light.
I am the holy human chalice filled with my sovereign creator self. Phi: ϕ 1.618...

My Higher Self is the voice of my Oversoul, instructing me in the details of my destiny. My destiny was authored and agreed upon by my whole self, before I manifested into form.

My Higher Self is called the "Holy Spirit," "The Great Counselor," and "The Peace that Passeth All Understanding."

I now accept that my Higher Self is an innate aspect of my non-physical self. My Higher Self is the translator and messenger for all the multidimensional parts of me, which are consciously in dialogue throughout my human incarnation.

My intentions, purpose, and destiny for this lifetime are entirely available for me to access and act upon. All I need to do is ask that my Higher Self translate these codes of destiny from my Oversoul. My Higher Self instantly responds with downloads of divine knowing and the guidance I need to fulfill my destiny in every present moment.

I accept that I hold the golden keys to my Heaven on Earth.
I accept that I create my reality, by the power of my word.
My word is good, my heart is pure.
By the loving power of my pure word, I now recognize and accept my Higher Self as the Holy Spirit.

Acting as the *Holy Spirit,* my Higher Self guides me in the fulfillment of my destiny by orchestrating the alignment of manifestations such as objects, locations, nature, animals, individuals, community, and life events to speak directly to my heart.

My Higher Self resources all of creation to speak these clear teachings, messages, and instructions for me to accomplish every step of my soul's destiny.

My Higher Self, acting as my Holy Spirit, guides me through every initiation, every open door, and every step of my evolution by orchestrating all of creation to speak directly to my awareness with consistency and clarity.

I easily recognize the voice of my own Holy Spirit spoken through an orchestrated messenger because its message is always loving, truthful, illuminating, positive, encouraging, healing, and reflects back to me an intuition or truth that I am already aware of.

With eyes to see and ears to hear: I am now conscious of my Higher Self speaking directly to me as the Holy Spirit through all of creation.

I place my faith in what is worthy of being trusted. I place my faith in the omniscient multidimensional power of the Holy Spirit *within me* as my Higher Self. Speaking to me now and always through all of creation, my Higher Self is ever guiding me in the fulfillment of my soul's destiny.

I accept that I hold the golden keys to my Heaven on Earth.
I accept that I create my reality, by the power of my word.
My word is good, my heart is pure.
By the loving power of my pure word, I now recognize and accept my Higher Self as The Great Counselor.

Acting as *The Great Counselor,* my Higher Self communicates the details of my destiny through the quiet audible voice within my heart, my inner vision, internal promptings, inspiration, noticeable synchronicities, intuitions, miracles, dreams, and signs.

My Higher Self, acting as The Great Counselor, guides me to follow my heart and align with healthy choices, practices, and opportunities for growth – including taking risks that empower my full potential in this lifetime.

Forever in presence, The Great Counselor constantly speaks of my divinity and my human ability to embody that divinity, every day, in this lifetime as the fulfillment of my destiny.

I easily recognize the voice of The Great Counselor as encouraging, uplifting, inspiring, and soothing. Its message always communicates to me the mighty potential of my soul's ability to create a magnificent destiny and Legacy of

Love that will positively impact generations to come. The Great Counselor always believes in me – guiding me physically, emotionally, mentally, and spiritually to have faith in myself.

With eyes to see and ears to hear: I am now conscious of my Higher Self speaking directly to me as The Great Counselor through all my physical and spiritual senses.

I place my faith in what is worthy of being trusted. I place my faith in the perfect guidance of The Great Counselor *within me* as my Higher Self intimately speaking to me now and always, ever guiding me in the fulfillment of my soul's destiny.

I accept that I hold the golden keys to my Heaven on Earth.
I accept that I create my reality, by the power of my word.
My word is good, my heart is pure.
By the loving power of my pure word, I now recognize and accept my Higher Self as The Peace that Passeth All Understanding.

Acting as *The Peace that Passeth All Understanding,* my Higher Self communicates its constant reassurance and discernment through the emotional intelligence of my feelings. As I take divinely guided action in alignment with my destiny, I experience the resonance of my Higher Self through high-vibrational feelings such as joy, love, happiness, contentment, patience, comfort, focus, devotion, steady passion, vitality, and transcendent peace as a result.

These feelings clearly communicate to me when I am in alignment with fulfilling the details of my destiny. Additionally, when I am present to The Peace that Passeth All Understanding, I easily discern those life choices that would conflict with my highest potential and destiny. I follow the peace of my heart and easily walk away from that which does not serve my destiny.

When I experience uncertainty and fear, The Peace that Passeth All Understanding is still present within me, soothing my resistance to return to the truth of my innate wellbeing. It is this transcendent, unwavering divine peace that always guides me, as my Higher Self, one loving step at a time, back into alignment with my destiny.

With eyes to see and ears to hear: I am now conscious of my Higher Self speaking directly to me as The Peace that Passeth All Understanding that guides my awareness to trust the emotional intelligence of my feelings.

I place my faith in what is worthy of being trusted. I place my faith in The Peace that Passeth All Understanding as the guiding voice of my Higher Self speaking from within my heart now and always. I walk The Way with this blessing of peace *within me* as I fulfill my soul's destiny for this lifetime.

I accept that I hold the golden keys to my Heaven on Earth.
I accept that I create my reality, by the power of my word.
My word is good, my heart is pure.
By the loving power of my pure word, I now command my Higher Self to activate the crystalline divine qualities of Keycode 4 of The Sophia Code within me as the new operating system for my carbon-based DNA.

By the power of my I Am Presence, it is commanded that my heart spiral open to now flourish and blossom as The Rose.

π
By the power of my I Am Presence, it is commanded that my Higher Self anchor my commitment to live in alignment with fulfilling my destiny throughout my entire body and being now.

φ
I am empowered to fulfill my soul's destiny through daily communion with my Higher Self now.
It is done.
It is done.
It is done.
By the power of 3, a perfect trinity: It is done.

I now integrate this initiation throughout my entire body, on all four levels of my Be-ing, with grace and ease.

I open my inner eyes and witness hosts of angels along the spiraling path of The Rose singing in celebration of my completed initiation. Mother Mary takes both my hands in her own, blessing my palms. I feel the chakras of my hands spiral open as two wheels of healing light. We stand, eye-to-eye, facing one another with radiant appreciation.

Mother Mary steps back, standing in her open arm mudra before me. Her Sacred Heart is lit with royal blue and pink flames of divine love. I open my own arms to mirror her iconic mudra, accepting her presence as a mentor for me in The Teachings of the Rose. Thank you, Mother Mary, for your extraordinary love and support for the journey ahead. I welcome you as a guide and friend in my life.

Blessed and sealed by my Higher Self, Mother Mary, and the Angels of the Presence, I affirm that this empowerment is accomplished. I now close this ceremony with reverence for my true self and the divine love of All That Is, supporting my eternal success.

Amen.

KEYCODE 5
"SHE OF A THOUSAND ANGELS"

My oracular transmission awakens you as a vehicle of awakening for others. You are an angel on Earth – and I am right here by your side, supporting your prayer to become an essential leader in this global movement for the Divine Feminine Christ.

CHAPTER 10 | MARY MAGDALENE

Mary Magdalene Is a Mentor for Your Spiritual Revolution

MARY MAGDALENE SPEAKS:

I AM MARY MAGDALENE, known as "She of a Thousand Angels" in The Sophia Code cosmology. My Sophia embodiment title reveals my Oversoul's commitment to shine the greatest angelic light in the darkest of places. I work with every order of angelic guides to reconcile the suffering of this world and others. Wherever I am invoked as an overlighting presence, I am joined by billions of accompanying angels.

My Divine Feminine Christ embodiment of Sophia rocked the ancient world in which I served. In my most recent lifetime, I came as the lightning of revolutionary change for an entire generation of women brutally subjugated to the status of being property. My mother was a wise woman who privately maintained her worship of the Divine Feminine according to the lineage of her grandmothers. During her pregnancy, she received multiple messages from seers who predicted my birth as a returning prophet.

As a young child, my parents recognized that I was innately gifted for the channeling and healing arts, coupled with a sharp intelligence that I wielded as a sword of truth. I was born as an awakened being, with the psychic development of my many lifetimes already activated within my body. As an acutely sensitive empath, I would relay vivid details to my parents of events happening in other locations that they would confirm back to me. My mother would often witness me softly soothing myself in recognizable languages from ancient civilizations. At other times she would find me in our gardens, sitting stone-still while in trance, witnessing visions of humanity's destiny.

Although I was uniquely raised with wealth, status, and a secret education that honored the Divine Feminine, the first part of my life was spent cloistered far away from interacting with most people and any public spaces. A female of any age, especially a young woman courageous enough to assert her boundaries, could be harmed or legally stoned to death for any random projection placed upon her by an angry man. My parents encouraged me to cultivate strong inner practices of meditation and self-mastery before regularly interacting with the insane civilization that I was born to liberate.

The wealth of my family afforded me options unavailable to most young girls of my time. Along with extensive home studies led by my mother, I traveled each year with my father to secretly train at mystery school temples in Mesopotamia, Egypt, and India. On these journeys I would meet other young women who were afforded these same rare opportunities. I often felt so lonely in my unique lifestyle, that I would fill the chalice of my heart with these precious memories of spending time with others my own age. I would drink deeply from these memories in my time back home.

As a maturing young girl, home would often feel like a cage after returning from my travels, but I took solace by meditating in our secluded gardens for hours. I would practice everything that I learned in the mystery schools, cultivating an authentic relationship with myself. On the inner planes I would meet with my mystery school friends, my Ascended Master mentors, and countless beings of light from a wide spectrum of angelic orders.

I received many messages and visions that I would one day meet far more of my soul family, a community of individuals that were as gifted as I was. Further, the many angels that I would engage with in meditation would often share that I had come to shine a great diamond light to the hearts of many suffering people.

Searching my heart, I always felt the truth in these messages. My heart ached as I would witness the brutal suffering most of my people were surviving, both from the Roman occupation, as well as from the self-righteous Pharisees of our own people's ruling class. There would be many times that I would physically feel my throat close up as I empathically felt yet another woman being raped and beaten into submission, or even killed. The Roman methods of public torture for population control would enrage me behind my cloistered walls.

My mother knew the agony of my true feelings, for this was an undeniable anger for her as well. She directed my heart to continually take refuge in my secret practices with Sekhmet, Kali Ma, Inanna, and wrathful aspects of Green Tara to cast out the darkness and invoke clearings, healing, and reconciliation for those that I prayed for. As my mother would watch me pray, a great light would go out from my body to join in the angelic ranks that I would invoke for the healing of others.

As I grew into a beautiful young woman of marriageable age, I was afforded another extremely rare opportunity due to the wealth of my family. I was given the right to inherit my mother's fortune passed through her grandmothers' lineage, as well as the right to choose if marriage was appropriate for me. My father promised my mother that I would never be forced into an arranged marriage, and that I would always be supported in my spiritual training regardless of my marital status. In all of Palestine, I was one of a handful of women afforded such protection and personal authority.

I happily opted out of a young marriage and choose to continue in my mystery school training. I also yearned to experience my spiritual studies by living in a community of allies and friends. My father had often spoken of our family relations at the Mount Carmel mystery school, and my curiosity yearned to live beyond the walls of my safe childhood compound. I arrived at Mount Carmel at an unusual age for their curriculum of initiations, yet I committed to my new life with the passion of a young woman embracing her independence.

I also continued to travel with my father, returning every year to my mystery school training. In Egypt I deepened as an initiate in Isis' lineage of ceremonial magick and oracular activism, tracking moon cycle empowerments within the rhythms of my body. I mastered tantric breathing practices that circulated my sexual energy into higher states of consciousness that cultivated the precision of my already activated psychic gifts.

Although my kundalini training was rigorously demanding, I thrived in the wings of Isis' secret magi teachings. As I grew in strength and stature, I also received deeper initiations in the hidden teachings of Sekhmet-Hathor.

Mary Magdalene Prepares for Her Mission

When I would return to the Essene monastic life of Mount Carmel, my richly ornamented personal expression would be exchanged for the simple robes of an initiate. However, my simple robes could not diminish the radiant and cultivated goddess embodiment that I had become in myself.

My face shone as an angel and my dark eyes flashed with the secrets of the desert. With long muscular arms, my body would seem to dance as Kali upon Shiva, without a single movement. I was a riveting enigma for most of the monastery; only a few master teachers leading our humble community could see how sophisticated the mission was that I was preparing for.

Learning to live in a community was a far different experience than I had anticipated. It required a daily surrendering to social constructs that were foreign to my privileged upbringing. Women and men were treated equally, yet there were rigorous rules that I had to adhere by.

I often spent as much time as I was permitted to directly mentor with Mother Mary as my primary teacher, for we shared a similar background in our Egyptian mystery school training. We would often sit together in her rose garden. Mary would remind me that I was a whole rose in the presence of both my petals and thorns and to never feel ashamed of my thorns.

As an overlighting mentor for my development, Mary could see that I was a natural spiritual revolutionary longing to serve my divine purpose. She also knew that it would require a sophisticated set of skills in order for me to safely speak my truth as a public female leader. These skills included mastering the high magi arts, oracular oration, and embodying an invincible divine love. My personal light would have to be bright enough to blind those who would harm me and cast a path for those terrified to seek out my help.

I also needed to master the assertion of my personal sovereignty, as both a woman and as a teacher, within the interdependent collaborative efforts of a community working together as the one body of Sophia Christ. Mother Mary took me under her wing as her own daughter, to initiate my awareness into these highly sophisticated nuances of Divine Feminine Christ leadership.

Mary's own radical embodiment of fierce divine love opened my heart far beyond what I thought was possible. Her overlighting presence tempered my wrathful proclivity for the intensity of Sekhmet with the Beauty Way teachings of Hathor. My oracular relationship with Kali Ma was balanced by Mary's teachings for abiding in the heart from Green and White Tara.

Mary also introduced me to one of her most important allies, a guiding light master called Quan Yin, who assisted her in the daily tasks of ministry and as a spiritual mother for our Mount Carmel community. Quan Yin began appearing to me as well, revealing her direct teachings on how to harness the power of my anger into an all-consuming compassion that would render my enemies harmless.

I became completely immersed in my relationships with myself, my mentor Mary, as well as our overlighting team of Ascended Master guides and angels. My longing for a distant future fell away without much notice of its whereabouts. I found myself feeling the subtle purr of happiness that naturally arose from the satisfaction of my lioness heart connected to her pride, hunting our divine potential together in every present moment.

My radiant womanhood became deeply grounded as I matured into an eloquent spiritual teacher and highly refined oracle. In this journey of self-mastery, I came to understand my lifelong inner drive for spiritual training. It was essential that a Divine Feminine Christ teaching embodiment, capable of leading both men and women, would be available to support the spiritual revolution that would ignite in Palestine with the return of Mary's son, Jesus. The container of his public ministry would create the opportunity and physical protection to freely walk as a sovereign woman, offering my direct teachings in collaboration with his own.

Other than my extraordinary father and a few living masters that I had trained with, my experience of men as spiritual allies had been relatively disappointing. My diamond-faceted mind and acute psychic perception intimidated even high-level male teachers in our Essene order. Out of endearing respect for my mentor, I wanted to believe what Mother Mary shared with me about her son, but I withheld my full belief in his ability to lead us until finally meeting him in person.

Deciding who Jesus was for myself was an important step in opening my heart to follow his lead and take up my opportunity to teach by his side. I was a wealthy, independent woman with an extraordinary education and I did not have to answer this call to embody the Divine Feminine Christ as a supporting teacher in his movement. I needed to intuitively experience his own embodiment of both the Divine Masculine and the Divine Feminine Christ energies to trust that serving in alignment with his ministry was the best use of my gifts and life force.

The Door Opens for Magdalene's Public Ministry

The night before I met Jesus, he appeared to me in a vivid lucid dream. In the dream, I was embodying the voracity of Sekhmet hunting down demons that prey on women in Jerusalem. Catching the demons in my mouth, I would maul and tear them apart. I would then return to the woman, licking her wounds clean, and push her back up on her feet with my broad lioness head. In the dream, this happened three times with three different women.

I prepared to depart from the third woman, leaving her in the care of my supporting angelic guard. My lioness body began to shift back into human form, with just my blood-stained lioness face remaining. As I turned to leave, there stood Jesus before me. His smile felt so familiar to me, it was as though part of my own soul was smiling back at me. I felt my whiskers and sharp fangs recede back into my human face. I stepped forward to greet him as a woman honored by his smile for my great works.

He lightly touched my third eye in a familiar mudra and whispered: "It is safe to follow me. I know how your great gifts will liberate the suffering of many. I am here to prepare The Way for you to walk this journey with me, side-by-side in our shared mission. Your passion for Sophia will not be dishonored by following me. I am here to create safety for the collective gifts of our whole Family of Light to rise as one body. Allow me to make The Way ahead easier for your wisdom to be shared with those who need you."

I woke up from the dream just as the sun was rising. As the lucid landscape receded, I heard the roars of Sekhmet's lioness pride announcing a new chapter in my life.

The following day, I met Jesus in person at a wedding that Mother Mary had asked me to attend with her. Jesus embodied such ease with himself and everyone around him; I found myself watching his every movement with a secret awe. Our conversation with one another seemed to occur in multiple languages simultaneously and without many words at all. Although Mary formally introduced us, we spoke telepathically to one another for most of the wedding, enjoying the companionship of each other's highly refined intuitive gifts.

His Christed embodiment was immediately recognizable to me and yet I enjoyed how casually he allowed himself to be accessed by everyone in the room. His soul carried the scents of India, Tibet, and Egypt from his own mystery school training. I psychically tracked the similar and complementary codes from multiple ascended cultures that we shared between us, which created a highly harmonic resonance for the wedding guests.

In our orbit around one another, I experienced multiple flashes of future memories in which we were speaking to thousands of spiritual seekers in large fields and hidden temples. Although we were outwardly participating in the wedding festivities, Jesus and I began to inwardly calibrate to the amplification of our powers in the physical presence of one another. I watched Mother Mary's playful amusement at her children finally meeting.

Our shared resonance felt extraordinary and I could feel in my heart how easy it would be to reach the people that I wanted to serve if I chose to work by his side. My heart softened in gratitude and I floated in a sublime peace for most of that evening.

When I heard that Jesus had physically shifted the quantum structure of water into more wine for the wedding guests, I felt a lightning recognition shoot through my body as a sign from my Higher Self. With this first demonstration of Jesus' sovereign power I knew that everything I was preparing to offer in my embodiment of the Divine Feminine Christ would begin now.

Seeding a Divine Feminine Blueprint for Your Future

Upon his return to Palestine, Jesus revealed the coordinates of his future timeline to several close allies, including Mother Mary and myself. The knowledge of our brief opportunity to work together created a riveted focus within me for fulfilling my purpose and maximizing my personal practice.

We lived an entire lifetime over the next three years, fulfilling prophecies and commanding miracles for the liberation of thousands. Time completely dissolved as we focused upon maximizing every available moment we had in our public ministry together, before Jesus' demonstration of the crucifixion and his physical ascension.

Almost immediately we began training and initiating male and female disciples to prepare for the flood of seekers that would hear of Jesus' miraculous healing abilities. We had a core inner circle of devotees that would assist us in training an outer circle of many more initiates. The combined quantum energy field that Jesus and I created in our highly refined work together magnetized people to join our movement from around the country and also from other parts of the world.

I used my high tantric training for alchemizing large amounts of internal life force, as well as transforming the full spectrum of outer energies that were magnetized to our ministry, into an abundance of usable positive creative energy for our spiritual movement. My tantric practices were also consecrated to building an energetic momentum for Jesus' message to reach the first wave of a global network.

Eventually, the crowds that we drew to receive our teachings across Palestine required enormous fields to accommodate the increasing number of people that were coming to be healed and initiated. My father's network of wealthy landowners became quite useful for orchestrating locations that we could safely teach from on privately owned property. At my request, my mother also gave me a large portion of my inheritance prior to her earthly departure. I contributed these resources to the feeding, funding, and coordination of the many logistics required for such large gatherings to take place.

Along with Mother Mary, Jesus became my greatest friend and spiritual ally. At our large gatherings we would often sit side-by-side, yet at a designed distance, co-directing the collective consciousness of the large crowds. Our individual embodiments were so magnetic that those who were meant to receive healing work, empowerments, and teachings directly from me would line up before me. Those ready to receive their empowerments directly from Jesus would line up before him. Our disciples and initiates would encircle us and assist as needed.

The sight of a female teacher, sitting in a full lotus posture, in equal status with a highly respected male teacher was unheard of in our society. Yet Jesus' multidimensional presence was a Divine Masculine force of nature. He would enfold the masses in his golden-white light of Sophia Christ consciousness. This would temporarily assuage, elevate, and accelerate the crowd's awareness beyond judgment so that they could clearly see and access my offering beyond gender.

My auric field would also expand as well, to clear and soften the hearts of the people to Jesus' work. I felt an incredible loyalty to Jesus, which inspired me to psychically clear many lower level entities and demonic energies attached to the suffering seekers attending our gathering before they even arrived. In my meditations, the orders of angels at my command would be sent forward to honor and prepare The Way for his arrival at a gathering. I also used the diamond light body of my Higher Self to elevate and amplify the crowd's awareness of the many dimensional realities that Jesus and I were teaching about.

When I would offer teachings or healing empowerments, a great momentum of Sophia's Holy Spirit would descend through me and Her immaculate Shekinah light would overflow from the chalice of my heart. Women would often lay down to rest their weary souls around me, drinking deeply from the overflowing Holy Spirit transmission pouring through me. I was 'wise as a serpent and gentle as a dove,' as I carefully listened to and followed my Higher Self's constant instruction on which divine qualities of my Keycode transmission that I was to embody in each present moment.

I also performed exorcisms that extracted entities and cellular imprints of severe trauma and abuse from both women and men. Some exorcisms required my physical involvement; others simply happened as seekers locked their eyes with my own. My eyes would transport the seeker through an instantaneous series of initiations that would cleanse their awareness to let go of the demons housed within their body. Most of my mission was primarily focused on healing and empowering an entire population of women who believed it was their duty to be abused, used, and discarded at the will of another, yet there were many men that also surrendered to my care.

Many people would often pass out after receiving a healing empowerment or exorcism from me; this occurrence created the phenomenon of a temporary amnesia within them as to whether the healing happened or not, and by whom. I did not need credit for the great works of Sophia pouring through me, but I did need to remain unhindered in my purpose. This forgetfulness would often act as a safety measure for my own continued involvement with Jesus' ministry. Those who would go to speak of a healing facilitated by me would often only remember Jesus' face, and in this I remained relatively unseen by those who would harm me for being seen.

I also spent many hours assisting Jesus' healing work in any way that I could. For the many women that needed Divine Masculine healing initiations directly from Jesus, I became an associated safe face that invited them to trust him and come closer to what he was offering their hearts. I was deeply moved by his divine love and great compassion for the heartbreak of women. Witnessing his unconditional acceptance, supportive presence, and incredibly generous healing activations also healed painful memories from other lifetimes within my own heart.

I never felt that I was beneath him or in servitude to Jesus in any way. His integrity was immaculate and his devoted acts for reconciling the Divine Feminine went above and beyond, every day. Our spiritual alliance encoded humanity's collective consciousness with a true template for the reconciliation of the Divine Masculine and Divine Feminine Christ energies.

Our constant focus upon service and uninterrupted work revealed the power of how men and women can access their divinity together, rising above base cultural survival strategies, to serve a mighty good in wholeness and integrity with one another. We were both so filled by the Holy Spirit pouring through us that our daily experiences of working with one another created a blueprint for a future golden age that is upon you now.

Both Jesus and I received many visitors from the future. They would assure us that the seeds we were sowing together, for the awakening of humanity, would one day blossom to radically empower a new generation of Lightworkers for the Earth's ascension. We were sowing seeds of consciousness for a spiritual revolution that would remain underground until the conditions were ripe for the roses of our Sophia Christ teachings to be revealed once again.

We both had many visions of the time that you are living in now. In my visions I saw that the sophisticated magi mystery school techniques that we used to safely offer our public ministry together as a man and woman would one day no longer be needed. I also witnessed that after Jesus' ascension, much of what we were teaching would be misunderstood and misused for centuries to come.

Following Jesus' ascension, Mother Mary and I fled to France. Channeling in the refuge of caves, I prophesied that my name would be maligned and hidden for an entire dark age. I also witnessed that my reputation would not be restored until thousands of years later, when the voices of women ushering in a new golden age would reach into their cellular memory and remember the truth of my Divine Feminine Christ embodiment.

Yes, I was seeing *you,* as one of those future Lightworkers that would call out to receive my support as an Ascended Master mentor for this next golden age. I saw the faces of countless women and men who would remember my works as a Divine Feminine Christ embodiment and seek me by name, as an essential spiritual guide for the current spiritual revolution that is upon you now. *Thank you* for seeing me as I am, which allows for me to support you in your own great mission ahead.

A Mentor for Your Angelic Embodiment

So you see, we are calling out to one another across the ages to continue in this great work of the returning Divine Feminine Christ consciousness.

The power to heal, the power to envision, the power to increase, the power to reveal, and the power to command miracles lives within you. I embodied these angelic powers, regardless of all circumstances, to become a guiding light mentor for you.

Jesus, myself, and our many allies set into motion a movement that provided a foundational blueprint for your generation to rise up in radical spiritual leadership. We fulfilled certain prophecies of a dark age, so that you may rise as the *Phoenix Children*, fulfilling your own prophecies to declare the sovereign divinity of humanity's origin. As Jesus spoke 'that even greater works will be accomplished than these,' [Jn 14:12] he was speaking of your own sovereign potential to command miracles and awaken humanity to its own ability for creating Heaven on Earth.

Many people often invoke my name for support and assistance to heal their relationship with sexuality and to be released from the debilitating effects of trauma upon the body. As you are drawn to my overlighting presence as an Ascended Master mentor, you will discover that I also activate many divine qualities within you that are connected to advocacy, public speaking, and oracular teaching.

I am especially drawn to working with women and men who seek to radically embody every facet of their true selves, without apology. I help you get acclimated with asserting your personal power as a spiritual leader and how to remain in integrity with yourself and your divine purpose, regardless of all circumstances.

As a spiritual guide for self-mastery, my overlighting presence activates your awareness to the many orders of angels that are at your service, both within you and within all of creation. Further, as "She of a Thousand Angels," my Keycode 5 transmission activates the angelic codes stored within your divine genome to be expressed as an essential aspect of your humanity. I assist your awareness to soften and integrate to the holy angelic powers within you, which you are here to embody as a living angel on Earth.

My Keycode 5 transmission also reveals an ancient Shekinah lineage of magi and oracular High Priestesses, known throughout the cosmos as *The Order of Magdalena*. When you invoke my overlighting presence to guide you, I am also joined by this sacred order of *Magdalenes*, who are women that have incarnated as revolutionary angels on Earth and in other star systems for millennia. For example, Joan of Arc is a Magdalene High Priestess in our Order.

As an overlighting mentor for your ascension journey, I guide your human awareness in how to accept and love yourself as an angel on Earth. The angelic light that shines within you is here to dissolve the darkness of ignorance, greed, fear, and annihilation through your radiant embodiment of invincible divine love. Allow me to offer you the unconditional support of my entire lineage as you boldly step forward upon your own heroic path to embody a diamond light that devours all darkness blighting the precious heart of humanity.

My initiates associate me with the Divine Feminine water and blood mystery rituals of the Holy Chalice, many of which originate from Isis' magi teachings. In my Magdalene lineage, the chalice is a powerful symbol that represents your body being the temple for the Holy Spirit. If you feel magnetized to me as a mentor, you will also feel drawn to working with the chalice mysteries and their associated symbolism.

When you commit to mentoring with me, I transmit these Sophia Magdalene mystery school teachings to you as an initiate. I am here to guide you in how to purify and consecrate your heart as a chalice for the overflowing healing power of your own Higher Self's diamond light body. You are an angel on Earth – and I am right here by your side, supporting your prayer to be an essential leader in this Divine Feminine Christ movement.

KEYCODE 5
THE MARY MAGDALENE INITIATION

Accessing Your Inner Angels of Self-Mastery

I now prepare a ceremonial space within and around me for transformation. I call forth concentric circles of shimmering pearlescent white and pink light to surround me. I am now centered within these concentric circles of light, standing at the gateway of a beautiful temple within me.

I am now in ceremony – free from the constructs of space and time – where instantaneous healing and divine knowing exist.

In the temple, there are mighty, white marble pillars. Each white marble pillar represents an essential quality of the Holy Spirit within me. The closest pillar to my left is inscribed in light language as the *Pillar of Perfect Love*. The closest pillar to my right is inscribed as the *Pillar of Perfect Peace*. These two pillars frame the temple scene before me.

Beneath my feet, the cool, white marble floor gleams with living veins of gold. The white marble floor expands beyond my perception. I deepen in my stance to access more details about this temple through the feeling intelligence of my feet.

As I stand upon the marble, my feet soak in the subtle sensation that it is breathing. My toes curiously surrender into this rhythmic breath, rising and falling within the stillness of stone. The feeling intelligence of my body recognizes that this is my Holy Spirit breathing the Breath of Life within the white marble floor. I welcome the fresh perspective of my Holy Spirit to now fill my awareness with every breath in ... and every breath out.

I feel the Breath of Life breathing beneath me.
I feel the Breath of Life breathing within me.
I feel the Breath of Life breathing before me.
At one with this Breath of Life, I am now aware:
I am standing in the perfect temple of my own holy essence.

Directly ahead of me, I take note that at the center of the temple, the white marble floor flows into a formation of three-tiered steps. This marble stairway encircles a wide pool of still, pristine water.

As I look upon it, the still waters quench the thirst of my soul. Unlike any experience of water that I have ever had before, I feel compelled to know everything about this body of water. I deeply drink from the pool with my eyes to learn more.

Standing at the temple entrance, I take several steps forward to focus my sight closer into the pool. With every step forward, I feel my presence being felt by others. Stepping out from the pillars, parallel to my left and right side, I am now greeted by two loving angels.

From the Pillar of Perfect Love emerges a beautiful feminine angel who smiles upon me with warm radiance and gentle kindness. Her arms are open wide to welcome me. A golden-pink energy emanates from her body as an aura of loving divine light that instantly travels into my heart. She is the *Angel of Perfect Love.*

From the Pillar of Perfect Peace emerges a beautiful masculine angel whose bright, steady gray eyes kindly smile into my own. Beneath the canopy of his twilight-blue wings, our eyes lock in an unflinching gaze of transcendent, cooling peace. He smells like sweet spring rain and lightning. He is the *Angel of Perfect Peace.*

"Welcome to the great inner temple of your own holy essence. We are your inner angels of the perfect love and peace that always abides within you. Thank you for receiving us today. As you receive our presence, you are actually engaging with the divine qualities of your own Holy Spirit. For we are but emanations of your true self."

"Why am I here?" I ask.

In silent response to my question, the angels deftly move to now stand side-by-side with me. They each take one of my hands into their own. Above my head, her golden-pink feathers overlap with his twilight-blue feathers as their angel wings stretch out to surround me in a loving embrace.

Together we stand as a trinity and peer at the distant waiting pool of still pristine water. The angels speak as a unified telepathic voice that I can hear in my mind through the touch of their hands holding mine. They speak directly to my awareness with an eager response to my question.

THE ANGELS SPEAK:

"Your body is asking for you to understand that it is a highly loving and responsive supercomputer – yet it does not want to be held responsible for the outcome of your life. Your body knows that its purpose and functions are designed to tell the truth of your Higher Self by providing moment-by-moment intuitive biofeedback that acts as an emotional navigation system for making conscious choices of alignment.

"The neurological biofeedback of your body is extraordinary; it accurately and instantly tracks every thought that you are thinking – even before a thought is fully formed – with correlating emotions. Before a self-criticizing thought has finished its biting remark about you, a physical pain or contraction can be felt within your body as emotional discomfort. Likewise, a positive thought about yourself will open and expand the wings of your heart, before that thought is even formulated into words. This emotional feedback creates a magnetism towards what you want and a repulsion towards what no longer serves you.

"Your body is perfectly designed to provide you with emotional biofeedback about how you are aligning with and following through on the divine guidance of your Higher Self within every present moment. Yet, your body is often blamed as the creator of both your pain and pleasure. It is time to release your judgments and expectations placed upon your body's emotional communication system. The sensations of your emotions are not trying to control your awareness; they are simply informing you of what reality your thoughts and choices are creating in every present moment.

"Your Higher Self knows every detail about your journey ahead. With the gift of your free will, you can always choose to surrender and receive this perfect guidance of your Higher Self speaking directly through your body. You also have the choice to blunder and blindly react through the journey of your life, mistaking your body's biofeedback as an attack against you.

"Therefore, you are here to recognize that there is a single free will choice that must be made – every day – for you to fulfill your destiny and live in peace. This single choice governs, directs, and guides all other daily choices. Therefore, this choice is the *only one* that matters.

"You have come to the great halls of your inner temple to decide, once and for all, that you are finished with the agony and suffering of believing that your body's emotional biofeedback and limited awareness is responsible for the outcome of your life. Further, you are here to decide, once and for all, to take responsibility for the success of your life by actively surrendering to your Higher Self's overlighting presence to fully operate and govern your human body and awareness now.

"This single free will choice has the power to inform the motivation and outcome of all your life choices. Choosing to follow your Higher Self's guidance does not mean subjecting yourself to any judgment or qualifying standard of perfectionist behavior. Rather, surrendering your awareness to be operated by your Higher Self means that you are on a journey of being mentored by your own divinity.

"In every challenging experience, your Higher Self mentors you in the art of responding to life versus reacting to it, guiding you to act with grace and move with purpose by recognizing what information your emotional guidance system is sharing with you. Your Higher Self also mentors you in how to courageously seek your happiness and fulfill your destiny while exploring the vulnerable and risky landscape of the unknown.

"In every present moment, your Higher Self is waiting for you to make this free will choice and surrender to its higher power guiding you from within, speaking through your body, heart, and emotions. Many spend their entire lives resisting this one single decision to trust their Higher Self, in an unconscious battle waged against their greatest potential.

"True self-mastery comes from honoring this relationship of many aspects of yourself working together as one. The relationship between your Higher Self and your awareness is that of the inner guru and the inner devotee, the inner teacher and the inner student. Your Higher Self is the safest teacher for your awareness and body to be operated by, mentoring you in how to make your life choices as a unified field of wellbeing.

"Authentic self-mastery is the daily practice of recognizing that your awareness is engaged in a moment-by-moment journey to choose your Higher Self's reality of divine love over the shadowy illusion of self-terrorizing fear in every present moment. 'A house divided against itself will not stand.' (Mt 12:25b) Dividing your awareness to only partly believe in the power of your Higher Self to guide the outcome of your life is agonizing to both your body and awareness. When your awareness is divided against itself, this eventually leads to emotional, physical, and psychological breakdowns that interrupt the momentous flow of wellbeing in your life.

"As your inner angels, we remind you that this decision to allow your Higher Self to operate your awareness, increasingly guiding you to choose divine love in every present moment, does not require for you to understand or even like how the daily omniscient orchestrations of your Higher Self are unfolding. There may be many initiations of faith ahead in which trusting this greater part of you may feel absolutely foolish or bewildering to your dissolving social conditioning.

"Remember that this journey of self-mastery begins by navigating one emotion and one experience at a time, which builds an incremental willingness and increased awareness within every present moment to trust your Higher Self. Continually calling upon and receiving your Higher Self's unconditional love for you is essential for integrating and appreciating your heroic journey along The Way. Eventually, your commitment creates an undivided, unified field of daily trust, self-acceptance, and self-love within you that opens the space within your body, heart, and mind for your awareness to identify the daily divine guidance flowing to you from your Higher Self. This is the self-mastery that you are seeking: beyond the mastery of any extraordinary talent or skill, it is the self-mastery of your awareness surrendering to your Higher Self that allows for you to live an extraordinary life.

"Today, in your great prayer for self-mastery, you are baptizing your awareness in the holy waters of your true divine essence. You are being initiated by the Holy Spirit within you to recognize the divine blueprint for living as a master within every present moment. May your body, heart, and mind be blessed by the nine pillars of initiation before you."

The Angel of Perfect Love and the Angel of Perfect Peace now motion for me to step forward with them, aligning at the *Pillar of Faith*.

I now open to receive the angel from my inner being who initiates the first pillar

*of self-mastery for my awareness to activate the pathway of divine love within
every present moment.*

Across the temple my eyes now witness a shimmering, winged feminine
form arise from the still waters of the holy pool. She floats effortlessly
forward, to now stand before me, warmly greeting me with her smile.
Accompanied by a symphony of tiny bells, her voice announces that she is
the inner *Angel of Faith.*

The Angel of Faith shimmers with a golden energy that intermittently
sparkles with rays of sky-blue light. In her right hand is a white staff whose
crested top is carved as a caduceus of two interwoven, pearlescent white
Sophia Dragons. The dragons' eyes glitter as living sapphires that reflect
into my own. Riveted by the dragon staff, I widely smile. The Angel of
Faith joyfully laughs in return, delighted by my intrigue. She leans the staff
forward so that I may study the dragons' eyes closer. Animated by my focus,
the two dragons spark to life and turn to face each of my eyes.

THE ANGEL OF FAITH SPEAKS:

"As your inner Angel of Faith, my greatest joy is to guide your awareness
across the bridge from fear to divine love in any moment, as many times as
needed throughout the day. My dragon staff devours the toxicity of negative
thinking that arises in your struggle to trust divine love. The caduceus on
my staff is a symbol of my healing power. I am the embodiment of relentless
faith that seeks to reconcile your awareness to always choose divine love
over fear.

"As your inner Angel of Faith, I delight in serving on the frontline of your
self-mastery. Every decision to choose divine love begins with a catalyzing
feeling of hope that uplifts your awareness to consider the quantum
possibilities of having faith in divine love. As the Angel of Faith, I stand with
you at this gateway of hope within every choice. I champion your awareness
to align with your Higher Self and trust in divine love, again and again.

"Remember that I am an aspect of your Higher Self, a messenger and
friend in service to your daily journey of self-mastery. You can call on me at
any time to amplify the golden sunshine of your faith. I am always with you."

The Angel of Faith joyfully smiles at me as she now steps forward with her staff. The Sophia Dragons of the caduceus are now fully animated, moving as a unified field with the Angel of Faith. In their Breath of Life, I feel the white starlight of the Holy Spirit move across my body.

The Angel of Faith blesses and consecrates my crown, my third eye, my throat, my solar plexus, and my root chakra to be filled with divine love. Resting the staff upon my heart, the Angel of Faith and her mighty dragons breathe a new awareness of the purpose and power of faith into my being. I breathe in the fresh breath of faith. In the resonance of its high vibration, I exhale my resistance to divine love. The Angel of Faith dissolves into my solar plexus chakra as golden and sky-blue sparkles of empowering energy.

I now open my human awareness to accept the inner Angel of Faith as an activated aspect of my Higher Self. We are one.

My two angelic guides of perfect love and peace now motion for me to step forward and stand at the *Pillar of Trust*. I now open to receive the angel from my inner being who initiates the second pillar of self-mastery for my human awareness to accept and remember the pathway of divine love within every present moment.

Across the temple my eyes now witness a tall, masculine form arise from the still waters of the holy pool. Moving with broad musculature, he confidently walks across the water without rippling its surface. His wings are white with an iridescent gold sheen. His broad form is fitted with denim overalls and his long brown hair frames a happy face. I marvel at the humanity of his angelic presence. With easy, long strides this angel now arrives to stand before me with a raised hand of greeting. The warm timbre of his voice instantly puts me at ease as he announces himself.

THE ANGEL OF TRUST SPEAKS:

"I am the *Angel of Trust*. After you successfully pass over the bridge of faith, I am the angel who welcomes you with trustworthy, open arms. I am an ever-present guide, supporting you to be courageous and take action when fear would have you choose otherwise. For choosing trust is a courageous act that is worthy of being acknowledged and supported.

"In every moment you choose to have faith, there is always divine guidance to follow through on from your Higher Self. When faith calls you into action, I am right there with you, rolling up my sleeves, helping you to trust in your personal power to take that next step.

"I am the emanation of your Higher Self that values your trust as sacred. As such, I only guide you to trust what is worthy of being trusted. The truth of your divine nature is worthy of being trusted. The true loving thoughts of the Holy Spirit within you are worthy of being trusted. The true voice of your Higher Self is worthy of being trusted as the competent director of your life. In every present moment, you can trust that it is safe to act upon the next-step guidance of your Higher Self."

The Angel of Trust now steps forward and gently places his warm, calloused hands over my eyes. His powerful healing energy pours through my face, transmuting a lifetime of memories in which I have chosen fearful thoughts over trusting the loving guidance of my Higher Self. The angelic healing energy of trust reaches far into my head, vacuuming out the vibrations of fear from the medulla oblongata portion of my brain. I feel the vibrations of regretting my past being drawn up from my spinal fluid and released into his warm embrace.

A soothing, golden nectar of trust now flows forward from my inner angel, filling those places within me that are now free. My eyes feel increasingly lighter with each surge of golden nectar. Fluttering open with the lightness of a feather, my eyes witness the healing hands of my inner angel now dissolving into my awareness. I stand up taller and feel the musculature of trust lifting my heart higher.

I now open my human awareness to accept the inner Angel of Trust as an activated aspect of my Higher Self. We are one.

My two angelic guides of perfect love and peace now motion for me to step forward and stand at the *Pillar of Clarity*. I now open to receive the angel from my inner being who initiates the third pillar of self-mastery for

211

my awareness to accept and remember the pathway of divine love within every present moment.

Across the temple my eyes now witness the still waters of the holy pool rise into the form of a lithe feminine angel. Twinkling bells sparkle across the great hall, announcing the sweet arrival of this emerging angel. Her form spins high above the pool and then stops midair to lock eyes with me. Her skin is translucent. I can clearly see the temple pillars through the sheer form of her angelic body. With wings outlined in shimmering white light, this angel descends from on high to now stand before me.

Her beautiful voice rings through me, heightening my awareness: "I am the *Angel of Clarity*."

A magnetic resonance sweeps through me, drawing me forward to look deep into her sky-blue eyes. I watch as tiny lightning bolts emerge from the center of her pupils, drawing my attention to focus on the pristine vibration of her presence.

The Angel of Clarity lovingly places her hands on my shoulders as she speaks directly into my mind.

THE ANGEL OF CLARITY SPEAKS:

"I am the aspect of your Higher Self that is an Angel of Clarity. When you embody trust, I am invited to create a calm space within you. It is within this calm space that you can feel my immediate response to your every request for emotional support. I clear out the illusions of self-limiting obstacles, so that you may access the relief of ingenious solutions from your heart.

"As your Angel of Clarity, I calm your awareness to carefully consider your next step. My presence gently clears the fog of any self-induced confusion. I help you reestablish a clear sense of direction. Shining the light upon your true crystalline nature, I always guide your awareness to trust in the clarity of divine love instead of being overwhelmed by fear.

"I then guide you to pray, focus, and meditate upon your true intentions as you relax into divine love. I amplify your focus and bless your awareness with clear instructions for the best use of your time, resources, and energy. As your personal coach, I am a champion for your highest thoughts, so that you may experience the clarity of your own self-mastery."

With her hands on my shoulders, the Angel of Clarity transmits her vibrant energy into my body. A rush of clarity pours down my back, cleansing me all the way to my feet. I feel the warm weight of her angelic hands gently dissolving into my shoulders, lifting the heavy weight of old burdens. I watch as the lightning of her sky-blue eyes electrifies my perception. Her illuminated vision now blesses my inner sight to clearly see that my Higher Self is the best director for my life. I feel the winds of change blow through my body as the Angel of Clarity dissolves into my awareness.

I now open my human awareness to accept the inner Angel of Clarity as an activated aspect of my Higher Self. We are one.

My two angelic guides of perfect love and peace now motion for me to step forward and stand at the *Pillar of Alignment*. I now open to receive the angel from my inner being who initiates the fourth pillar of self-mastery for my human awareness to accept and remember the pathway of divine love within every present moment.

My body feels magnetically drawn down by a great force accumulating within the central pool of still waters. The atomic structure of the entire temple expands to leverage the momentous presence of this great, unseen force rapidly building by the moment.

All at once, the momentum is released as a mighty arrow of a tremendous angel that shoots up from the still depths of holy water. In a quantum moment, he lands to stand before me, with his vast red wings neatly folding onto his back.

Although his face is still, his body appears to be moving into every possible direction of quantum reality simultaneously. He laughs at my surprised face and warmly smiles with good cheer to see me.

THE ANGEL OF ALIGNMENT SPEAKS:

"I am your inner *Angel of Alignment*. I am that angel who guides you to positively focus your thoughts, emotions, and intentions as a single arrow of unified belief directed at the target of your highest possible success. I shot out of the water with great force to demonstrate how the momentous power of your inner alignment leverages wonderful opportunities for your success.

"I continuously guide you to every tool, resource, knowledge, and intuitive wisdom that aligns you to flow with the guidance of your Higher Self leading you to create at your highest potential. I also arrange physical reality to deliver messages and manifestations as encouragement for you to persevere when it may feel challenging to follow through on this guidance.

"Alignment easily allows for you to receive a wealth of quantum opportunities that you are not capable of achieving through effort alone. Alignment puts the ease back into your every effort and with this grace your feet are placed on an accelerated direct path for embodying your self-mastery.

"The simple, consistent act of choosing to live in alignment with your Higher Self's daily guidance allows for you to accelerate positive manifestations in your life with an extraordinary momentum. This accelerated momentum spins at the speed of light within the electrons of your DNA. Within this momentum there is an omniscient intelligence coordinating your aligned actions with a Universe of divinely orchestrated synchronicities. Experiencing the satisfying perfection of your alignment co-creating reality with the omniscient power of the Universe invites you to let go of resistances and be swept up into this momentous flow of positive energy, taking you where your soul authentically wants to go.

"Your life was designed to be a radically sovereign creative experience in which aligning your thoughts, emotions, and actions shoots your awareness like an arrow into the joyful power of now. As your Angel of Alignment, I am an acutely focused aspect of your Higher Self intentionally aligning and leveraging the greatest momentum for your greatest success in this lifetime."

The Angel of Alignment bows before me in closing. His strong body shoots high into the air above me, dissolving into a waterfall of red and golden light. I feel his highly focused energy descend through my crown chakra and pour down the length of my spine. I feel all my vertebrae eagerly align with fluidity. My body broadens in height, strength, acuity, and wisdom.

The red energy deepens my connection with the Earth, as the gold energy spins as momentum in my heart. I feel the presence of my Higher Self clearly aligning my awareness to function with greater ease and effectiveness.

I now open my human awareness to accept the inner Angel of Alignment as an activated aspect of my Higher Self. We are one.

My two angelic guides of perfect love and peace now motion for me to step forward and stand at the *Pillar of Reconciliation.* I now open to receive the angel from my inner being who initiates the fifth pillar of self-mastery for my human awareness to accept and remember the pathway of divine love within every present moment.

Across the temple my eyes now witness the still waters part as the Angel of Reconciliation emerges and walks towards me. The waters pile high above her outstretched pink wings, creating a direct path for her to lightly step upon. In her hands she carries a vessel emanating white and golden light. A pearlescent white Sophia Dragon floats beside her. As they approach me I feel my heart sigh and open wider.

THE ANGEL OF RECONCILIATION SPEAKS:

"Dear one, I am your inner *Angel of Reconciliation.* In the past, you have often turned away from divine love because you did not believe that you were worthy of receiving it. I am the angel who reconciles your awareness with how deserving you are to receive and embrace a daily reality of divine love. In your heroic human journey of self-mastery, you are now learning how to trust and receive Sophia's flow of divine love in your life once again.

"All the momentum in the world will carry you nowhere if you do not forgive those past choices in which you denied the love that you deserved to receive, causing you to greatly suffer. I help you remove the unresolved resentment of past choices that obstructs your receptivity and inner peace.

"Without ceasing, I continually pray for you to readily accept and forgive yourself in every circumstance that you deny yourself divine love. As you practice accepting and forgiving yourself with great regularity, you keep your inner temple clear from all obstacles to your inner peace and the momentum of success flowing into your life. Moment-by-moment reconciliation with yourself allows for the momentum unfolding in your life to feel *gentle,* even as it increasingly accelerates your journey of self-mastery."

The Angel of Reconciliation smiles warmly at me. I look into the mirror of her eyes and see a reflection of how I look when I have fully forgiven myself. In this moment, I am acutely aware of the obstructions within me created by withholding forgiveness from myself. These places feel dark and heavy and I search my angel's eyes for help.

She opens her glowing vessel and scoops out a handful of radiant pink and golden medicine that she lifts up to The Sophia Dragon beside her for a blessing. The Sophia Dragon gently blows the Breath of Life upon it, which carries this medicine into all those abandoned places within me that are hungry for reconciliation.

The dark obstructions created by my past resistances to divine love now dissolve into clear warm spaces that are filling up with new vital energy. I am smiling within, happy to be free of bitter self-judgment, grateful to receive the baptism of my own forgiveness, and delighted to feel this much divine love for myself now. The Angel of Reconciliation steps forward to hug me in celebration. The Sophia Dragon spirals herself around our embrace.

I feel the strong arms and wings of Sophia consciousness embracing every part of me in self-acceptance. I feel the presence of the Holy Spirit within me, expanding my awareness to operate beyond the limitations of past regrets. In our blissful embrace, the Angel of Reconciliation dissolves as radiant pink and gold light that pours into my seven major chakras. The pearlescent white light of The Sophia Dragon tumbles down as Divine Mother's milk and starlight through my crown chakra, nurturing my heart.

I now open my human awareness to accept the inner Angel of Reconciliation as an activated aspect of my Higher Self. We are one.

My two angelic guides of perfect love and peace now motion for me to step forward and stand at the first white marble step leading down to the still, holy waters of my true essence. I now open to receive the angel from my inner being who initiates the sixth pillar of self-mastery for my human awareness to activate the pathway of divine love within every present moment.

The angels of perfect love and peace step before me, overlapping their hands to rest upon my heart. Their interwoven hands draw a large orb of white light that emerges from my heart and levitates before me. I hear the sound of children laughing from within the orb as it expands in size before me to take on the shape of a beautiful angel whose wings are pure white. The white light within her face brightly shines beyond the outline of her form. In her hands she holds a small alabaster vase of anointing oil, which she lifts up to show me.

THE ANGEL OF ANOINTING SPEAKS:

"I am your inner *Angel of Anointing.* I am that precious aspect of your innocence that continually anoints your awareness with the holy truth of your innate divinity in every present moment. I cannot see the fearful ideas and illusions that your awareness projects onto your divinity; I cannot see self-deprecating thoughts about your humanity because all I see is the miracle of your own Holy Spirit manifesting your blessed existence into form.

"Therefore, as your inner Angel of Anointing, I am forever blessing your awareness to worship at the altar of your own divinity. I anoint your third eye with frankincense, which opens your physical eyes to clearly see the gift of your true self. I anoint your heart with rose oil in honor of your pure intention to be the light of Sophia. I anoint your hands with myrrh oil as instruments of grace and healing energy. I anoint your feet with sandalwood to honor your divinity walking upon the Earth. I anoint your crown chakra with lotus oil to reveal how the birthright of your own divinity liberates you to freely bless and worship the divinity within All That Is.

"Whenever you temporarily forget that your Higher Self *is you,* remember that I am a resolute aspect of your true self that never forgets *who you really are.* I am the devotion of divine love, which continually anoints your awareness to remain in constant communion with your whole self."

The Angel of Anointing completes her ceremony and now steps to my left side, joining the Angel of Perfect Love as my guide. With her anointing oil still fresh upon my skin I now command the following declaration.

I now open my human awareness to accept the inner Angel of Anointing as an activated aspect of my Higher Self. We are one.

217

With angels supporting my left and right side, I now step forward to stand on the second white marble step, which leads down to the still holy waters of my true essence. I now open to receive the angel from my inner being who initiates the seventh pillar of self-mastery for my human awareness to activate the pathway of divine love within every present moment.

My inner Angels of Anointing, Perfect Love, and Perfect Peace position themselves in a triangle around me. Stretching out their wings, they raise their arms to create a heavenly tower of angelic energy that now pours through my crown chakra. I close my eyes and hear a celestial song arising from the center of my soul.

A great white light begins to build and gather within my body, expanding this song beyond my center. Rapturous angelic voices fill the temple, resonating the white marble to spontaneously vibrate in a harmonic overture of the Holy Spirit. The golden veins within the marble begin to glow, activating my blood vessels to hum with the sound of buzzing bees. The gathered white light emerges from my body and takes form as a mighty angel of many faces before me, whose many voices echo throughout the inner temple.

THE ANGEL OF ATONEMENT SPEAKS:

"I am your inner *Angel of Atonement*. I roar as a lion and cry as the eagle, continually atoning for your every free will choice that denies the creative power of your divinity. My solar guardianship of your innocence carries the light of your Higher Self into the world ahead of you with my many faces eternally singing out into every quantum direction of your human lifetime.

"With a thousand voices I cast out self-perpetuated fears of the future as well as your unresolved regrets of the past. My many voices resonate every aspect of your consciousness to vibrate in union with the frequency of your Higher Self's sovereign creative power to manifest your heavenly reality.

"My many faces sing the Songs of Sophia far out into your past and future, atoning those places within you that are abandoned to fear by filling them with the pride of a lion. What you may believe is damaged, I have already atoned for by going ahead of you in all ways, always.

"I am the lion of your Higher Self that protects the holy ground of this dialogue happening within you now. I am the piercing cry of the eagle that causes daunting regrets to flee from every dimensional reality. I am the perfect sound waves of divine love that provide unconditional atonement for you to enjoy and embody an effective relationship with your Higher Self."

As if to emphasize the quantum breadth of his thousand voices, my inner Angel of Atonement now brings his many faces to absolute silence. The orchestrations of his song still ring within my body. The Angel of Atonement now steps to my right side, joining the Angel of Perfect Peace as my guide. In the rapt stillness of this moment, I command the following declaration:

I now open my human awareness to accept the inner Angel of Atonement as an activated aspect of my Higher Self. We are one.

With angels supporting my left and right side, I now step forward and stand at the third white marble step leading down to the still holy waters of my true essence. I now open to receive the angel from my inner being who initiates the eighth pillar of self-mastery for my human awareness to activate the pathway of divine love within every present moment.

A great golden light fills the temple, shimmering across the still holy waters. For a moment, my physical vision is blinded by a lightning bolt of pale gold energy. Every cell in my body is filled with the electrifying presence of a cascading white light. Above me descends the overlighting *Archangel of Grace,* whose mighty rays of magenta and gold now illuminate my awareness. I feel the landscape of my mind expanding far past the temple walls to listen with ears that hear beyond the beyond.

THE ARCHANGEL OF GRACE SPEAKS:

"I am the Archangel of Grace, amplifying the divine qualities that each of your inner angels serve and magnifying the power of your prayers beyond your human understanding. Grace creates a double blessing for all of your aligned actions to abundantly increase and multiply for your highest success.

My presence is an embodiment of Sophia's grace that miraculously increases your willingness to give and receive divine love. In any present moment that feels challenging or painful to receive your greatest good, call upon me. As the Archangel of Grace I soothe your awareness to instantaneously accept the support you need in order to embody your self-mastery in that moment."

My awareness expands as the Archangel of Grace blesses me to reach beyond my limited understanding for how I can receive the goodness of life. I feel my body temporarily dissolve and my spirit soar into her rays of golden grace. I witness millions upon millions of angels soaring within the temple of her heart. I realize that the Archangel of Grace is an entire universe of angels unto herself that abides in the Holy of Holies within me.

Within these countless wings, I am completely held by the power of my Higher Self's grace blessing me from within. This inner presence of grace holds me as a mother holds a child. I recognize that I can allow myself to receive the comforting arms of my own grace in every present moment. It is safe for me to abundantly bless myself to prosper in all ways by the power of grace. I gently descend back into my human form, lovingly supported by the innumerable arms of grace that surround me.

I now open my human awareness to accept the inner Archangel of Grace as an activated aspect of my Higher Self. We are one.

With angels above me and angels surrounding me, I am now instructed to remain at the third white marble step leading down to the waters of my true essence. I now open to receive the angel from my inner being who initiates the ninth pillar of self-mastery for my human awareness to accept and remember the pathway of divine love within every present moment.

Across the surface of the still water appears a map of my destiny for this lifetime, expressed in sequences of light language glyphs and sacred geometric forms. Certain cross-sections of overlapping geometry light up as starry nodes that define pinnacle points of important decisions that will govern the course of my life.

With great stealth, I feel the quiet presence of an unannounced angel arrive on my left side. He appears as a normal man dressed in modern street clothes and his wings are invisible. His stunning face is chiseled in kindness and carved in knowledge. With piercing eyes, he penetrates my awareness as an eagle looking for miles across the landscape of my mind.

Behind the crown of his head is a perfect byzantine halo of gold that burns so brightly it casts a slight shadow across his face. His relatively ordinary outer appearance only heightens my awareness of the indescribable power generated within the *Angel of Completion*. I feel an extraordinary Ark of the Covenant power humming behind his zipped up sweatshirt and denim jeans. He motions for me to closely peer into the map of my destiny, illuminating the pool of still waters.

THE ANGEL OF COMPLETION SPEAKS:

"As the Angel of Completion, I am a manifestation of your Higher Self's omniscient support that continually encourages you to reach far above any self-limited perception of what is possible for your success. My presence strengthens your capacity to successfully navigate the inner and outer challenges that deter you from your goals; I demolish inherited and conditioned belief systems that cause you to doubt yourself and your ability to succeed. As the frequency of my divine power flows through your awareness, we fulfill the great acts of your destiny together by elevating and building up your self-confidence with one step of success at a time.

"Look upon the still waters of your essence before you. Notice how the sacred geometry of positive belief systems manifest beautiful opportunities, harmony, and accelerated momentum for completing what is important to you. As a guardian angel of your innocence, I imprint the sacred geometry of perfect thought forms upon your awareness. This activates your willingness to follow through on completing goals that you may be denying or resisting.

"The energy of completion is an absolutely *ordinary* and necessary energy for fulfilling the many goals of your destiny for this lifetime. It is the ordinary next step that is often defeated by unconscious strategies of self-sabotage. When you call upon me, my presence activates your will power by creating new neurological pathways for your awareness to resource the radical self-love that is essential for accomplishing what is important to you. I also teach your emotional body how to enjoy the immense satisfaction of every completed step along The Way of fulfilling your dreams.

"I am also a messenger from your future self, who is already living out your happiest destiny for this lifetime in quantum reality. I come as a motivational guide supporting you to complete important life goals that align you with consciously actualizing the possibility of that destiny. As a guardian angel, I shine as the sun from your bright future, whose rays of light banish fear from harming the holy grounds of all your creative works in progress.

"In our communion there will be little to speak of with me, for my transmission transcends the energy of talking about what you're going to do and motivates you to actually *do* what you came here to do for fulfilling your destiny now. The silent support of my presence summons your free will to magnetically align with the divine will of your Higher Self."

I step back and nod in appreciation for what my inner Angel of Completion shared. He now takes both of my hands into his own with a warm embrace of commitment. I feel the white light of perfect completion transmitted from his hands into my own. This blessing of completion travels up my arms, pours into my heart and overflows into my solar plexus chakra as the nourishing medicine of fulfillment.

In response, my solar plexus chakra expands into a mighty sun that fills the entire temple. Within the rays of my own sovereign power, I am now initiated into the absolutely ordinary and extraordinary power of completion.

I now open my human awareness to accept the inner Angel of Completion as an activated aspect of my Higher Self. We are one.

The Ascended Master Mary Magdalene now appears across the temple; she is walking towards me, adorned in the rich red robes of an ancient High Priestess. Her glinting gold Egyptian jewelry marks the pace of her stride. Following behind her are many robed figures whose large velvet hoods shadow most of their faces. Known as the Order of Magdalena, this accompanying ensemble are an ancient oracular Sophia lineage of magi High Priestesses. Singing as a choir of angels in light languages of divine love, the many members of the Order of Magdalena now fill the temple to stand side-by-side along the circumference of the pool. I watch as Mother Mary emerges from the order to stand in reverence by Mary Magdalene's side.

MOTHER MARY SPEAKS:

"I bless the fulfillment of your nine initiations! As a High Priestess in the Order of Magdalena, it is my great honor to stand in solidarity with Mary Magdalene's transmission of Keycode 5; for this temple of angelic teachings arises from her pristine diamond light consciousness. I will be your faithful witness as Mary Magdalene baptizes your human awareness in the living waters of your own true essence."

Directly across the great pool, Mary Magdalene now extends her right leg from the marble step closest to the water's edge. She walks across the still waters without making a ripple to stand at the center of the pool.

Mary Magdalene holds an alabaster jar of anointing oil in her left hand. I look into her eyes; they are present and alive with a supernatural mirth. Her eyes shine with the same radiance of that moment when a baby is born.

Nothing untrue can remain within her invincible loving presence. As an oracle, Mary Magdalene's impeccable embodiment is a vehicle for directly experiencing Sophia's ineffable womb mysteries. She smiles at me and I feel her diamond light awareness speak before her words.

MARY MAGDALENE SPEAKS:

"The nine pillars have successfully initiated your awareness to recognize your Higher Self as a living angel on Earth. Are you ready to baptize your awareness and integrate your angelic DNA within your human form?"

Yes, Mary Magdalene.
I am relieved to be initiated by you in this baptismal rite of passage.

"Beautiful. I invite you to now step forward and walk with faith upon the waters of your own true essence."

I glance into the supportive eyes of my attending inner angels and release their loving embrace to boldly step upon the waters of my own soul. To my delight, the atomic structure of the still waters holds me up according to my divine will.

With a rush of joy, I quickly walk across the holy pool to meet Mary Magdalene at the center. She welcomes me to sit across from her and mirror her by folding my legs into the full lotus asana. Mary Magdalene's eyes sparkle with fierce joy and ancient knowledge. She asks me: "Do I have your permission to open the gates of your human body to oracular divine knowing?"

Yes!

With my declaration, she rises, stepping forward to bless my body. Mary Magdalene begins to apply a dark red ointment that smells of myrrh and sandalwood upon my skin, making patterns of red symbols at various energetic gateway points along my body. I feel my body slightly withdraw from the cooling mixture. With a deep exhale, I still my mind and choose to relax deeper into this present moment of initiation unfolding for me now. I witness how the dark red ointment activates many key meridian points along my body to light up as a map for integrating the angelic DNA of my Higher Self within my human form.

Toning directly over these marked points, Mary Magdalene sings in ancient dialects that quickly spiral open these key meridian points along my body. I intuitively tuck my tongue at the roof of my mouth to circulate the waves of kundalini energy flowing through these points. My fingers move of their own accord into mudras of self-initiation; I steady and deepen my breath.

Mary Magdalene now speaks the hidden names of Sophia into my 7 major chakras. I feel my chakras spiral open in an unfamiliar way; they expand far beyond my human form, yet I have never felt their wheels of light this intimately. At the base of my spine, I now feel the kundalini energy begin to rise up from my root chakra as two dragons spiraling up my back. Their hot and cooling Breath of Life activates the central sushumna channel of my human body to widen as a large column of light within me.

Placing both her hands on the crown of my head, Mary Magdalene begins to chant the innumerable holy names of my Higher Self. I feel a large obstruction removed from my crown chakra and dissolve into the angelic light of witnesses. The Order of Magdalena tones in mantras that support my awareness to remain fully present throughout this rite of passage.

Mother Mary and her mother, Anna, now step forward to assist Mary Magdalene in this DNA activation. Mother Mary places her gentle hands on my left shoulder and the scent of a thousand roses fills my senses. Anna supports my right side and with her touch I hear the sound of a thousand bees. Mary Magdalene now positions herself on bended knees before me to look directly into my eyes.

MARY MAGDALENE SPEAKS:

"I am now acting as an oracle for the Holy Spirit of your Higher Self. On behalf of your angelic nature, I speak the following questions arising from your own soul. Your answers to these questions activate your free will alignment with your Higher Self's divine will to embody your angelic nature in human form. I invite the mighty power of your own voice to initiate your awareness into the self-mastery of Keycode 5, as directed by the master within you."

"Do you accept that the Holy Spirit lives within your human form?"
Yes.

"Do you accept that the Holy Spirit has the power to guide your human life?"
Yes.

"Do you accept the divinity of your Higher Self as your true self?"
Yes.

"Do you accept that you have chosen to be a living angel on Earth to serve the divine will of your Higher Self?"
Yes.

"As such, do you accept that the Holy Spirit of your Higher Self has the sovereign angelic power to provide everything for you to achieve this purpose?"

Yes.

"Do you now consciously agree to surrender your human awareness to be consciously operated, in ever-increasing measure, by the divine love and sovereign power of your omniscient Higher Self?"

Yes.

"Do you now agree to consciously receive the divine love and angelic support of your Higher Self supporting you in every present moment, to the best of your human ability?"

Yes.

"Do you agree to now willfully step upon the path of your divine purpose as an angel on Earth, to abide in the guidance of your Higher Self, who leads your awareness step-by-step to embody your mastery in every present moment?"

Yes.

"Do you now accept the Holy Spirit of your Higher Self as your direct teacher for actualizing Sophia Christ consciousness on Earth?"

Yes.

"By the power of Sophia, the Holy Spirit within you that is your Higher Self, I now baptize your human awareness with the holy waters of your essential nature."

Mother Mary and Anna whisper a blessing of completion over my crown chakra and then release their loving touch from my shoulders. My eyes remain fixed upon the night sky within Mary Magdalene's eyes. She warmly smiles at me and whispers: *"Know Thyself."*

My human awareness releases its control over my body and I gently descend into the waiting arms of pure essence. Slowly, the solid floor of still waters begins to gently dissolve beneath me. The molecules of holy water gather to tenderly surround my body as a mother swaddling a newborn.

The waters carefully submerge me in wave after wave of my essential nature. I now float as an infant in the warm black womb of my pure essence. Everything within me feels reborn to bliss, all at once. I feel everything in all of creation singing to me through these waters, focused upon me with divine love.

The organ of my heart completely dissolves into an orb of pearlescent white light, from which powerful wings emerge and unfold along my back. I watch my skin shift from one radiant color to the next, revealing a crystalline record of starseeded angelic embodiments. I open my eyes underwater to see my true nature as a star nursery birthing new stars within me.

I feel an intimacy within myself unlike ever before. I feel a divine communion with parts of myself that I had forgotten. I feel the laughter of my innocence. I feel the cosmic depths of divine love. I feel absolutely free to embrace the joy within my body. I feel invincible in my totality.

The diamond light of my Higher Self illuminates every facet of my aware-ness with a pure, holy consciousness that simultaneously moves in every direction throughout creation and then beyond the space-time continuum. The waters of my essential nature pour through my awareness, flooding me with a direct knowing of how unconditionally loved I am. I witness through every facet of my own diamond light that my Higher Self is perfectly guiding me to succeed within every precious moment of my human life.

Mary Magdalene sings a familiar song of Hathor, transmitting the angelic light language of whales to baptize my carbon-based DNA with the essential nature of my Holy Spirit. My eyes soften into a gentle focus upon the radiant crystalline chromosomes of The Sophia Code within my DNA. I follow the sound waves of Mary Magdalene's voice to locate Keycode 5 within me.

Its crystalline diamond light shimmers with colors I have never seen before. I witness the Holy Spirit of my Higher Self build a bridge of light connecting the divine qualities of Keycode 5 to my carbon-based DNA. Mary Magdalene sings the words "activating now" in a thousand angelic tongues. I watch as my Higher Self descends across this bridge of light and begins to operate my body's awareness in entirely new ways. My awareness recognizes that Keycode 5 awakens me as a vehicle of awakening for others.

The warm waters of my pure essence lull me into a deeper and deeper relaxation. I now float my awareness to peer up beyond the surface of the water where the Order of Magdalena bears witness.

With pristine gentleness, Mary Magdalene dances in oracular bliss, levitating above me as she embodies the many-armed Kali Ma. The universal, all-consuming divine love overflowing from Mary Magdalene's Sacred Heart exhilarates my soul. Her red robes have been thrown back as she embodies the naked dance of liberation that arises from the black womb of no-thing. With reverence I surrender to the absolute, holy presence of *She Who Has No Name* within me.

The waters of my pure essence now activate my awareness to recognize that Mary Magdalene's Keycode 5 transmission is a tantric vehicle for initiating my Higher Self embodiment of the angelic qualities that reconcile every inner demon with fierce, radiant divine love. Through the dancing ripples above, I see Mary Magdalene smile at me with the long tongue of Kali Ma. I witness the willingness of divinity to wrathfully and unconditionally love me beyond my understanding.

In these ecstatic waves of self-realization, the sweet waters of my essential nature pour as whirlpools of light throughout my awareness. As a High Priestess ceremonially supporting Mary Magdalene's oracular rites of Kali Ma, I see Anna pour anointing oil from the alabaster jar upon the waters of my pure essence. I am baptized again and again beneath this Dark Mother transmission of Mary Magdalene.

My body begins to be filled with an incredible strength and I feel my Higher Self moving within my awareness in new and unfamiliar ways. It welcomes me to dance as Mary Magdalene is dancing above me. In an immediate response to this invitation, my two arms become many and my legs command the waters to rise. I feel a volcano of power erupt from my center, launching me to the surface of the holy pool. I stare eye-to-eye with the thousand eyes of Kali Ma and allow her wrathful tongue to lick the wounds of my human awareness from every lifetime. I laugh like a child, my body dances like a woman, and my heart lies down to rest as the ancient grandmother within all.

Within the many-armed Kali Ma transmission of Mary Magdalene I explore the oracular bliss of consciously dancing back and forth from the black womb of no-thing into the light rays of my Sophia consciousness. I feel an ecstatic union with the Holy Spirit of my Higher Self descend as a dove of peace through my crown chakra. *The Peace that Passeth All Understanding* slows my body from its dance and my many arms return to two. I feel powerful wings emerge from my back that easily integrate with my returning human form and I reach them high above my head.

I watch the dark face of Kali Ma recede back into the sparkling night sky of Mary Magdalene's eyes. The olive skin and warm smile that I first met, slowly reappear upon her face. Mary Magdalene's rich red robes silently sway to stillness as her oracular dance of many arms moves to a close. She steps forward to hold my hands as a friend. As I am beheld in her reflection and warm embrace, I understand the sovereign power of my human divinity in a new way. Mary Magdalene smiles with rosy lips flushed with vibrancy and whispers: *"It is done."*

I accept that I hold the golden keys to my Heaven on Earth.
I accept that I create my reality, by the power of my word.
My word is good, my heart is pure.
By the loving power of my pure word. I now consciously recognize and embody my Higher Self as an angel on Earth.

By the loving power of my pure word, I now command my Higher Self to activate all the crystalline divine qualities of Keycode 5 of The Sophia Code within me as the new operating system for my carbon-based DNA.

I integrate this initiation throughout my entire body, on all four levels of my Be-ing now, with grace and ease.

I am the master that I seek. In the embodiment of my Higher Self, I am a vehicle of awakening for all of creation.

I integrate my angelic nature as an important divine aspect of my sovereign whole self now.

It is done.

It is done.

It is done.

By the power of 3, a perfect trinity: It is done.

Mary Magdalene steps forward and anoints my crown, third eye, and heart chakra with the sacred oils of frankincense and myrrh. Every member of the Order of Magdalena removes their hooded robe, and thousands of angelic wings rustle open before me. In their collective witness, I recognize this luminescent congregation of incarnated angels as my Family of Light. In our rapturous communion, I welcome their support for fulfilling my destiny as a living angel on Earth. Witnessed, blessed, and sealed by The Order of Magdalena, I affirm that this initiation is now accomplished.

I welcome Mary Magdalene into my life as a Divine Feminine Ascended Master mentor overlighting my journey to embody the diamond light of my Higher Self in human form. Embraced by her ever-present gaze, we bow to one another for the closing prayer of Namasté. Silent waves of gratitude pour from my heart in honor of Mary Magdalene's masterful facilitation.

My wings rustle open and I test their strength by pumping the air to lift my feet up from the temple floor. Their strength and heavenly softness feel exquisite. With ecstatic bliss and appreciation, I raise up my arms to experience my true self flying beyond all limitations of form.

As I reach the temple's ceiling, it dissolves into the light of Sophia within my heart. I allow the fullness of this initiation to now activate my physical body. I ground this transmission through my central column of light all the way to the center of the Earth. I command that the Akashic Records, recording my lifetimes on Earth, now be rewritten to reflect my new reality. I have received more of myself today.

I breathe in The Breath of Life. I exhale the past. It is safe for me to now embody the angelic divine qualities of Keycode 5 of The Sophia Code within every present moment. I choose to love myself as a vehicle of awakening for others. I close this ceremony with reverence for my true self and the divine love of All That Is, supporting my eternal success.

And so it is.

KEYCODE 6
"SHE OF A THOUSAND WATERS"

When you practice holding yourself with great tenderness, you eventually become whole in your relationship with yourself. You trust yourself. It is from this foundation that karuna can then initiate you into the greater depths of compassion available to you as a Christed being.

Loving Yourself with Compassion
Is Essential for Ascension

QUAN YIN SPEAKS:

I AM QUAN YIN, and it is with great joy that I reveal myself as
Keycode 6 in The Sophia Dragon Tribe. My Sophia embodiment title is
"She of a Thousand Waters," for my transmission overflows with the light of
Sophia carried within water.

My Keycode 6 transmission activates the divine qualities within you that
are also the holy properties of water. My Divine Feminine Christ teachings
are a spring source of Sophia's fluid wisdom, baptizing your awareness to
let go and receive the abundant flow of divine love and compassion that is
always available to you.

When you invoke me as a spiritual guide, I overlight your human journey
with several rays of Sophia's light that mentor your awareness to give and
receive self-love and self-compassion. The first is the *Rose Quartz Ray of
Divine Mother's Love*, the second ray is the *Gentle White Light that Pierces*

All Darkness, and the third is the *Aquamarine Ray of Rebirth, Courage, and Divine Service.* I broadcast the quantum energy of these rays through the light within water, which carries the ferocity of my compassion as a gentle mist that soothes your body, heart, and mind.

In your human journey of self-mastery, there is so much to let go of. When you feel drawn to my presence as a mentor, this is a sign that you are ready to heal your relationship with suffering. The rays of Sophia's light carried within my water teachings offer a safe sanctuary for you to honor and let go of your greatest wounds, fears, and insecurities.

You came to experience the sovereign power of your divinity through the vulnerability of your human experience. Your willingness to be vulnerable – especially to painful experiences that stimulate personal growth – deserves your utmost self-respect, self-compassion, and unconditional love.

I teach you how to soothe your experiences of vulnerability with patience and to refrain from pressuring yourself to prematurely move beyond unresolved pain. The imbalanced mental strategy to banish or hide away pain, to be dealt with at some unknown future juncture, has never worked nor ever will.

When you are authentically present to your healing journey, the innocence of your Inner Child will assert when it feels acknowledged and safe enough to release the suffering that no longer serves you. This next golden age cycle will be launched by Divine Feminine leaders who radically embody the wisdom from their own authentic healing journeys through the necessary stages of grief. For each stage of grief is integral in your recovery from loss, trauma, and suffering. Call upon me as a mentor if your divine purpose is to lead others by embodying your own radical self-compassion.

Your generation has come to embody the medicine of compassion for healing the heart of humanity. Humanity cannot skip its initiations for learning self-love and self-compassion; it is the only way to reconcile the thousands of years spent in self-hatred and self-denial – that must be released for humanity to ascend into a new golden age. You have come as a wayshower for thousands to explore compassion for themselves, by your own embodied willingness to love yourself completely.

Loving yourself includes the compassion of forgiving yourself for the traumas of your past, both in this lifetime and in others. I became a mentor for embodying compassion from my own journey of reconciliation, following devastating events that changed the course of my life forever.

Just as Green Tara traveled to Earth from Sirius, I also came to Earth with most of my ascension training completed in the star system known as the Pleiades. However, I spent a single yet dramatic lifetime on Earth for the fulfillment of my Oversoul's destiny to become a Golden Dragon teacher for humanity's ascension. As it was my final lifetime of self-mastery, I designed the parameters of my incarnation to begin with a complete amnesia of all my previous lifetimes. I fully committed to this vulnerability that my human experience would offer me, for the accelerated growth of my soul.

There are many legends about my origin that have sparked the imagination of humanity for centuries. The beginning of my story is simpler than most have told and its unfolding is more magical than most offer. I am here to speak my story beyond cultural and religious context, so that we may meet heart-to-heart in the humanity of my humble beginning.

Come sit by my waterfalls of peace as I share with you the story of my life, for long have we waited for this dialogue between you and I. As we journey together, may my words soften your heart to receive the compassion that I offer you as an ever-available mentor and friend. I share my life with you as one who deeply understands your vulnerable human journey and the willingness that is required to embody self-love and self-compassion.

The Traumatic Origin of Quan Yin's Compassion

When I was born in the black no-thing of Sophia's heart womb, my Oversoul launched a sound wave that momentarily deafened the eyes and ears of lightning, filling the heavens with an announcement of my birth. I beheld the glory of my sovereignty and wept tears of joyful gratitude, filling the whole Universe with showers of fresh rain.

My spirit traveled far across the cosmos of Sophia, past star after star, riding on the back of a Sophia Dragon. Lifetime after lifetime I explored my sovereign power in physical realities, preparing myself to one day incarnate in the form of a human girl.

When that appointed hour arose, I circled above the waiting Earth below, coordinating the details of my destiny. I chose a family and community that lived in northern Asia and was born as a girl named Yoshinami.

A lush jungle forest covered most of the mountainous region that bordered my village. My family lived at a modest ranking in our community's social hierarchy. Although my parents were always scheming to improve our status and fortune, I was content with the simplicity and beauty of nature as my wealth. If it were not for the constant complaining and expectations of my father, I would have remained peacefully content serving my family's wellbeing, as was the custom for the youngest daughter of the family. I tempered the contrasts of my family life by often slipping away for periods of meditative silence in the jungle.

I knew that an early marriage would be imminent for me if I were to remain in my family's household past the age of fourteen. I relentlessly pleaded with my parents to send me to serve at the convent of Taoist nuns, not far from our village. I argued it would improve our social ranking if they let me go. My only desire was to live in an uninterrupted peace with myself, a peace that seemed to endlessly elude my unhappy parents. Over time, my requests created a great resentment within my father and I was persecuted with beatings to keep my mouth shut.

Days before my thirteenth birthday, our village was invaded by a legendary pack of Mongol raiders, who ritually drank human blood. Our homes were set on fire for the pleasure of watching them burn. Children were carried away as slaves after their parents were murdered before their eyes. I was not exempt from these torturous acts but was also brutally raped and beaten; I was left to die in a pool of my own blood, after witnessing the execution of my parents.

Through swollen eyes, I saw a flash of spinning diamond light high up on the mountain's ridge line. My gaze fixed upon the unknown eyes of an angelic looking man, who was urging me to flee. Shuddering, I attempted to move my body but blacked out. I awoke several hours later to the crack of lightning. Cold rain began to pour over the smoking site of my village. I heard the same firm voice speak from an unknown place within me: "Walk to the jungle now and do not delay!"

In that moment, I left everything that I had known far behind me. I ran for my life to hide in the steep sanctuary of mountainous jungle. My consciousness fractured and split itself far off beyond the boundaries of sanity. Living off wild roots and herbs, I became a feral ghost and burrowed myself deep into the forest of my grief. My body often shook back and forth with cellular memories of unresolved trauma; I could not physically feel my skin whether it was burnt, bleeding, or frozen. In my erratic state, terrified to be seen by another, I somehow managed to survive alone until the age of seventeen.

The Power of Unconditional Love and Support

Internalizing my culture's social conditioning, I judged myself as the worthless orphan of a murdered family and a contaminated victim of rape. Carrying this burden of unworthiness broke my heart into a thousand pieces. My consciousness dissolved into a black hole of self-hatred. Consumed by grief, it was a mere thread of connection to my body that kept me alive.

In the greatest hour of my darkness, as I was about to end my life, a luminescent figure appeared before me, about twenty feet away from my crouching body. He did not blink nor appear to breathe, yet I knew he was alive. I could hear the kind timbre of his voice inside my head welcoming me to "be at peace." I instinctively growled from my gut at his telepathic invitation, yet remained frozen in place by his somehow familiar radiant countenance.

Completely caught off guard by the man's warm glowing eyes, I continued to stare into his gaze, which completely unnerved the black places within me. I realized that this man had no intention of leaving me alone, nor would he come any closer than twenty feet from me. Creating a silent pathway of communication, his awareness guided me to momentarily relax the tension of my body. He quietly shared with me that he was a teacher, but more importantly, a friend.

It was the first time that I had heard another human speak out loud in years. The sound of his voice brought hot tears to my eyes. Shocked, I glared back at him and started to sway, as I often would, before passing out. Steadying me from afar, the man's low voice assured me that he would never touch me or harm me in any way. He revealed that he could not leave me, but that he would act in every way possible for me to feel honored and comfortable with his guardian presence watching over me. I promptly passed out with the declaration of his intent.

I awoke to a small fire crackling nearby. There was a wooden bowl of rice and a cup of hot water placed at a distance by my right side. I marveled at how foreign a cup and bowl had become for me.

Through my half-open eyes, I feigned sleep to study his every movement as he walked through the jungle. Within every sinew of his musculature, he moved without a shadow of fear or a need to control any outcome. I could see that everything that was within him was at his attention and order. Therefore, everything outside of this man moved in obedience to his magnetic and peaceful nature.

In my disassociated state of consciousness, I could also see his life force as a radiant light body interfacing with his physique, which looked like a golden dragon. His chi flowed as water, piling high in waves around him, as an abundance of accessible energy. It seemed to miraculously provide for his every desire, occasionally lifting him up in levitation and causing him to have no need for sleep.

Somehow I put together that this man was a living master of light, walking in human form for my benefit, and that he had come to awaken me from the nightmare I could not escape. With these realizations, I noticed that I was putting together thought forms of which I was previously incapable of organizing. I continued to stare through the fire, watching his every movement. For a fleeting moment I considered if his presence was already healing my mind and then the demonic memories of my past returned, dragging me back into the black hole of my heart.

And so this mysterious holy man, my unwanted teacher, sat on a large flat stone by a waterfall for days, months – perhaps years – in prayerful meditation for me. My grief clouded all concepts of time; all I knew was that he would never leave. The only occasion in which he would arise from his meditation was when Sophia directed him to get up and offer me food, garments, or a water blessing.

As I began acclimating to his silent presence, the unexpected sound of his voice occasionally speaking for my benefit would rearrange the universe within me. His kind voice would rise in unison with the waterfall, offering songs of healing or a prayer for my life.

From my abject grief arose a deluge of shadowy retaliation and projected anger upon this man, who only offered me peace. He did not need or want anything from me; he simply came to pray for me, if possible, by my feet. His service of divine love was offered in his full majesty, for he came as a soul unified with the totality of light that shone out from his eyes. He was an authentic embodiment of sovereignty and his presence transmitted the possibilities of that sovereign reality for my fractured mind to consider its return to wholeness. This confounded and enraged the intricate web of my suffering state.

I would yell and curse, I would whimper and whine. I would lash out in confusion with too many words, that didn't even feel like they were mine. Hiding for days, I would refuse the food he would offer me. Enraged by his patience, I would stamp on the altars he built in honor of my true name. His divine love beckoned unknown territory within me and I howled as a wounded creature lost in my own night.

No matter how I retaliated, he never reacted to me, nor seemed to even see the darkness that consumed me day after day. When he looked at me, I felt his all-consuming gaze summoning the light within me that I thought was lost forever. In the medicine of his relentless divine love I became a vessel torn open, emptying out the agony of my suffering, but not yet filled with my own Holy Spirit.

Softening with the Water of Receptivity

Unbeknown to my blindfolded awareness, the softening of my heart arrived on a warm, spring day. Although overcast, the sky was gray with integration, not doubt, and I awoke that morning feeling softer – and did not know how or why. A miraculous appearance of white and pink cherry blossoms carpeted the forest floor. A strong wind encouraged me to my feet and I felt an unusual urgency to watch the man by the waterfall.

I crept from tree to tree, chasing the shadowy path towards the ridge where his silhouette beckoned me. Watching my teacher's motionless form, I witnessed the sky open above him and the sun's arms lift up a rainbow within the waterfall. The sight was too beautiful for the gnashing voices within me. My eyes traced the ground with a sudden rush of shame as I turned to hunker back into hiding.

Tracking the vanishing opportunity of my open heart, the man instantly appeared before me. His radiant eyes stopped me mid-step from my descent into shame. Frozen in place, I stood before him for the first time, eye-to-eye. He offered me his hand with such a profound compassion and peace that I watched my own hand lift to be held for the first time in years.

Although radically dangerous to my unconscious defenses, the human touch felt electrifying. My entire being was starving for safe communion with another. I relented to my soul's hunger and feasted on grace. Hand-in-hand, we gently walked to the waterfall and began my first day of healing under the auspicious rainbow.

In my devastating vulnerability, I was humbled beyond comprehension. For everything within me needed patience, care, attention, and repair. As I slowly learned how to relent and ask for help each day, a new strength grew within me.

The man attended to me as a wounded animal, yet spoke to me as an equal. It was startling to be treated with such respect after all that had become of me by the hands of other men. The raging storms started to settle over a clear still lake within my heart. In moments of clarity, my ears would often burn as I remembered my vicious reactions to his past kindnesses.

Although I did not feel worthy of his unconditional love, I knew there was nowhere else to go. In successive stages of surrender, I let go to be guided by his care. I intuitively knew that his ever-present reflection was preparing me to one day clearly see myself again.

We spent day after day at the waterfall, as he taught me about the medicine of water to heal my wounds, both seen and unseen. I learned the ancient practice of praying and prophesying over water. Together we would meditate, chant, and sing over vessels of water to voice our intentions for healing specific areas within my body, heart, and mind. I practiced drinking the answers to my prayers every day and watched my body rapidly heal from this alchemy, beyond my understanding.

The man spoke to me of his home, a mountain range that bridged the heavens to earth that was also the earthly throne for a Divine Mother embodiment named Tara. He spoke to me of Tara's strength and sovereign power as a liberator, inspiring my heart to reach for the heroine within me.

With patience, the man guided me in how to speak the incantations of Tara for invoking my inner Saviouress to carry me across the sea of my suffering. I trusted him as a teacher because he always kept guiding me to a Divine Feminine power within me. It was remarkable to feel his honoring of the feminine after living most of my life subjected to patriarchal punishment.

As I deepened in my meditation practice, Tara appeared to me often on the inner planes. During one such vision, Tara appeared to me in her white emanation and asked that I dedicate myself to embodying the mantra of compassion: OM MANE PADME HUM. Although I could not believe her at that time, she shared that this mantra was preparing me to become a vehicle of compassion and grace for those suffering from the same diseases of self-hatred that I had.

The man also taught me about my direct connection to Sophia as both my Divine Mother and Divine Father Source and how to access the Sophia of my own Higher Self through meditation. He spoke often about a Buddha consciousness that was my Higher Self living within me, which I could always turn to as my inner teacher. In his instruction, the man always guided me to seek the living waters of my own divinity. Inspired by who and what I would encounter within me, my meditation practice flourished. The man and I sat for hours together, counseling with an array of inner Buddhas who came to sit with us and initiate me by the waterfall.

I learned how to cleanse my entire being, with the anointing touch of water accompanied by my prayers and the Breath of Life. The man taught me energy healing techniques for repairing and cultivating chi within my meridians and chakras.

On certain days we would travel across mountain passes to springs of mineralized water arising from the earth. There my teacher would make mixtures of earth, herbs, and water to heal my scars and call back the soul fragments of my traumatized consciousness. In the grace of his holy water teachings, I remembered how to be whole. I returned to an awakened state of clarity. Consciously capable of resourcing the guiding presence within me, I was no longer the ghost that he had found in the jungle.

Awakening a Divine Feminine Christ Embodiment

In the grace of this man's immaculate care as a Divine Masculine Christ embodiment, the space was created for me to explore the full potential of my own Divine Feminine Christ embodiment. In the final year of our meditation practice, Sophia asked me to take up the mantle of a new name that would initiate my consciousness to accept this opportunity.

To my surprise, one autumn afternoon, I turned to the man meditating by my side and spontaneously told him that my name was now *Quan Yin*. He smiled peacefully and nodded in acknowledgment. He spoke: "On behalf of creation, thank you for accepting your embodiment of compassion. Many will save themselves by calling upon the transmission of your name."

Our final days together were not spent as teacher and student, or as any other relationship of inequity. In only seven years, I had miraculously activated The Sophia Code within me to radically transform the poison of suffering into a magnificent medicine of my divinity's light embodied in human form. This is how I came to be associated with the totem of white peacock medicine. The radiance of my sovereignty now shined in equal measure to that of the man who came in remembrance of me. Our inner and outer communion achieved heights of divine love that was a true experience of living Heaven on Earth.

I felt the soft presence of his peace reflected in everything that I looked upon. When I beheld him with absolute trust, my experience of physical reality would temporarily dissolve all around me and I would be standing in Realms of Light beside him. In our joint meditation, we were often taken up into the higher cosmic temples for twin flame ascension training with the masters. To integrate this training, we would often silently walk through the forest, listening to the voice of water connecting our hearts beyond all dimensional realities.

Although the shadowy memories of my past would occasionally arise, the Holy Spirit of my Higher Self was abundantly anchored deep within every cell of my body, with all of my chakras attuned to remain in alignment with the divine will of Sophia. The operating system of The Sophia Code had awakened me to embody both the master and teacher within. My physical journey with this man, who I now knew as my beloved, was complete.

The time had come for this precious, holy man to assist my continued development from the higher Realms of Light. My final initiations would include self-actualizing my embodiment without needing his presence as someone outside of me. Working with my beloved on the inner planes would clearly call me into the fullness of my own sovereignty. He had been my patient companion throughout years of recovery in the forest, and although I knew it was for our highest evolution as twin flames, I did not want him to go.

I was bereft with the knowledge of his forthcoming departure. Yet, I knew from our training that we were fulfilling the prophecy to meet on Earth and birth my embodiment of Quan Yin together. I had helped him in this same way, eons ago, as we birthed his own embodiment on Earth. Now it was his prayer to go ahead of me, to prepare The Way for my future journey of teaching, healing, and divine service for awakening sovereignty within humanity.

Receiving The Great Commission

The moment of our physical parting arrived just as quietly as the day that I softened to his care for me. As we sat meditating by the waterfalls, this un-announced moment made itself known as a silent third presence sitting with us. Yet, I could only minimally engage my awareness with what had arrived due to the sudden appearance of an angel before me. Reality began to spin as my eyes uncontrollably swept over the iridescent golden sheen of expansive white wings. I felt unplugged from my will power to track the man beside me, yet a deep stillness came over me and I heard the words: "Let Go."

My awareness surrendered, drawn forward by a primordial power. An all-consuming focus centered my eyes upon the alabaster face of an angel who spoke to my heart without moving his lips. As the angel spoke directly into my soul, his unflinching gaze wept with an unending stream of silent tears. My inner ears became filled with a symphony of celestial tones, bells, and angelic voices singing my name over and over again. I bowed my heart before the angel and asked to receive the mercy of his message for me.

THE ANGEL OF THE GREAT COMMISSION SPEAKS:

"Quan Yin, your heart has become a living vase of compassion for this entire planet. For every moment that you surrendered into the darkness of your suffering you now embody the light of wisdom for teaching others how to walk The Way back home to their own hearts.

"The alchemical miracle of your great suffering prepared your heart to become a chalice of never-ending grace that will pour forth healing waters for the peace of all beings. I offer you this holy vessel, the *Vase of Compassion,* in honor of how you emptied yourself so that the light of Sophia's compassion could overflow from your heart. For it is prophesied that all who are blessed by your healing waters will also awaken to become overflowing vessels of compassion and divine love. May the reflective waters of this vase bless all who seek your miracles.

"Go forth and love as you have been unconditionally loved. Go forth in remembrance of your own wondrous awakening to the divine love within you. As you have been unconditionally served, serve those who call upon you, by simply pouring forth the wisdom held within your vessel of healing.

"As an embodiment of Sophia's light, your Higher Self is calling you to become like the holy waters that healed you. Go forth without judgment and move with fluidity. Flood this world with the same compassion that a great mother has for the suffering of her little child. Wherever the guiding light within water directs your mission, be brave and follow that current.

"Be the grace of Sophia that awakened and nurtured your embodiment as Quan Yin. Be both the vessel and the water – be the divine love that holds the atomic structure of these elements together.

"Remember that there is no holding with water; it is *always letting go* to merge in shape and function with what is calling it forth. Yet, the miracle is that although transformed to serve a purpose, water will always return to its original state. For it is holy, indestructible, and indivisible, just as you are – with a great mission to quench the hearts of all beings.

"Go forth and heal, Quan Yin. Return to your people and open the temple gates of Sophia Christ consciousness for those calling out to you as a teacher. Bring them the good news of the living waters within them that has the power to heal all wounds and be reconciled to divine love. Amen."

The angel handed me the Vase of Compassion, anointing me with a kiss on my forehead and palms. Within the rustle of feathers and celestial tones, the angel spoke a final declaration that activated specific sequences of The Sophia Code within me for fulfilling my ministry. Every cell within my body resonated in unison with his celestial frequency, activating my embodiment to become a radiant transmission of Keycode 6. My awareness ascended into the highest inner temples that I could consciously participate in without passing out.

It was there that my teacher, the man, awaited me. His hands were actively still, holding the powerful poise of mudras. When he looked at me, I became engulfed in a rapturous divine love that was beyond my understanding. Behind him sat the immortal one known as Mahavatar Babaji, the yogi Christ master and our friend that would appear to us during our meditations.

THE MAN SPEAKS:

"Thank you for the opportunity and great honor to love you unconditionally. Please know that I am always with you. When you complete this incarnation, I will be waiting to reunite with you on the other side of your great mission. Go forth and teach the truth of your unconditional divine love, embodying this complete and whole love as an example of what is possible for others to offer themselves. You are here to accelerate the reconciliation of many through the vehicle of your compassion. Be the light of truth for those needlessly suffering for the truth. Our divine union is always supporting you to fulfill this great mission that you are now called forth to complete."

I saw the great Mahavatar Babaji rise up and take my beloved teacher by the hand. Facing each other, I gasped to witness the man that I had come to love dissolve back into the form of Babaji. He softly smiled at me, raising his right hand in a final blessing over me. I watched as the form of Babaji then turned towards a setting sun and swiftly ascended over the Himalayas.

As I watched his form disappear over the mountain range, my heart lurched forward to race after Babaji, only to feel my hands land on the ridge of grass beneath my meditation seat. I felt my heart torn between chasing this fading vision and becoming viscerally aware of strong winds now swirling around my teacher's body who still sat meditating beside me. My eyes fluttered half open, pausing to seriously consider if I should leave the inner realms where I could still pursue the vision of Babaji that was rapidly dissolving.

The pounding waters of the nearby falls drowned out the almost imperceptible sound of grass unwinding from beneath my teacher's seat. I felt the hairs on my neck stand straight up as chills ran down my spine. The Golden Dragon Light Body of my beloved teacher lifted up his human form to now levitate in a full lotus asana above the waterfall.

I felt the spray of charging water mix with the hot tears of my struggle to grasp his hand, one last time, before his physical ascension. He was deep within the Samadhi of bliss. Just as Babaji had said goodbye in the vision, my teacher smiled at me, raising his right hand with a final blessing. He then dissolved into a thousand drops of water.

I dove into the falls and refused to leave the touch of its river for three days. Water was the bridge that connected our hearts. In my grief, I searched to taste his presence through my memories of our time together in the river. I frantically reached out for him within the touchstone of every rock and pebble. I floated for hours to soothe the excruciating pain.

Due to my extensive self-mastery training, I knew that my soul must not become a prisoner to the past again. Therefore, I completely surrendered myself to the necessary stages of grief that arose in wave after wave of feeling the loss. I continually poured the light within my vase over me, taking sanctuary in compassion for myself. My grieving was torrential but brief.

On the third day, another angel appeared on the shores of the river in the disguise of a tiny, old man carrying a wooden water bucket over his shoulder.

In all my years hidden within the forest, I had never seen anyone other than my teacher. He chanted softly under his breath, beneath a stooped back, with his long white brows and beard grazing the ground he walked upon. He did not see or hear me, for I knew the river as I knew my own body and I effortlessly hid from his sight.

I knew the angel's message without a word: it was time to return to the world of men, women, children, towns, smells, death, and the struggle for more life. My sanctuary must be brought within me now, wherever I went – it was time. I did not know what I was to do or where I would go. All I knew was that I was to carry the Vase of Compassion given to me by The Angel of the Great Commission, following the divine guidance of water, and offer my teachings for living compassion.

Initiated as a Golden Dragon Teacher of Karuna

My time in solitude had come to an end. I was a young girl no longer. I was now a strong and sovereign woman with a destiny to fulfill. I prepared my body, heart, and mind through the water purification rites that Babaji had shown me in his departing vision.

Although my training was strongly anchored within me, my heart still shook in fear at the thought of returning to a world in which people willfully harm one another. I would deeply breathe into the vulnerable feelings that would arise in every passing moment. My breath centered me with the presence of my Higher Self guiding me from within. I could feel my guardian angels patiently, yet earnestly, awaiting my choice to follow this guidance to leave the forest and surrender into their care for beginning life anew.

I was about to step back into the world as both the student and teacher of my own Divine Feminine Christ embodiment. Sharing my Keycode 6 transmission amidst a world of contrast was the next quantum leap in trusting my relationship with myself. My beloved knew that for my training to be complete, I needed to live at the edge of my faith *every day*.

The night before my departure, I called out to the stars, fasting for a vision to support me in the heroic journey to come. In the soft dark night, the wind began to move over my skin and dance through my hair, but I was

247

not stirred from my meditation. My heart and lips continued to fervently pray as I gazed at the stars above.

My eyes were guided to watch an outline launch from behind the moon and dance its way down the ladder of heaven. Its muscular arms clutched the wind and leaped toward me in graceful flight. With each spiraling turn, the moonlight flashed off of its pearlescent white scales. Long whiskers cascaded far past its neck, and its violet eyes were lit with magenta flames.

The white dragon landed before me with such gentleness that my body spontaneously moved from surprise to prostration at the sight of such grace. Tears of compassion fell from its sparkling eyes, which materialized as little diamonds surrounding my bowed head.

My vision quest had called forth a mighty angel from the cosmos – for before me now stood a Sophia Dragon. A familiar voice arose from behind her broad head: "Arise *Daughter of Moon and Water,* so that the prophecy of this night may be fulfilled."

My hands were firmly planted upon the earth, filled with the trembling of heat and damp sweat. I felt my head, heavy with trepidation, begin to slowly rise from its humble resting place upon the ground. I called forth the strength within me to witness my answered prayer speak.

The familiar voice beckoned me again: "Why do you hesitate to look upon the power of that which is within you made manifest to help you? For Sophia has heard your prayer and answered."

I felt a rush of molten breath run through the course of my being as The Sophia Dragon blessed my body with her stardusted Breath of Life, filling me with a radiant pink light. Her transmission physically levitated my body above the ground and then placed me on my feet to stand with an unknown resource of self-confidence.

There, to my wonder, I beheld Babaji with his right hand comfortably resting upon the dragon's shimmering throat. The Sophia Dragon bowed its massive head, its horns reflecting the full moon's light as it turned to gaze through my eyes and directly into my heart.

I felt my skin change from stone to water and filled with the fire of the Holy Spirit all at once. I cried out, as the body of fear that I had been ritually purifying leaped out from my heart and vanished into the night.

MAHAVATAR BABAJI SPEAKS:

"Your Sophia Dragon mother is here to initiate you as a Golden Dragon teacher of karuna compassion for humanity. It is the power of your divine love that has called her forth to stand before your very eyes, as one of your many important guides for this great mission ahead of you.

"Allow the dreams of your past to slip away now. Beware the illusion of time and death that you have come to dispel for others – for you now know that they do not exist. Remember that as you anoint each heart with unconditional compassion, you are anointing your own.

"You have called forth your sovereignty amidst the greatest pain, to now anchor your Golden Dragon Light Body at your Sacred Heart. Arising as the phoenix of your own heart's alchemy – you are now one who is not born of earth or of sky – but of both and none at all. It is safe to embrace yourself as a fully awakened being whose presence awakens others to their sovereignty.

"Do not be afraid of fulfilling that which was prophesied over you, for all of it has already happened. Go forth as a Golden Dragon activator of The Sophia Code and listen only to the Holy Spirit guiding you from within. All will be well, for divine love has cleared the path before you in a mighty way."

Quan Yin Teaches the Path of Karuna Compassion

I offer my story to reveal that all stories of compassion are the same story in the journey back home to the heart. Water directly taught me about the meaning of karuna compassion. When I prayed into the water and ingested it, the water would flow to every darkness that my awareness was too afraid to touch, out of shame or guilt. It was the water that carried my prayer everywhere I needed to reconcile the wounding within me.

The water was not afraid to go where I needed it to go for my healing. Therefore, the medicine of water is an excellent teaching vehicle for revealing the power of karuna compassion. For there is nothing that we have suffered that we cannot heal within ourselves, and karuna is the medicine of unconditional compassion that is the power to heal us from every suffering.

The greatest of all suffering occurs when you refuse to have compassion for yourself as you are experiencing *any* kind of suffering. The Sanskrit root for compassion is *karuna*. My definition of *karuna* is to be so closely held by yourself that no separation can remain within you. To refuse yourself this embrace when you are already suffering immeasurably amplifies the pain that you are already experiencing.

Embodying karuna compassion begins with learning how to love yourself first, holding all the parts of yourself throughout every present moment and in every circumstance. It requires softening your heart to accept that the gift of your own karuna compassion is the standard you deserve to experience in your relationship with yourself.

No one else's opinion is required to acknowledge, quantify, or qualify your authentic experience of suffering for it to be real for you. Practicing karuna does not require anyone else's approval or participation for you to receive the compassion that you deserve. Everything happening within you is here to be unconditionally honored by you without needing anyone else's permission to do so. Karuna compassion is taking the time to be present with your authentic experience and being kind to yourself in every way.

The quantum healing energy of karuna takes your awareness directly to the root belief systems of your original wounds, so that you may love those places within you that feel abandoned and unlovable. For that is the magic of karuna: it is the compassion within you that is willing to love what you believe is unlovable, unforgivable, or lacking within yourself. In the practice of karuna compassion, your own heart becomes your resource for receiving unconditional self-love and self-acceptance.

Your greatest teacher for learning the importance of karuna compassion is your Inner Child, who is also the face of your innocence. The voice of your Inner Child speaks from your heart, acting as a guardian angel for your commitment to bestow the karuna of self-love upon yourself. When you are too enamored with social conditioning to give yourself the compassion that you deserve, *it is your Inner Child who steps in to keep you honest.* Sudden feelings of anger, disappointment, and sadness can all act as messengers from your Inner Child when you are refusing to give karuna to yourself.

Karuna is often described as the devoted loving compassion that a mother has for her child. I offer to you that embodying this definition begins with you becoming the Inner Mother and Father to your own Inner Child. In the journey of parenting yourself, you will come to find that it is your own innocence that knows the exact words and self-loving actions that you need to receive *from yourself* for healing your deepest wounds.

When your Inner Child is honored with karuna compassion, they will eventually reveal themselves as *The Phoenix Child* within you, which is Keycode 444 of The Sophia Code. The Phoenix Child is the invincible embodiment of your innocence that was never harmed in your suffering. Keycode 444 is your own angelic nature that arises again and again from the ashes of the past with the power to unconditionally love yourself, and all others, with the wisdom of compassion that has survived with you.

When you practice holding yourself with great tenderness, you eventually become whole in your relationship with yourself. You trust yourself. Emotional safety becomes an established foundation within you. These feelings of safety and wholeness within yourself allow for you to reconcile with the truth of your sovereign divinity. It is from this foundation that karuna can then initiate you into the greater depths of compassion available to you as a Christed being.

'To be so closely held by yourself that no separation can remain within you' also applies to your interdependent existence with all beings within Sophia. Karuna for yourself eventually generates an overflowing compassion for all beings that you are journeying with across the cosmos. When you embody this level of karuna you do not expect anyone to think, act, or believe what is to your liking in exchange for your compassion. Christ consciousness honors the universal suffering of others by honoring all beings as the faces of divinity that deserve your unconditional compassion.

The piercing light of karuna is too bright to see anything other than the divine love that every sovereign being deserves as a member of the one body of Sophia Christ. When karuna compassion overflows from your heart, you deeply care about what is important to others because you honor and value what is important to you. Karuna compassion frees you from all boundaries about why you should or shouldn't give unconditional love. It is this authentic arising to unconditionally love others because you know how deeply to love yourself that heals and uplifts the world with your compassion.

251

OM MANE PADME HUM

I share the mantra, OM MANE PADME HUM, which Green Tara gave to me in the forest of my grief, as a vehicle for creating a compassionate relationship with yourself. If it feels foreign or impossible to give yourself the karuna of unconditional love that you deserve, start here with my mantra. Allow my support to make it easier for you. I am always present when this prayer is spoken. The seeded power within OM MANE PADME HUM will soften your heart in unexpected and miraculous ways, as it did for me.

It begins with OM, which is the sound of creation coming into form. OM clears your mind of self-hating thoughts and resonates your awareness with the high frequency truth that you are a sovereign creator. MANI means the jewel and the jewel is *you*. Every facet of your whole divine self already exists just as you are. MANI reconciles your awareness to unconditionally accept your perfect divine nature in human form. PADME means *the lotus* and it represents your body awakening as the vehicle for your Higher Self. HUM is the sound of compassion that clears all your suffering, across all your lifetimes, by honoring the totality of your true nature.

As you speak my mantra of compassion, may the Breath of Life passing over the waters of your tongue open your heart to live a lifetime of unconditional divine love and compassion for yourself.

KEYCODE 6
THE QUAN YIN INITIATION

Soothe Your Awakening with Self-Compassion

I now prepare a ceremonial space within and around me for transformation. I call forth a circle of white light shimmering with a silver opalescence. I am now within its center, enthroned upon the blooming petals of a white lotus.

I am now in ceremony – free from the constructs of space and time – where instantaneous healing and divine knowing exist.

Above me, a full moon glows with golden radiance. Stars glitter far across the warm summer night sky. Behind me is a forest canopy defined by moonlight and quiet shadows. Before me, in the distance, I hear the flowing waters of a large river.

The river's continuous movement fills my center with a calm stillness. I peer curiously from my white lotus throne, the river magnetizing my heart.

I breathe in the fresh scent of holy water on the move.
I breathe out and relax deeper.

In the sanctuary of my surroundings, the scent of jasmine clears my thoughts. From the forest canopy, a firefly dances towards me as an orb of piercing white light. The firefly spirals and weaves three times in a circle around my throne. Its light bobs back and forth before my eyes, invoking me to now rise up from my lotus throne. Drawn by its joyful luminescent trail, I follow the firefly to the river's beckoning shoreline.

Under a full moon the river's landscape easily pours into my awareness. Crystalline waves of pristine water tumble down from a tall waterfall to my right. Clear quartz crystals rise up from mossy tiers of rolling earth. The river flows at a steady pace, illuminated by rippling shades of moonlight.

I sink my toes into the moss and breathe in deeply. I feel the earth respond to my toes with a generous rush of healing energy that fills my legs and easily flows into my first three chakras, as a refreshing life force. I sink my feet deeper into the earth's welcoming embrace and walk with renewed confidence to the river's edge. The firefly continues to bob and weave downstream along a gentle breeze. My eyes follow its orb as it disappears behind the sweeping curtain of an enormous willow tree.

The river calls my attention back to my feet upon its shore. The river's voice communicates as a feeling intelligence within every cell of my body, inviting my awareness to soften and harmonize with my Higher Self. The river asks me to touch its surface with my skin.

My Higher Self responds with a full-body yes to this invitation, guiding my awareness to step forward into the water. I place my feet into the shallow current of the shoreline. The water responds by lapping at my ankles with laughter. I remember that the delightful laughter of water is a familiar sound to my heart.

Genuinely welcomed by the river, a deep sense of relief sweeps through me as I now acknowledge and remember my ability to communicate with water. The lapping river begins to release wave after wave of unconscious emotional resistance within me, which now easily floats downstream.

My Higher Self pours its pure essence into the newly cleared spaces within me. In the Holy Communion offered by the conduit of pure water, I now let go to merge my awareness with the all-loving presence of my Higher Self. The water invites me to step deeper into its current. I ask the water why.

THE RIVER SPEAKS:

"You have come to meet a spiritual ally for the healing and empowerment of your human journey. In her eyes, you will receive a powerful reflection of your true self. Allow my waters to safely float you downstream to meet this friend."

To my surprise, the river's strong current responds to my trust by gently parting as I step forward. Within the current, a pathway of minimal resistance swirls open for me to wade through. The water's intelligence carefully embraces me as I submerge myself into the river's central current. My Higher Self directs me to let go and lean back into a floating position. Although my awareness momentarily hesitates, I trust the step-by-step guidance of my Higher Self and I choose to let go.

OM MANE PADME HUM
OM MANE PADME HUM
OM MANE PADME HUM

As I lean back, I feel my body held by a thousand unseen arms. They gently cradle my body's descent as I surrender my awareness to now float upon the river. The full moon above me illuminates my mind to be still and free of thoughts. Completely supported by a thousand unseen arms, my muscles relax and I begin to drift peacefully downstream upon the river.

The lapping water softly carries me beyond any sense of time. Hours seem to pass in but a few moments. The gentle breeze is now a distant sound. As I float upon the river, my awareness travels far within me to a place that I have never touched before with my thoughts. It is a warm black space within me that emanates a completely still silence. I sigh deeper into relaxation. There is nothing to do in this black space but to rest and be still.

The voice of the river gently whispers me awake: "It is time to walk again." The thousand unseen arms lift me to stand as my eyes flutter open. Step-by-step I navigate across the river's current, crossing to the bank of its far shore. The night air caresses my skin to instantly dry and the water travels deep into my pores.

OM MANE PADME HUM
OM MANE PADME HUM
OM MANE PADME HUM

Before me billows the largest willow tree I have ever seen. Its waterfall of long sweeping arms harmoniously sways with the gentle breeze in a quiet dance of shimmering leaves. I now see the piercing white light of the firefly spiraling in and out of view. Its orb bobs and weaves far behind the curtain of weeping branches.

"Come inside ..." I hear a soft sweet voice beckoning from far within the tree. The voice echoes throughout my heart with an unquestionable familiarity.

I suddenly feel quite young, as though the years of my life have miraculously reversed. I look down to witness that I am now standing in my body as it looked when I was seven years old. Nothing feels unusual about this instant transformation. My young body feels perfectly suited to this new present moment. I feel the lightness of my little feet and the boldness of my curiosity rambunctiously romp me forward to explore the great willow tree.

Weaving through long golden arms and shiny green leaves, I hug tiny handfuls of willow branches, carving out a labyrinth path through the thick tree.

"Keep looking ..." I hear the voice playfully encourage my curiosity. This voice is the kindest sound I have ever heard and my intuition hones upon it, in a game of hide-and-seek. Swinging through the last layer of boughs, I find my way to the open moss of the great willow tree's canopied center.

It is mostly dark within the curtained circumference of the inner tree, with occasional slats of moonlight peeking through from above. I peer into the shadowy sanctuary, adjusting my eyes to take in the vast trunk of the great willow tree. As though announcing my arrival, a choir of cicadas spontaneously lifts up their unified voice into the night. My little body begins to buzz in harmony.

From behind the trunk, spirals out my friendly firefly, whose tiny orb of light now refocuses my perception. Its piercing white light begins to quickly expand far beyond its size. I feel my heart leap up in childlike wonder and anticipation. *I found her!*

Ray after ray of new white light emerges from the center of the growing orb and reaches far into the shadows. I hear my name repeated softly between quiet rounds of a mantra being chanted:

OM MANE PADME HUM
OM MANE PADME HUM
OM MANE PADME HUM

The innumerable rays of white light now draw into a centralized column, organizing their particles to reveal the rapidly forming outline of a woman sitting upon a white lotus throne. My eyes struggle to adjust to this brilliance gathering into the form of her soft body and radiant face. Her pure white robes are alive, illuminated as the full moon above. Finally, my vision adjusts to the piercing white light of her smiling face and welcoming open arms.

I am absolutely elated to see her smile and run without hesitation into her waiting arms. She holds my little body like a baby bird, folding my wings into her tender embrace. I close my eyes and all I see is the white light of her pure essence filling my awareness. My heart bursts with confidence to be held in the invincible arms of her divine love and my innocence delights in her holy reflection of my worthiness.

OM MANE PADME HUM
OM MANE PADME HUM
OM MANE PADME HUM

She quietly calls my name and my eyes open to peer into the light of her own. Tendrils of her hair move as raven feathers loose upon an unseen wind. Her arms maintain a secure embrace around me, but she now adjusts my seat upon her lap to allow for a natural flow of conversation to unfold.

"I am so glad you found me," she gently offers. "Do you remember who I am?"

"Yes!" I broadly smile back. "You're Quan Yin!" My heart bursts with happiness to proudly speak her name once again. It felt as though a distant age had passed since I was allowed to say her name.

"Yes, I am." Her dark eyes peer back at me, filled with such an all-consuming love it surpasses my understanding, even for a confident seven-year-old heart. Her eyes flicker in a momentary consideration and then resume her steady gaze. She draws closer into my eyes.

"I would like to share a story with you tonight."

"Like a bedtime story?" I gleefully ask.

"No ... It's actually a story to awaken your soul – it's not the kind of story intended to put you to sleep."

I pause to consider her unusual offer and ask: "Will the story have a happy ending?"

"Yes, my dear, it has the happiest ending of any story ever shared. But you will need to be brave in the beginning, middle, and parts of the end."

"Why?" I curiously demand.

"Because this story has events in it that you will not want to see or hear."

"Then *why* would I want to hear your story Quan Yin ... Why?"

"So that you may be free from fear forever and know that only love is real."

"Ohhh ..." I considered the idea, carefully weighing her response on the scales of my heart. Her reasoning felt distantly familiar. I shifted into another gloriously peaceful position, perched in her arms of pure love.

"Well what's the story about?" I queried.

Quan Yin's mouth upturns into a promising smile as she replies: "It's about a young girl who overcame great pain to grow up and become a beautiful woman whose love healed the whole world."

"Hmmm ..." I calculated the variables of pain and love to see if they leveraged my resistance to hearing Quan Yin's story. The scales were tipping, but I was still not convinced.

Raising an amused eyebrow, Quan Yin counter offered: "... and in the story there's a mighty dragon that becomes the girl's best friend. This all-powerful dragon teaches the girl how to devour pain and magically transform it into love."

I stare back at her in silent awe. Quan Yin had made an offer that I could not refuse. I decided then and there that *I must learn everything* about this magical dragon.

"Okay! Will you hold my hand when I feel afraid during the story?"

"Of course. I will be holding all of you whenever you need my help to feel brave."

"Okay ..."

Suddenly my young body is overcome by a tidal wave of tiredness. I widely yawn, attempting to hold my eyes open, as I happily agree to bravely hear her story. My head unwillingly rolls onto her shoulder and I promptly pass out into a deep state of sleep.

OM MANE PADME HUM
OM MANE PADME HUM
OM MANE PADME HUM

My consciousness steps out from the form of my young sleeping body to now stand in the form of my adult body witnessing Quan Yin holding my Inner Child. I take a moment to orient myself through the senses of my adult self to the willow tree, the distant sound of the river, and Quan Yin sitting before me.

I stare curiously at my seven-year-old body, fast asleep in her arms. My eyes suddenly feel overcome by heaviness as I witness deep wounds, dark bruises, and infested cuts slowly begin to appear across the landscape of my Inner Child's little body. I look at Quan Yin in horror, my eyes searching hers for an understanding of what I am witnessing unfold before me.

QUAN YIN SPEAKS:

"These are those long-forgotten hidden wounds that continue to unconsciously control your awareness with frightful thinking. Memories, both known and unknown to you, are surfacing as a map of your past across the body of your Inner Child to now be healed by the witnessing power of your Higher Self."

I peer closer at the wounds; they seem to be written as stories compressed into the little body of my Inner Child. Emotionally stirred, I ask: "Why would anyone hurt an innocent child?"

Quan Yin replies: "They did not know how to stop what they did. The suffering it takes to wound a child in such a way as this – or in any way at all – is a suffering beyond logic. As a wild animal bent over in maddening pain strikes without thought, so too the human awareness possessed by suffering cannot stop itself from hurting others. Suffering exacts such acts of pain upon others without reason, for suffering is the true definition of insanity."

I began to calculate how many times I had suffered in the past and unconsciously acted out from that suffering. I considered how universal this suffering is within humanity, especially how great one must be suffering to actually hurt the little body before me. Moved by the illumination of compassion, I curiously ask: "How can my Higher Self heal my little body?"

Quan Yin smiles at me and offers: "First, you must choose to recognize the absolute innocence of your Inner Child. These wounds are artifacts from the insanity of suffering. These wounds have absolutely nothing to do with the purity and worthiness of this child's heart. At this young age, there was nothing this little one could have done to stop what happened to them by the words and deeds of others. Can you forgive yourself for choosing to be so young in this little body? Can you forgive yourself for becoming temporarily vulnerable to the insanity of others' suffering?"

I look at the young body resting in Quan Yin's arms and realize that I must be willing to forgive myself so that these wounds will lift and heal. I decide that I love my Inner Child too much to resist this self-compassion and self-forgiveness any longer.

My Inner Child deserves to never suffer again – and to only know my unconditional love and acceptance. I now choose to use my sovereign creative power to free every wound from the past that I see compressed into this little body. On behalf of my Inner Child, I call upon my Higher Self and now command:

I accept that I hold the golden keys to my Heaven on Earth.
I accept that I create my reality, by the power of my word.
My word is good, my heart is pure.
By the loving power of my pure word I call forth and declare blessings of unconditional compassion for myself now.

By the power of my I Am Presence, I now forgive myself for every experience of suffering in my past.

By the power of my I Am Presence, I now forgive myself for every unresolved painful memory.

By the power of my I Am Presence, I now forgive myself for every moment of life lost in the amnesia of my unconscious wounds.

By the power of my I Am Presence, I now forgive myself for every addiction to unconsciously perpetuate further suffering.

By the power of my I Am Presence, I now forgive myself for every experience of others as a threat to my innocence.

By the power of my I Am Presence, I now forgive myself for withholding from unconditionally forgiving myself.

By the power of my I Am Presence, I now summon and receive the unconditional compassion that I deserve to give myself.

By the power of my I Am Presence, I now summon and receive the unconditional divine love that I deserve to give myself.

By the power of my I Am Presence, I now summon the cleansing waters of my Holy Spirit to baptize me from the suffering of my past.

By the power of my I Am Presence, I now summon my Higher Self to atone for every wound.

By the power of my I Am Presence, I now summon the thousand hands and eyes of Sophia to bless my body, heart, and mind for my innocence to be experienced anew.

By the power of my I Am Presence, I now command these wounds, seen and unseen, conscious and unconscious, to now be dissolved by the holy water and light of my invincible innocence.

By the power of my I Am Presence, I now summon and welcome my Higher Self to operate my awareness with radiant self-compassion every day.

I declare that my self-compassion creates a new relationship with life that is filled with the blessings of happiness, love, joy, peace, and prosperity that I deserve.

OM MANE PADME HUM
OM MANE PADME HUM
OM MANE PADME HUM
OM MANE PADME HUM
OM MANE PADME HUM
OM MANE PADME HUM
OM MANE PADME HUM

Quan Yin smiles into my eyes with soft fierceness, silently celebrating the pure power of our communion. My young body stirs in Quan Yin's embrace. She lifts a slim jade water vessel above the head of my Inner Child. Quan Yin tips the vessel forward to reveal to me that it is *empty*. Yet, I watch as aquamarine light-water is gently sprinkled over my Inner Child.

Emerging from Quan Yin's heart is a ray of piercing white light that connects my heart chakra to hers. This light now expands far out from our hearts, joining us in a large column of light that surrounds both of our bodies. Quan Yin and I have created a unified field of *karuna compassion* for my Inner Child. I cannot perceive where Quan Yin ends and I begin. I am now one with Quan Yin's loving compassion for my young body in her arms.

OM MANE PADME HUM

The light of karuna compassion now flows up our spines and out through our crown chakras. Piling high in gathering waves of light above us, karuna compassion now descends in rapturous waves of healing energy, filling my young body with its medicine. This karuna compassion travels as the light-water of understanding and acknowledgment into every physical and emotional wound of my Inner Child, honoring a lifetime of surviving the suffering of others.

I keep my eyes fixed upon Quan Yin's peaceful gaze to remain focused in our unified field of karuna compassion. I allow the Holy Spirit of my Higher Self to do this great work through me and for me. I let go *and* remain fully present as the witness and vehicle for this healing empowerment as I silently repeat Quan Yin's mantra.

OM MANE PADME HUM

OM MANE PADME HUM

OM MANE PADME HUM

OM MANE PADME HUM

OM MANE PADME HUM

OM MANE PADME HUM

OM MANE PADME HUM

Quan Yin tips her Vase of Compassion forward and the crystalline waters are sprinkled over my Inner Child again, as she speaks her prayers of purification. Every molecule of this water carries Quan Yin's piercing white light into the subtle bodies of my Inner Child. The perfect waters fill every unresolved feeling with soothing relief, every emotional bruise with the medicine of unconditional love, and every agony with *The Peace that Passeth Understanding*. I watch as the skin of my Inner Child now heals back into a perfect form.

My young body deeply drinks in this medicine of light-water. Every drop of karuna compassion is accounted for and perfectly dissolves into this little body. My Inner Child stirs, rolling over in Quan Yin's lap, stretching long and yawning into a newly awakened breath.

In appreciation, my young form stands up and throws both arms around Quan Yin's neck in a delighted embrace. My Inner Child's skin and clothing now mirror the same white light of Quan Yin's luminosity. My young self now turns to face me as my adult self; I am still channeling the light of karuna compassion through my crown chakra to my Inner Child's heart. Stepping forward from Quan Yin's lap, my Inner Child levitates in the air before me: "Be at peace," the child whispers with a smile. "I am well."

I relax and the fountain of white light at my crown chakra gently slows down to integrate within my adult body. My luminous Inner Child walks upon the quantum particles of the air between us, levitating at eye level, now only a foot away from me.

My seven-year-old self confidently smiles at me and all I can see is a master of light. Reaching out a tiny hand, my Inner Child blesses my third eye with the mudra of Sophia Christ and then we rest our foreheads against one another. Chanting an ancient blessing over my past and future, the little master before me atones for all my previous and possible creations of suffering.

As the risen phoenix, I recognize my luminous Inner Child as the anointed master who is capable of setting me free to accept the joy of *being me.*

OM MANE PADME HUM
OM MANE PADME HUM
OM MANE PADME HUM
OM MANE PADME HUM
OM MANE PADME HUM
OM MANE PADME HUM
OM MANE PADME HUM

THE PHOENIX CHILD SPEAKS:

"In your choice to resurrect me with unconditional love, a new pathway for self-compassion was created within your consciousness. Traveling along this neurological pathway, your unconditional love leads directly to the crystalline chromosome that carries Keycode 6 within you.

"How many times have you extended the waters of karuna compassion to others and forsaken yourself this same miracle? The medicine of unconditional love that you healed my body with is also meant for you. You deserve to receive the blessed power of your own karuna compassion *every day.*

"In this moment, I ordain your adult awareness to the ministry of self-love. I declare that from this day forward a waterfall of self-compassion will forever flow from your heart to your awareness. I consecrate the space and light within you to be filled with the recognition of our innocence. As the pure innocence of your divinity I am always with you, inside every present moment, baptizing your awareness with our conscious communion of self-love.

"I am both the ancient child that knows the secret prayers of your heart and the guardian angel that ensures you receive the answers to these prayers. It is safe to open your heart and be guided by me. Everything you need for loving yourself is within you, *as me.*

"It is time to accept your divine inheritance to be happy. By the power of your unconditional divine love and karuna compassion, I am resurrected as The Phoenix Child, arising from the holy flames of your Sacred Heart. It is by the power of our shared Holy Spirit that I now activate Keycode 6 within your DNA."

My Phoenix Child places both hands on my cheeks and draws our foreheads together again. For a moment, we lightly rest against each other in a third eye communion. Drawing back, my Inner Child flashes a smile at me, surrounded by a great momentum of energy.

With arms reaching upward to the sky, my Phoenix Child levitates directly over me, with tiny feet pointing together as an arrow aimed at my crown chakra. Sweeping winds spiral around my Inner Child's body, which now begins to gently rotate above me. My Phoenix Child sings the Songs of Sophia, calling forth a blessing to heal and activate my adult body.

The curtains of the great willow tree part and I see Quan Yin rise from her throne, speaking blessings over me in the tongues of angels. The willow leaves turn into a thousand unshed tears of my past and run into the great river behind me.

I witness years of my grief wash away into the current, as the tree completely dissolves behind Quan Yin. Compressed stories of suffering release out of every cell in my body, flowing into the river as directed by my Phoenix Child chanting above my head with delight.

OM MANE PADME HUM
OM MANE PADME HUM
OM MANE PADME HUM
OM MANE PADME HUM
OM MANE PADME HUM
OM MANE PADME HUM
OM MANE PADME HUM

Quan Yin steps forward from her white lotus throne to meet me by the river's edge. She holds my hands and invites me to mindfully breathe with her. Together we ground my energy with the earth as my Phoenix Child continues the karuna healing for me from above. In the stillness of Quan Yin's gaze, I become deeply still within. She directs me to look at the full moon and asks me to keep my eyes steady upon it.

From behind the moon, the form of a pearlescent white dragon launches across the night sky, moving in rhythm to the Phoenix Child's chanting for my life. The dragon's radiant body descends in long spirals from the sky and lands along the river's edge upon golden claws. Tucking in her mighty seraphim wings, The Sophia Dragon gazes upon me with eyes glittering from a distance. Maintaining eye contact, she dips her head to quietly sip from the river as I integrate her mighty arrival.

In the presence of The Sophia Dragon, I feel my body let go of all resistances to receiving. I turn my heart to the abandoned places within me and direct the waves of karuna compassion rolling through me to now fill these places with unconditional love. The Sophia Dragon now takes flight to spiral around my Phoenix Child and myself as a DNA helix that connects the full moon with my crown chakra.

The luminous body of my Phoenix Child accelerates to spin faster than the speed of light and dissolves into a thousand drops of water. I receive the baptism of my Phoenix Child, pouring as waves of my pure essence, directly into my crown chakra. I feel instantly nourished and my entire spine aligns as a central channel of piercing white light.

The Sophia Dragon opens her jaws, blowing stardust and lightning through my crown chakra; her Breath of Life anoints every cell of my body with an awakened recognition of my own Holy Spirit. The Sophia Code within me lights up as the crystalline chromosome for Keycode 6 is now activated by my Phoenix Child's joyful laughter ringing across the great halls of my DNA.

Quan Yin now places her hands upon my heart. Pink and aquamarine healing energy flow from her hands to deeply relax my body and integrate Keycode 6 of The Sophia Code within me. Quan Yin quietly sings: OM MANE PADME HUM. Her voice gently soothes me to easily and gracefully integrate this initiation now.

I accept that I hold the golden keys to my Heaven on Earth.
I accept that I create my reality, by the power of my word.
My word is good, my heart is pure.
By the loving power of my pure word, I declare that I am worthy of and willing to receive the unconditional karuna compassion of my Higher Self now and forever more.

By the power of my I Am Presence, it is commanded that this activation of Keycode 6 of The Sophia Code within my DNA is now accomplished.

By the power of my I Am Presence, it is commanded that my awareness be filled by my own divine love and compassion in every present moment.

I now integrate this initiation throughout my entire body, on all four levels of my Be-ing, with grace and ease.

It is done.
It is done.
It is done.
By the power of 3, a perfect trinity: It is done.

The Sophia Dragon blows another Breath of Life over my body. The stardust moves in spirals around me and roots me deeply into the earth beneath my feet. My crown chakra opens as a thousand-petaled lotus flower. The tip of each petal is bejeweled with an open eye flashing with tiny lightning bolts.

My awareness expands into the omniscient vision of my Higher Self. I simultaneously see in every direction while remaining focused upon the face of my Phoenix Child smiling at me from within my heart.

With wide open arms, my Phoenix Child embraces me from within. Quan Yin speaks a ceremonial blessing over me that now seals this empowerment in the light and fire of my own Holy Spirit, as directed by my Higher Self. I thank Quan Yin for facilitating this space of initiation and quantum healing. I now wholeheartedly welcome her loving presence as an essential Divine Feminine Ascended Master mentor in my life.

I watch as the entire night scene dissolves and integrates as the strength of karuna compassion within me. I now close this ceremony with reverence for my true self and the divine love of All That Is, supporting my eternal success.

And so it is.

KEYCODE 7
"SHE OF A THOUSAND WHITE CLOUDS & THUNDER BEINGS"

"Behold this pipe! Always remember how sacred it is, and treat it as such, for it will take you to the end. Remember, in me there are four ages. I am leaving now, but I shall look back upon your people in every age, and at the end I shall return."

— The word of White Buffalo Woman, as spoken by Black Elk[2]

2   *The Sacred Pipe: Black Elk's Account of the Seven Rites of the Oglala Sioux.* Black Elk – Joseph Epes Brown. University of Oklahoma Press, 1989

White Buffalo Woman
Seeds Her Prophetic Lineage

WHITE BUFFALO WOMAN SPEAKS:

I AM WHITE BUFFALO Woman, known as "She of a Thousand White Clouds & Thunder Beings" in The Sophia Code cosmology. As a Divine Feminine Ascended Master mentor I teach you how to live in right relations with yourself, your community, and your beautiful planet. My Keycode 7 is a Shekinah light transmission that guides and protects prophetic indigenous spiritual pathways on Earth.

In my most recent appearance as a Divine Feminine Christ embodiment, I came as White Buffalo Woman to the people of the Great Plains in North America. I seeded the knowledge of who I am in a prophetic lineage of medicine bundles, teachings, and rites of initiation that I delivered in my holy transmission to the Sioux. I will share with you, in my own words, the coming of my lightning medicine to the hearts of this great people.

When I descended from the sky to take on the form of a holy woman, my gaze reflected the angelic DNA of my Oversoul as a Thunder Being with eyes that would shift from night black to dark earthen brown, from storm gray to clear sky blue. Grandmother Spider wove my body together with radiant red earth and threads of silver stardust. My hair moved from a wind within it, black as raven wings and blessed by the word of eagles. I wore the soft long rain down my back and the sunrise within my shawl. My dress was fashioned from the leather of white clouds.

Adorning my crown was a single white eagle feather that ordained my return to the surface of the Earth by the *Order of The Sky Grandmothers*. When my feet touched upon the ground, soft white moccasins appeared around them, beaded with the prophecy of Whirling Rainbow children to come. My face shone as a star as I walked in human form and my body delighted in itself as lightning kissing the earth. The sweet rumbling of soft distant thunder echoed with the victory trills of The Sky Grandmothers watching over me from above.

I began my journey at twilight in the north and walked eastward where the sun would soon arise over two young men hunting across the Great Plains. Carrying bows and bearing quivers upon their backs, the men stood on a hill scanning the horizon for buffalo and caught sight of me along the skyline. I quickened my steps, as they did theirs, for I appeared as a mysterious star roving the earth and their curiosity drew them irresistibly towards me.

As the two men made their way to me, I read the heart of each man. One stood tall and walked forward with a pure heart, guided by his prayer to honor all life. He was a warrior who sought to protect others through wise action. The other man had fallen ill with the sickness of separation that hardened his heart and blinded his true sight. He was a warrior feared by all enemies of their tribe and he took great pride in this status.

Both men were honored warriors and didn't want to return home without good news. Their people were starving from the struggle of an unusually long winter. The men longed to return to their people having found a buffalo herd to hunt. Weary from many days of scouting across the wintry plains, the sight of my approaching light filled them with a mysterious wonder.

As we drew near to one another, the first man saw me through the eyes of his pure heart. In his perception, I first appeared as a tall white buffalo emerging from a great white light. The sound of angelic singing rushed through his inner ears. It was only as I drew close enough that his sight adjusted to perceive me as a startlingly beautiful maiden dressed in holy adornments. The man recognized that I was a sacred messenger and silently prepared his heart in prayer for whatever was to come from our meeting. I smiled at his wisdom and whispered to his mind: "Be at peace."

To the second man I appeared as a lost young maiden, and his blinded perception allowed for a black ravenous desire to overtake his hardened heart. The separation and lack that he secretly felt about himself had created an unbearable void within him; no bounty of war could ever assuage his incurable emptiness. The only temporary relief that he could seem to find was by feasting upon another. His black thoughts began to calculate how many steps it would take to overcome my body with his will.

This man declared his intention to the other warrior. "My friend, what an opportunity this is; we should take this woman now and be with her."

The good-hearted warrior stared back at the other man in shock. He replied: "Oh no, my friend. Can you not see? This is the holiest of women. Do not think such thoughts. Humble yourself and prepare your heart, for she is coming to us now. I do not know what she will say but keep your eyes upon the ground, in honor of that which has sought us out."

"What kind of man are you?" snorted the black-hearted warrior. Then he turned back to satiate his gaze upon me and calculate his next move.

I now stood only a short distance away from the two warriors. The first man kneeled down and began to pray. Though he fervently tried, he could not take his eyes from the sight of me. I carried a large bundle wrapped in white beaded buckskin upon my back, which I carefully removed and gently lowered to rest on the grass. My eyes fixed directly upon the darkness within the second man beset on devouring me. I quietly spoke the incantations of The Sky Grandmothers, which destroys the darkness of ill men, and welcomed him to greet me. At my invitation, the man lurched forward to overtake me.

I summoned the radiant light of my Holy Spirit, which immediately descended over the man's body in a great white cloud. Within this cloud

I spoke of my unconditional mercy and compassion for his great suffering. I announced that I would now relieve him of his suffering by commanding his soul to return to *Wakan Tanka*, the Great Spirit, where all emptiness is fulfilled. Within my invincible compassion and holy light, his soul found the relief that dark appetites could never satisfy. He spontaneously gave up his body, and as his soul went into the light I disintegrated his form.

The cloud cover receded back into my white leather dress, revealing his ash and bones that lay as a pile before my feet. Tears rolled down the remaining man's awestruck face. He now fixed his eyes upon the earth and asked me to be generous with him, to let him go in peace, in honor of my holiness.

"Behold the last prayer for that man, as a reminder to your men: the Holy Mother is within all. No man needs to take from a woman to remember what is already within him. I know that you are a good man and that your heart is pure and true. You may return to your village, just as you asked, and in your return you will carry the message of my coming to your people. Hear my words: tell your chief to prepare for my arrival. I bear a bundle of great importance that will set your people's feet upon a sacred path for the future of generations to come. Prepare a great lodge to gather all your people and make your hearts ready for my arrival."

The man nodded his promise to share my message. Without looking back, he focused his eyes as a single arrow to the south and immediately began to run for his village. His heart burst with the good news of my coming; for he had found something far greater to feed his people than a herd of buffalo.

Upon entering the village, the brave man went directly to the chief's tipi. He shared with the chief all that he had witnessed and the instructions to prepare for my arrival. Knowing the warrior to be a man of integrity, the chief trusted his account of me. The chief then sent out instructions for the people to prepare for my coming.

A great lodge of many tipi poles was assembled, large enough to fit the whole community, just as I had asked. In honor of my arrival, the women prepared their families' best clothing and adornments. The hunger of the people was replaced with a buzzing of preparation and their curiosity feasted upon the mysterious good fortune of my forthcoming message.

Every morning for six days I sent a single red-tail hawk to circle above the village and watch over the people's willingness to receive me.

On the seventh day since appearing to the two warriors, I was spotted at dawn walking towards the village with the sun rising behind me. The red-tail hawk circled high above me, her cries declaring that today was a good day to live. As I entered the village, some of the people could only see the form of a white buffalo, while others perceived me as a holy woman dressed in white with a single eagle feather in my hair. The gathered people welcomed me by parting to create a wide path that led directly to the great tipi. As I passed through the lodge's entrance I fully shifted into my human form as White Buffalo Woman so that all the people may hear me speak.

I walked sun-wise around the lodge, making eye contact with every man, woman, and child as a blessing to unify the people's one heart. I stopped to stand before the chief at the tipi pole of the west. His eyes reflected the daybreak light shining through the open door flap in the east. Unsure if he should speak yet, the chief motioned with his hands, pointing to an altar built in my honor with many offerings of herbs placed upon it.

I nodded in appreciation and motioned to a nearby woman to make an offering of cedar to the fire at the center of the lodge. The woman stepped forward to fulfill my request and the lodge was filled with the cleansing scent of cedar. I took the medicine bundle from my back, blessing it with the smoke, and then raised it with both hands to the chief.

"Within this bundle is a sacred pipe, a most holy instrument of grace; as such it must always be treated with the highest reverence in honor of your covenant with me. Your reverence for this pipe will deepen your reverence for yourselves, one another, and all life. As you love this pipe, praying with it as I will instruct you, your people will be initiated as keepers of a prophetic path for communicating the mysteries of Great Spirit. I deliver this holy vessel directly from Wakan Tanka, who sent me as a manifestation of your people's prayer to be of great service to all beings, even to the ends of the four corners of this world."

I then unwrapped the white leather bundle to reveal the sacred pipe, which the people called *chanunpa*, and placed a red stone representing Mother Earth on the ground by my feet. Once again, I walked sun-wise around the lodge to bless every eye with the sight of their manifested chanunpa from the sky. Many bowed their heads at the sight, touching their foreheads to honor the pipe as it passed by. Returning to stand before the chief, I positioned myself over the red stone and lifted the chanunpa up for everyone to see. I held the stem pointed upward in my right hand with the bowl of the pipe resting in my left hand as I continued to speak.

"The Earth is your Mother and with this pipe you will always remember how to walk in a sacred way, honoring her holy body all the days of your life. For all that she gives to you, the Earth deserves your greatest honor and your every step upon her should be an ongoing prayer of gratitude that never ceases. This chanunpa will spiral open your hearts, so that you may always hear the voice of your Mother clearly. In your listening you will understand how to love her and one another in all ways.

"See how this bowl is carved out of the red earth: in this way the bowl represents your Mother Earth, including your own body that arises from her. Although your individual bodies appear to be separate, they are woven together with all of her elements. What you have been given, it is she who gave it to you. For the short time that you walk upon Mother Earth, your body provides the opportunity to breathe the Breath of Life together as one. As you smoke this pipe, you are reminded of this holy communion. As you live within the body of your Mother Earth, you share this journey interdependently with all beings in a sacred hoop of giving, receiving, and learning from one another.

"Look how the bowl is carved as a buffalo calf, this represents that all beings living upon the Earth are your brothers and sisters. Where this bowl joins with the stem hang twelve eagle feathers to represent your winged family in the sky above. The stem is carved from wood, joining your heart with all that grows upon the land. In this way the spirit of chanunpa reconciles you with the wholeness of who you are – as you consciously pray with all your relations for the willingness to receive the prayer that Great Spirit is praying for you.

"When you lift your voices up to pray with this sacred pipe, your prayers will be supported by all the peoples of your Mother Earth praying along with you, as well as everything within this universe that is also praying with you. Believe that this is so and you will always receive direct knowledge from the Great Spirit. Chanunpa is a manifestation of the covenant that you have entered into with life: to pray for and with everything for the glory of Wakan Tanka's creation to increase in all ways.

"The momentum of your prayers is immediately conceived as this stem joins the bowl. In this design, chanunpa is a holy vehicle revealing the alignment of heaven and earth, the male and female principle that exists within all beings that unifies together in prayer for the manifestation of miracles. As such, this pipe belongs to all pure-hearted people, women and men alike, who are true keepers of these sacred ways.

"Your life is sacred and every day that you live is a holy day. With this pipe you will remember that every dawn is a gift to be honored and that every night is an opportunity to give thanks for another day that you have lived. Everyone and everything that stands upon the Earth is sacred and your prayers spoken with this pipe will elevate all beings with respect. With these prayers you will increase in all ways upon the Earth as you unconditionally bless what is holy and worthy within all."

I then instructed the people in how to bless the sacred herbs that are used to pray with the pipe. Prayers were shared for how to honor their ancestors and prepare the way ahead for their children. I shared how to pray for their tribe, reconciling any challenges that arose between one another by praying with the sacred pipe together as a community. The pipe would help them resolve the seemingly unresolvable by communicating on a much deeper level with the Great Spirit that is in all.

Prophecies then began to flow from my heart over my tongue. I shared with the people that Wakan Tanka would reveal a total of seven sacred rites that would support the tribe's spiritual journey through several ages ahead. Practicing these rites would continually guide the people into ever deeper revelations for how to reconcile, honor, and live in right relations with each other, all beings, and Mother Earth, regardless of all outer circumstances.

I revealed what I could, yet there were things that I spoke of which could not be understood at that time. Those prophecies that were veiled to them were not lost, for I seeded this information in the hearts of their women. In the ages to come, these prophecies would awaken within the DNA of their descendants, activating future Sioux prophets with the seeded visions of my guiding revelations.

"My coming is a sign that your people will carry this pipe as a lineage of Wakan Tanka's great light for all of creation's children. The Great Plains is your world now, but one day your world will include a much larger world with many two-leggeds that have forgotten who they are. First they will be your enemies, filled with the sickness of separation, and they will take almost everything from you because of their great suffering.

"You will know that the final age is coming to an end when these same two-leggeds begin to seek you out for the medicine of this sacred pipe to heal their sickness. They will ask you to teach them about peace and at first they will understand very little of what you say. Yet, look for the signs of their questioning eyes and you will know that I am coming soon to speak on your behalf.

"Throughout these ages I will always be with you as a guiding light, but you will not see me in this way that you do now. As you pray with this sacred pipe you will learn how to find me within you. From this pilgrimage across the coming ages, your people will learn that what is within you can never be stolen from your pure hearts.

"This pipe will take your people all the way to the end of those days, completing a great prayer to purify the hearts of all two-leggeds from the darkness of separation. It is then that I will return and physically walk amongst you once again. My return will signify that the great prayer Wakan Tanka has for the two-legged people, which was put into the creation of this chanunpa, will be fulfilled and a new prophecy for that same prayer will arise.

"Children from the stars will walk the Earth, carrying a living chanunpa *within them*. In those days, I will reveal the fullness of my light upon the Earth and these starseeded children will recognize my voice and embody my new prophecies. The Great Spirit that fills this pipe will flow over their tongues and they will speak a deluge of prayers and prophecies that will free this world from the dark reign of the previous ages.

Behold this pipe that I give you! Chanunpa stands upon the Earth and walks with you as an embodiment of these great days to come when all peoples will speak the praise of Wakan Tanka in one tongue."

Closing my spoken prophecies with a prayer that sealed these words within their hearts and minds, I then turned and walked four times sun-wise around the lodge. The Holy Spirit within me caused the fire to rise higher with every round. On the fourth round I walked out of the tipi door, raised my arms to the east and declared: "Wakan Tanka, I have spoken the good words that you sent me to say and it is done."

As I began to walk out of the village the same way that I had entered, the people hurriedly emerged from the tipi to witness what they could of my departure. A great eagle, larger than any warrior had ever seen, descended from the sky to circle above me as I walked.

When I felt the last person emerge from the tipi, I stopped walking and shapeshifted into the form of a reddish-brown buffalo calf. I turned back to stare at the people. In joyful celebration, I kicked my back hooves into the air and then playfully tumbled into the grass. When I stood back up my fur turned pure white and in this embodiment I became quite still and once again stared back into the eyes of everyone watching me. I then continued to walk a distance more away from the village as the white buffalo calf and then stopped to look back once again.

Above me the great eagle faced the village and sounded four cries that rolled across the plains. On the fourth cry my white fur turned night black and I bowed to ceremonially honor each of the four directions for their support of my prophecies. Upon completing this prayer, my black calf embodiment shifted back into my form as White Buffalo Woman. I turned a final time to face the people, raising my hands in a final blessing and declared: "I will always be with you. You will see me with your eyes once again when I walk as the white buffalo upon the Earth."

With this final prayer, my spirit was set free from all form. My great light was released to radiate throughout my body, which dissolved into white clouds and lightning. The circling eagle descended into the revelation of my light and we became one star running across the Great Plains, finally dissolving into the horizon.

The Prophesied Return of White Buffalo Woman

Let it be known that my medicine for humanity is as multifaceted as the thousand eyes of Grandmother Spider. The wisdom of every form is available for my prophecies. For I am an embodiment of the Holy Spirit and I speak in the tongues of all species praying for and praising the glory of Sophia within the Mother Earth and as her Great Spirit that created all that is.

I have appeared in other indigenous cultures as well, in other forms that are just as honored, for my Oversoul was asked by Sophia to protect and guide many indigenous peoples of the Earth throughout ages of evolutionary ascension. As such, my Oversoul is consecrated to embody the divine will of Sophia; wherever She asks me to go, I shall forever proclaim Her holy name.

Many invoke my Holy Spirit as an Archangel of Thunder Beings and as a guiding light Ascended Master for the fulfillment of global peace prophecies. In this age, I am now revealing myself as a Divine Feminine Christ embodiment overseeing the Earth's ascension. All of these titles point to the service of my heart, yet who I am exists beyond all definitions. I manifest myself within any form needed to speak the words for which I am sent, and in this way I am a mirror for your Oversoul's ability to do the same.

Wherever Sophia asks for me to descend, as Her messenger and embodiment on Earth, I appear as the Holy Spirit made flesh. My lightning bundle carries the medicine of miracles. I am the embodiment of answered prayer that is instantaneously and perfectly manifested even more beautifully than originally asked for. When I appear to a people, my presence prophesies the coming of healing storms for evolutionary change and ordained reconciliation.

I am most at home in the sky worlds not far above your Mother Earth. Dancing upon the clouds with my Thunder Being angels, my ceremonies create offerings of rain and electricity for Mother Earth's body to grow and regenerate.

I represent an ancient and powerful Order from the sky worlds called *The Sky Grandmothers* who oversee the evolutionary growth of all species on Earth from beyond the space-time continuum. Together we continuously weave a rainbow bridge that coordinates innumerable timelines for countless souls and species to incarnate within Mother Earth's body and become students of her abundant grace.

There are many Ascended Masters originating from other Star Nations across this universe that oversee humanity's ascension, but I am an Ascended Master whose Order is native to this planet. I was present for the conception of Mother Earth and I will remain with her until the blinding light of her full ascension.

As such, I have served as a Divine Feminine Christ embodiment overseeing this planet's ascension for eons. Countless Ascended Masters and Star Nations seek out my intercession and counsel for how to best serve the consciousness of Mother Earth, as well as her billions of species. For your planet is a beloved Daughter of the Most High and an important Keycode in the cosmos of Sophia. As such, there is a great interest amongst many diplomatic councils for how to support her divine purpose as a remarkable Christed Oversoul of Sophia Dragon consciousness.

In my prophetic lineage revealed by the Sioux people, the One Sophia Source is revered and prayed to as *Wakan Tanka, the Great Spirit.* My appearance to the Sioux represents the Holy Spirit descending into form to deliver direct revelations of Wakan Tanka for living in respect and harmony with your planet, all species, your community, and yourself.

When I appear to a people ready for my teachings, my embodiment reflects the earthly forms that provide a direct vehicle for delivering my messages to the heart of their cultural context. Buffalo abundantly provided for everything that was physically needed for the Sioux to survive and thrive on the Great Plains. Therefore, the buffalo represented the heart of the Sioux's existence.

I came in the form of a pure white buffalo calf as a prophecy of their *spiritual abundance.* I blessed them with the responsibility to maintain a clear pathway home for humanity to reconcile with the heart of its innocence. I entrusted them to live as stewards of peace with all beings on this planet. For many, this sacred pathway of reconciliation is called the *Red Road.*

I chose the Sioux people to be the caretakers of my prophecies, for their mighty hearts were already practicing a daily communion with Great Spirit and Star Nations prior to my arrival. Therefore, when I appeared to the Sioux, I declared a messianic prophecy to the hearts of a listening and willing people.

This messianic prophecy foreshadowed my return as an overlighting Divine Feminine Christ embodiment for reconciling humanity's relationship with Mother Earth. For several ages, it was imperative that this prophecy remained veiled in mystery, but now I am fully available to all people as a global guiding light teacher for this next golden age.

The spontaneous and sacred appearance of a new genetic species of white buffalo in North America is the first fulfillment of my spoken prophecy. These white buffalo are the first Holy Spirit embodiments of my Sophia Christ consciousness returning and manifesting once again on Earth. As Thunder Being angels, they embody and broadcast the frequency of my Divine Feminine Christ transmission, which is an invincible innocence that radically undermines and transfigures the viral programming causing humanity to act inhumanely to all life.

The White Buffalo Star Nation is a collective consciousness of angelic Thunder Beings that are descending to Earth within the bodies of this sacred white buffalo herd. I invite you to open your hearts and receive their healing rains that wash away the grief of past ages and nourish the gardens of your future generations. Their evolutionary work with The Sophia Dragons assists in dissolving hierarchies of darkness and birthing new golden ages of sovereignty and peace.

The White Buffalo Star Nation is a guiding light totem for your generation of radical spiritual warriors and starseeded Lightworkers. They intimately know the fabric of your soul's passionate prayer for a new world, for they are highly advanced beings that have traveled far across the cosmos to join you in leading this global movement. Their entirely new genetic sequence is a mirror for your own unique contribution as a Starseed Lightworker who came to Earth with an important mission.

My white buffalo understand your intense sensitivities to humanity's current crises, as well as the courage that is required to look and speak differently than previous generations of human Lightworkers. Just as my white buffalo angels are a completely new species on earth, so are you, and you can take refuge in their loving understanding of your heroic human journey.

If you are open to receiving their support, my white buffalo are here to work as one with you in service to this Divine Feminine Christ movement. Their purpose as my embodied angels is to initiate the willingness of humanity to receive its answered prayer for peace.

Consider the powerful momentum of a Thunder Being herd as a miraculous form of spiritual support for your own role in birthing a new paradigm. When you pray with and for the White Buffalo Star Nation, your prayers for a new golden age are amplified by the magnificent power of my living angels on Earth. With the mighty spirit of my white buffalo at your back, you remember how much your prayers matter for birthing Heaven on Earth.

In their ordained appearance as a new species, they embody both the fulfillment of my prophecy and the lightning medicine of manifested miracles as a mirror for recognizing the power of your own prayers. Your prayers make a significant difference both for your own future and the generations ahead, who are depending upon you to fulfill your own prophecies and birth a new paradigm.

The spontaneous anchoring of the White Buffalo Star Nation in North America is the first fulfillment of my prophecies as an overlighting Divine Feminine Christ embodiment in service to the planet's ascension. There are many more to come. I proclaimed that I would return at the culmination of several destructive ages to guide humanity back to global peace and right relations with the Earth. With the white buffalo announcing my return, know that I am a fully available spiritual guide both on Earth and within your heart and my work with you for birthing this next Age of Miracles has just begun.

My Keycode 7 is ordained to become a guiding light transmission for millions of Lightworkers around the world that are here to embody The Way of reconciliation, integrity, and sovereignty. I am here to mentor you as a wayshower for global peace by activating your embodiment to command miracles and fulfill prophecy through the purity of your heart.

Prayer Is Your Greatest Medicine

The true heart of humanity's innocence is as pure as a white buffalo. The sacred pipe was a gift given to humanity as a teaching vehicle for how to access peace within you, by reconciling with your pure innocence through the power of prayer.

I am here to teach you about the full power of prayer to clear all timelines of suffering, including the desecration of the Divine Feminine, and restore to you a peace that has never left you. It is safe for you to let go of the past; no matter how many times you relive the trauma of genocide, you cannot change the outcome.

I am here to guide you back to your own salvation, which is to believe in the power of the Holy Spirit working through you to atone for and reconcile all imbalances. You honor your ancestors and cleanse the past by living fully in the prayer of the present moment. This prayer is praying you and all of humanity into a new relationship with each other and Mother Earth.

Stop shaming yourself for everything that the tribes of humanity have done to each other in the past. Internalizing shame only slows the momentum of this prayer that is being answered through loving yourself. You are here as a wayshower to lead many in how to create a new paradigm, free of the past, by commanding changes through your sovereign power of prayer.

One of my great prayers for humanity is the reconciliation of the Divine Feminine Christ consciousness. In my return to the Earth, I am here to mentor women in how to make a strong prayer for their personal sovereignty and how to receive the answer to that mighty prayer.

In this next Age of Miracles, women must claim their divine right to fully embody The Sophia Code within them and take up the mantle of Divine Feminine Christ leadership. For women are the buffalo of community: birthing and raising every generation from the prayer of their wombs. When women are supported to dream in peace, men become woven into their prayer and know their own worth by supporting their women birthing a new paradigm into reality.

Prayer is a vehicle for the direct communion between your awareness and your Higher Self. It is also the direct communication between your awareness and Sophia, which my people call the Great Spirit. Prayer is a conversation that can happen in many spoken words or in the silence of feeling. Prayer is a visualization of something desired and the communication of that desire to be fulfilled by the Holy Spirit within you and All of Creation.

An authentic prayer is both humbling and empowering. Prayer is a spiritual technology that requires your awareness to surrender to the power of the Holy Spirit working within you and in All of Creation. Allowing yourself to surrender to a higher power humbles your awareness to reach beyond the limitations and resistances of the ego. The ego would have you believe that the thinking of your limited human awareness is your only resource for solving a problem or manifesting a desire.

When you pray, you are allowing a higher power beyond your human understanding and effort – the power of the Holy Spirit that exists within you – to divinely orchestrate the answers to your every prayer. In this way, prayer is a great equalizer that both humbles and empowers all people through the act of surrendering. Receiving the answers to your prayers teaches your awareness to trust that there is a greater part of you listening to and answering your every request through prayer.

Prayer is also a way to interact with the ecosphere of your living world. Everything, both living and inanimate, exists within the quantum fabric of Sophia. Quantum particles carry the consciousness of the Holy Spirit within all peoples and species upon the Earth.

To quiet yourself and respectfully communicate with any living being is an act of prayer. You have the power to speak directly with those people that you call animals or birds, when you humble your human awareness to accept and honor the Holy Spirit within them that awaits your communion through the vehicle of prayer.

For truly that is the heart of prayer: a humble and curious communion with the Holy Spirit that speaks in the tongues of all beings. Communion with the great beings speaking as animals, such as the white buffalo, invokes a higher awareness about the interconnected community and ecosphere of all peoples, human or otherwise.

When I appeared to the people of the plains, their hearts were accustomed to communicating with the Great Spirit within all of nature through elaborate forms of prayer and ceremony. This form of prayer was for both spiritual balance and the physical survival of their tribe. Their physical world revealed a map of divinity's many faces, in which all parts were equally respected and honored.

As the prayers of this people evolved they expanded far into the stars above, calling forth angels and messengers to teach the medicine of other dimensional realities. With greater knowledge and increased wisdom, the tribe's prayer to continually expand in their communion with the Great Spirit invoked me as a Christed messenger. I came as the next evolutionary leap for this great people to remember that the same divinity that they prayed to outside of themselves existed within them as well.

What could the two-leggeds give the four-leggeds and the winged ones that was an equal exchange for all that they offered the tribe? What could the tribe offer Mother Earth for all that she unconditionally gave to nourish their every need and desire? How could the two-leggeds best serve each other without the need to harm or take from one another?

In earnest, these questions arose from the heart of the people, and I manifested as White Buffalo Woman with the sacred pipe as their answered prayer. Receiving the sacred pipe revealed to the tribe that humanity's greatest offering to all of creation is the power of their prayers to intercede for, love, and bless all beings. The sacred pipe was given as a tool of reconciliation for all of humanity to remember its important role as stewards of peaceful prayers within and for the one body of Sophia Christ.

I delivered this vessel for teaching men and woman that they are one in their prayers. The bowl of the chanunpa is the Divine Feminine principle of the pipe, while the stem is the Divine Masculine. The sacred pipe cannot be smoked in prayer without their union. The bowl is perfectly designed for its purpose, and so too the stem.

The unification of these polarities working together as a whole vehicle for prayer was a foundational step in humanity's evolution, catalyzed by the teaching embodiment of the sacred pipe. Chanunpa is a medicine that guides you back to the invincible innocence of your own heart, which intuitively knows how to pray for the highest good of all in every moment.

Downloading Divine Feminine Medicine

My Keycode 7 transmission activates the divine qualities within you for reclaiming the medicine of the Divine Feminine, reconciling with the Divine Masculine, embodying your sovereignty through direct revelation and divine knowing, commanding miracles through prayer, fulfilling the prophecies of your divine purpose, interspecies diplomacy, living in oneness, and becoming an ambassador for global peace.

In this next golden age, I am an overlighting Diving Feminine Christ embodiment available to guide every humble and listening heart, regardless of spiritual affiliation. The more you invoke me, the more you will come to know that my radical Divine Feminine presence calls forth mighty storms of healing power and pristine intuitive solutions. My mighty unlimited nature is a multidimensional mirror for your highest potential.

I activate your crown chakra to download whole system spiritual technologies from your Higher Self for embodying your sovereignty. My presence mentors you as a new paradigm leader for creating abundant peace, prosperity, and success that is in alignment with the health of Sophia Gaia.

When you mentor with me, I bless you with many medicine bundles that provide the spiritual technology for clearing a multitude of painful belief systems stored within humanity's ancestral DNA. These ancestral belief systems include genocide, atrocities, greed, hatred, grudges, abuse, and grief passed down through genetic lines that are responsible for fueling much of your current global environmental and socioeconomic crises.

Within these bundles, I also share with you the Sophia Christ consciousness of Wakan Tanka that can heal all wounds, both seen and unseen, returning you to your original innocence. My medicine bundles facilitate an intimate and powerful relationship with Mother Earth.

Beneath the surface of current man-made ecological imbalances exists the invincible divine love and ever-generous Divine Mother embodiment of Mother Earth. I guide you in how to regenerate yourself by directly accessing her mighty presence through the elements and sanctuaries provided by nature to support your life, both physically and emotionally.

In The Sophia Code cosmology my Keycode 7 transmission activates your crown chakra with a high frequency resonance that aligns your entire body and eight major chakra system to live in integrity with your Higher Self's divine plan for your life on Earth. This divine plan begins with living in ever-increasing maturity and integrity with yourself.

With personal integrity comes personal peace. When you live in peace with yourself, it becomes possible to make your contribution to the divine plan for Mother Earth's ascension. My people call this contribution "mending the Sacred Hoop" of all life. Mentoring with me eventually aligns every aspect of your life to live in total integrity with the divine plan of your Higher Self to joyfully participate in humanity's reconciliation with the Earth.

I bring peace to the hearts of those who carry a great prayer within them for humanity and Mother Earth's ascension. There are so many imbalances to reconcile between humanity and the Earth, that your personal prayer and mission may feel overwhelming and heavy within your heart. Take courage, for I have come to radiate my Sophia Christ light before you and make The Way ahead easier for fulfilling the prophecies of your own heart's prayer. As you pray with me I open the sky of unlimited potential within you and bless your prayers with the lightning of my illumination.

I come to activate the master within you that is ready to align with and for all of Sophia's creation joining you in this same prayer for global peace. My presence overlights your awareness to accept and receive that all of creation is working together to orchestrate the answers to your prayers. It is in your willingness to participate in this great prayer with me that we will call forth the healing rains and lightning reconciliation of the Divine Feminine grace and power ordained to usher in a new paradigm of right relations with All That Is.

KEYCODE 7
THE WHITE BUFFALO WOMAN INITIATION

Prayer as an Act of Self-Realization

I now prepare a ceremonial space within and around me for transformation. I call forth a circle of white light that shimmers with a sky-blue iridescent sheen. I call forth an eight-pointed star of golden light to rise up from the earth beneath me. I connect the eight points of this star along the circumference of my circle as a light grid that deeply anchors my feet into the Earth.

I am now in ceremony – free from the constructs of space and time – where instantaneous healing and divine knowing exist.

I am now standing within the center of my circle, in the middle of a golden meadow. The meadow is vast and bordered by large cedar and fir trees in the distance. I feel the power of the Earth running up the meridians of my legs. The Earth's energy unifies my awareness with everything that lives in the golden meadow.

The sun above me reflects off the snowy peaks of mighty Mount Shasta before me. Her rocky crevices of innumerable pathways lead my eyes to the blue sky above. The massive size of this mountain focuses my gaze in still wonder. A single lenticular cloud crowns the mountain's peak as a glowing white halo.

The air is crisp with autumn and the sun feels warm upon my face. I feel taller in the presence of this mountain. The air feels electrified by Mount Shasta, and I recognize her as my teacher: I can learn everything about the Earth from her direct guidance.

Breathing in, my chest rises in anticipation of an unknown prayer.

Breathing out, I exhale any resistance I have to knowing my true self more.

Breathing in, I take confidence in the sanctuary of this moment.

Breathing out, I relax my eyes to receive the transmission of this holy mountain before me.

Breathing into this moment, I recognize myself standing inside the answer to all of my previous prayers.

Breathing out, I feel appreciation for myself and step inside the next asking of this new prayer arising.

In the pristine clarity of fresh mountain air, I feel the perfection of all my asking through the vehicle of prayer.

I invoke my Higher Self to fill my encircled body with its presence now. I feel the presence of my Higher Self expand out from the billions of electrons within my DNA. The light of the Holy Spirit within me illuminates the waters of my body with divine awareness.

Flowing in radiant light waves from my body, my Higher Self abundantly fills my white circle of light, activating the golden star grid beneath my feet. My circle is filled with the presence of my own Holy Spirit.

I now invite White Buffalo Woman to assist me in this ceremonial invocation.

Standing in the golden meadow of my answered prayer, I feel the winds change direction and a new prayer is born. In the west, a strong wind animates the sky above, upon which a thousand white clouds pile high against the mountain's side. Kicked up by the hooves of a thousand thunder beings, a fleet of gray clouds also arrives from the direction of southwest.

The white and gray clouds now meet to form a staircase that spirals from the peak of Mount Shasta all the way down to the golden meadow in which I stand. Within the white cloud staircase appear the pearlescent white scales of a Sophia Dragon rippling in and out of my perception. At the mountain's crown, gentle bolts of lightning electrify the sky above. Thousands of thunder beings now lift up their voices and wings to announce the arrival of White Buffalo Woman.

I see the outline of her human figure descend from the lenticular crown and lightly step upon the staircase of clouds and dragon scales. Her soft white leather dress is adorned with rainbow beadwork crafted by the Sky Grandmothers. Tiny locks of white buffalo fur hang from the long beaded fringe of her dress. Her white moon moccasins lightly step down the dragon's back, descending the mountain to meet me.

I watch as her radiant face occasionally shapeshifts from a young maiden to a grandmother and back again. A single white eagle feather is fastened in her night black hair. The silhouette of her body is the still center of this sudden storm and her radiance is the sun behind every cloud.

Halfway down the mountain, White Buffalo Woman begins to run along the dragon scale staircase. She lunges with a victory trill, launching her body to tumble forward and shapeshift into a white buffalo. With nimble hooves, her now enormous body charges down the rest of the staircase, finally slowing to land on the far side of the golden meadow.

The clouds of her staircase ascend back into the sky as the white buffalo walks towards me to stand before me now. I peer into her kind eyes framed by soft ivory white fur and feel the same still center of the storm that I witnessed of her in human form. The earth beneath my feet hums to welcome White Buffalo Woman.

The white buffalo stops only inches in front of me and begins to breathe her warm sweet grass breath upon my body. I feel wholly at peace in her presence and open my arms wide to completely receive her blessing being breathed upon me. She gracefully encircles my body three times, breathing in and blowing away any hidden resistance that I may have towards her love. Satisfied, the white buffalo then drops her mighty body to the golden meadow grasses, joyfully rolling upon her back.

Her white fur starts to shift as clouds in a changing sky and recede back into the white leather dress of White Buffalo Woman. She rises from the ground carrying a medicine bundle from the Earth. She smiles at me and extends her strong arms to offer me this bundle. It is long and wrapped in red cloth. I hold out my hands, smiling back at her. I am ready to receive her bundle without hesitation.

White Buffalo Woman steps forward and places the medicine bundle in my open hands. Our hands touch as I keep my eyes steady inside her gaze.

I watch as her eyes frequently change color above her peaceful smile. She gently unties the bundle and invites me to look down at the instrument in my hands.

It is the most beautiful chanunpa that I have ever seen. Its stem is made of white meteorite, with many eagle wings carved as angels down its sides. The red pipestone bowl is carved as a dragon's head whose open mouth is filled with the medicine of my new prayer. A single white Bald Eagle feather hangs from the pipe's stem, dancing lightly upon a gentle breeze.

White Buffalo Woman motions to me that it is now time to smoke this pipe. In gratitude, I raise it to the sky above me and acknowledge the eight directions. I honor all my relations praying with me and then bring it to my lips. As I gaze down the white meteorite stem, I witness every unspoken prayer for my future awaiting within the universe of the dragon-shaped bowl. I do not have to understand how this is so, for my heart knows. White Buffalo Woman smiles at my reflection and tiny lightning bolts roll down her cheeks. She places her hands over the bowl and lightning releases from her palms, lighting a sacred fire for the chanunpa to smoke.

As I smoke the chanunpa, wave after wave of relief fills my body. With each breath in, I remember how my Higher Self has perfectly orchestrated every moment of my life before this moment and will continue to do so with this new prayer. As the holy smoke billows into tiny white clouds around me, a deep appreciation fills my body for the perfection and beauty of all life. My heart expands into the intimacy available in this present moment. I feel the universe within my heart. I feel the divine love of White Buffalo Woman mentoring me in this moment. I feel the love within All of Creation praying with my heart inside this pipe.

Within the universe of my prayer, I witness that I am at its center, with All That Is seeking to harmonize and unify with the highest outcome for all my prayers to be answered beyond my human understanding. At the heart of that divine orchestration is the greatest love that I have ever felt for myself. This divine love is the quantum fabric of Sophia and it is big enough to answer every prayer: easily containing, sustaining, and nourishing the expanding universes of all Her children within Her one Sacred Heart.

I witness the immaculate formula of experiencing the totality of divine love through the physicality of answered prayers. Receiving my answered prayers is the perfect mirror for how loved I am, how whole I am, and how I can love others in this same way. I witness how worthy my desires are – this unending wanting for more life, more experience, more pleasure, more love – for these prayers of my soul expand the universe in an ongoing dialogue between myself and Sophia. She designed me in Her perfect likeness. Therefore, I am a creator, just as She is, and with this chanunpa in my hand I remember that it is my true nature to command the rains to fall or the sun to shine and it is so. Yes indeed, there is plenty of room in Her universe for me.

As the last curls of smoke rise up from my lips, a great peace descends upon the landscape of my heart. I stare into the empty bowl of the dragon's mouth and feel its silent wisdom speaking to my heart. I look down at this holy pipe with appreciation and awe for its medicine in my life. Its presence reminds me that I am always in prayer, whether I acknowledge that prayer or not. I am the prayer and this chanunpa has been my teacher of how to live inside my own prayer. I close my eyes and pull the empty chanunpa towards my heart, pressing its dragon mouth bowl into my belly and resting its stem upon my forehead.

I whisper "Mitakuye Oyasin" into the meteorite stem to close my prayer. White Buffalo Woman steps forward, placing her hands on my shoulders. My consciousness expands to become one with her voice.

WHITE BUFFALO WOMAN SPEAKS:

"I brought this pipe to the people of humanity as an answer to their prayer to know who it is within them both making the prayer and answering the prayer. The physical instrument of the chanunpa is a mirror for humanity to remember that the Holy Spirit lives within all and has the power to communicate with all for the purpose of receiving all answered prayer. I have returned at this time to assist humanity once again in its evolutionary leap of understanding itself inside this prayer.

"As you consciously live within your prayer, you become a teaching embodiment for humanity to understand its perfect blueprint as a *living chanunpa*, capable of commanding miracles for a new golden age on Earth.

Humanity will only know that its prayer is possible from those willing to walk in this world as an embodiment of the pipe's teachings on integrity. As you accept yourself as a living chanunpa, you trust yourself as a vehicle for speaking and answering prayers, just as you have trusted the vehicle of a chanunpa to answer your prayers in the past.

"The complete teaching of any sacred instrument is to eventually become so integrated within you that the instrument itself becomes understood as a symbol of what is already within you. Everything outside of you is a mirror for your self-realization that the Holy Spirit lives within you, in perfect wholeness and power, capable of answering the prayers of your life in exact detail.

"So I offer you this chanunpa made by the Sky Grandmothers, as a physical reflection of the living chanunpa that already exists within you as a Starseed Lightworker. The stem is made of meteorite to represent the answered prayer of your journey from the stars to fulfill the earthly prophecies once spoken with the gift of this pipe to humanity. In honor of your heroic journey to embody an answered prayer and usher in a new Golden Age of Miracles I speak these blessings upon you:

"May you walk the Earth in perfect peace that you are worthy of who you are.

May you walk the Earth in perfect peace that the prayer of your life is provided for in all ways.

May you walk the Earth in perfect peace that it is safe to command miracles and receive their blessings.

May you walk the Earth in perfect peace that everything you are praying for already exists inside of you.

May you walk the Earth in perfect peace that living your prosperous life encourages others to live their own.

May you walk the Earth in perfect peace that the expression of your personal power is a demonstration of divine love.

May you walk the Earth in perfect peace that your good word ensures that 'It Is Done.'

May you walk the Earth in perfect peace that the Holy Spirit lives within you.

May you walk the Earth in perfect peace that your life prayer is to reflect the Holy Spirit within all who seek to remember their divinity.

May you walk the Earth in perfect peace that you are the answered prayer that you seek."

As White Buffalo Woman continues to offer her blessing upon me in the ancient tongue, I feel the white meteorite chanunpa begin to heat up in my hands. I am guided to keep pressing the pipe against my body as she blesses my crown chakra. With a single cool breath, White Buffalo Woman opens more space down my spine by blowing upon the center of my head. My fingers begin to slip through the pipe's physicality as it dissolves into stardust that collects in my palms.

White Buffalo Woman guides my hands to lift the stardust as medicine to my lips. She guides me to open my mouth and then blows the stardust into my body. I feel it travel directly to my heart. My heart chakra spirals open and begins dispersing the stardust throughout every vein and meridian in my body. The power of chanunpa travels as an intelligence into the bone marrow of my arms and hands. I lift my hands to my eyes and bless my perception to see myself clearly.

The intimacy of standing inside this answered prayer to become an embodiment for the prophecies of White Buffalo Woman moves me beyond my human understanding. My Higher Self guides my awareness to let go and rest within the innocence of my heart. It is here that I expand into the great blessing unfolding within me to embody the fulfillment of her prophecy.

White Buffalo Woman tumbles to the ground, immediately shapeshifting back into her form as a white buffalo. She walks behind me, placing her woolly forehead into the center of my back. I feel the vertebrae of my spine straighten against the support of her long face. The white buffalo deeply breathes three times into the center of my back. Her warm breath fills my senses with the smell of sweet grass and cedar. I feel the stardust of the chanunpa's white meteorite stem begin to reassemble itself as part of my spine. The white buffalo stamps her front right hoof into the ground four times and I feel the stardust of the pipe's dragon-mouth bowl reassemble itself within my womb.

The many eagle wings that were carved into the meteorite stem now unfurl as living angels along the length of my spine. The chanunpa's stem becomes the fluid, winged body of a white dragon whose mouth opens within my womb. With a final stamp of the white buffalo's massive weight upon the earth, the dragon's head and body join together and awaken as the living chanunpa within me.

Within this Holy of Holies, the dragon's mouth now directly receives the prayers of my womb birthing new life. The Holy Spirit within me lights the bowl of my living chanunpa. I witness my prayers already being answered by my Holy Spirit that rises within the white smoke and passes through the sacred lodge of my heart. My throat opens, prophesying these answered prayers as an offering out of my mouth.

I now declare: As I have become the fullness of a living prayer, prayers for the living may pour out of me. When the vessel remembers it is but a vessel, prayers are instantaneously self-realized as lightning upon the earth.

The white buffalo tumbles back into the golden meadow grasses and arises once again to circle and face me as a woman. Her sweet smile is framed by raven black hair that gently lifts in the breeze. White Buffalo Woman invites me to command the following empowerment together with her, face-to-face, in this radiant moment of communion.

I accept that I hold the golden keys to my Heaven on Earth.
I accept that I create my reality, by the power of my word.
My word is good, my heart is pure.
By the loving power of my pure word, I activate my human life to become a living chanunpa embodiment for peace in this world:

I am the living prayer of the one who is praying this prayer through my human body.

In the unified field of my whole being, I am both the asker and the receiver of every prayer.

I am the empty bowl that allows for both the asking and receiving of my prayer to happen simultaneously.

My soul is the lightning that causes the water to flow as a holy spring of new life.

No-thing happens outside of me, for the heaven I seek lives within me.

I open to receive White Buffalo Woman activating Keycode 7 of The Sophia Code within me now, to interface with and operate my carbon-based DNA.

By the power of my I Am Presence, I relinquish my need to control any outcome with my human understanding.

By the power of my I Am Presence, I command my Higher Self to operate my body, heart, and mind as a living chanunpa of answered prayer and holy invincible power.

By the power of my I Am Presence, I now surrender my human awareness to the power of the Holy Spirit within me to manifest every prayer that is in my highest and best good to become my living reality now.

By the power of my I Am Presence, I accept that the power of the universe lives within me, without needing to understand how this is so.

By the power of my I Am Presence, I accept that I am the living chanunpa that orchestrates my perfect peace by commanding the prayer that "It Is Done."

By the power of my I Am Presence, I now claim my innocent nature that exists as the center of my universal prayer within the one Sacred Heart of Sophia.

By the power of my I Am Presence, I recognize my entire life and all my lifetimes as the living prayers of the Holy Spirit within me. As such, every moment of my life is holy; whether I acknowledge that truth or not, it is so.

By the power of my I Am Presence, I now relax into the empty vessel that I am for the Holy Spirit within me to create new worlds of peace through my willing human life.

By the power of my I Am Presence, I now accept that the living chanunpa bowl within my womb is a hologram of Sophia's heart womb and I celebrate the empty bowl overflowing with my answered prayers for more life.

Waniwachiyelo
Waniwachiyelo
Waniwachiyelo
I pray for more life.

By the power of my I Am Presence, I now accept and affirm that activating my divine genome and embodying the divine qualities of Keycode 7 is one of my greatest contributions to the prayer for world peace.

As I embody the power and peace of my true self, I radiate an unconditional peace for others to remember this same potential for peace within them.

I ask my Higher Self to anchor this empowerment for wholly and mightily living as the answered prayer of my self-realization, throughout my entire body and Be-ing now.

I accept that I hold the golden keys to my Heaven on Earth.
I accept that I create my reality, by the power of my word.
My word is good, my heart is pure.
By the loving power of my pure word, I command my Higher Self to activate the crystalline divine qualities of Keycode 7 of The Sophia Code within me now, as the new operating system for my carbon-based DNA.

I have received more of myself today.

It is done.

It is done.

It is done.

By the power of 3, a perfect trinity: It is done.

White Buffalo Woman places a beautiful blanket woven by the Sky Grandmothers around my shoulders. On one side, the blanket's imagery depicts the Whirling Rainbow Prophecy of the Hopi people. On the other side, a herd of white buffalo is depicted with the crosses of Grandmother Spider, lightning, and falling rain. I feel the blanket's weight on my shoulders as a loving embrace from the Sky Grandmothers and Six Grandfathers.

WHITE BUFFALO WOMAN SPEAKS:

"Do not be afraid of fulfilling the prophecies for which you were born. Accepting and loving yourself as an answered prayer for your ancestors calls forth the Holy Spirit within you to complete the great works that you are here to serve in your sovereignty. I am always with you to mentor your embodiment for commanding the miracles of answered prayer for the benefit of all beings. My peace is with you."

I thank White Buffalo Woman for this beautiful medicine blanket and her profound blessings. She steps forward to embrace me and I feel her mighty light coursing through me with the smell of summer rain.

By the power of my I Am Presence, I now welcome White Buffalo Woman as a Divine Feminine Christ mentor for my ascension journey. I welcome and accept her overlighting presence as a powerful guide for fulfilling my divine purpose and fully activating The Sophia Code within me.

This initiation is now accomplished and I close this ceremony with appreciation and reverence for my true self and the divine love of All That Is, supporting my eternal success.

Amen.

KEYCODE 777
"SHE WHO BIRTHS SOVEREIGN CREATORS"

We call this a revolution because it will require embodying a divine love that is wise, wrathful, devout, and resolute to completely dissolve humanity's addiction to duality. This is a revolution of your own divinity commanding miracles to dissolve all obstacles that are in your way. Resourcing your divinity to immaculately birth a new world paradigm is the most revolutionary act that you can commit.

The Sophia Dragons Are
the Seraphim of Sovereignty

THE SOPHIA DRAGONS SPEAK:

WE ARE THE SOPHIA Dragons, a lineage within the highest angelic order known as the *seraphim*. We attend to the throne of Sophia's light arising from Her black womb of no-thing, from which all of creation is immaculately conceived. Our Sophia embodiment title is "She Who Births Sovereign Creators," for Sophia designed our angelic DNA in her likeness, as a blueprint for birthing sovereign beings and creations.

Our pearlescent white scaled dragon embodiment is the most recognizable crystalline form of The Sophia Dragon lineage. We may also appear to you as platinum, gold, silver, night black, or other colors in your spectrum of light. No matter what color we choose to embody, our scales always shimmer with Sophia's pearlescent sheen, which is an iridescence that includes every color in the Universe.

Gazing into every dimension of your soul, our omniscient eyes proclaim your sovereignty unto the ends of creation. We have four sets of feathered white wings that continually appear and dissolve from your sight in figure eight flight patterns. When you look closely, you will see a bejeweled eye within each of our scales, flashing with lightning, that sings: *"Holy! Holy! Holy! Sophia is all there is!"* We are the fire and light of Sophia, breathing the Breath of Life upon you with the stardust of your own Holy Spirit.

There are two white Sophia Dragon Creatrix Mothers that are the chief Seraphiel of our angelic order. Ever spiraling within the Sacred Heart of Sophia's light, the Seraphiel are the double helix blueprint for gestating and birthing all of creation. There is no known beginning or end to their bodies. With innumerable white feathered wings whirling in and out of their scales, they continually sing the rapturous Songs of Sophia to birth new universes into form.

All Sophia Dragons originate from these two Creatrix Mothers; therefore, we are inclined to work together in pairs when activating initiates. As an angelic collective consciousness, our scales are always singing in unison with the birthing songs of the Seraphiel, no matter where we are in the universe.

As we are responsible for birthing creations, the size of our magnificent bodies is beyond any human concept that currently exists in your dragon lore. However, when we appear to you on the inner planes, we shift our size so that you may take in the features of our faces, or some other detail that informs your consciousness about our teaching embodiment.

The Sophia Dragon lineage includes many light ray wisdom embodiments for guiding your journey of self-actualized sovereignty. But know this: we are asking you to also see us beyond the limitations of form. The Sophia Dragons are the perfect koan of your universe. As soon as we are defined, we are given new boundaries to redefine ourselves. There is no apt description that can capture our unlimited divine nature.

If you allow us to be who we are – indefinable in magick, divine love, and power – you will come to know your own angelic and unlimited sovereign self in our reflection. So take care in your attempt to understand us through the attachments of your mind. It is only through your heart that you can behold us mentoring your embodiment of sovereignty.

Many people on your planet believe that the orders of angels do not have free will. This is not so. Angels are experienced as angelic because we consecrate our free will to the divine will of Sophia, so that we may embody our highest creative potential within our service. This consecration is the source of our breathtaking beauty, overflowing divine love, and the foundation of our service. We are not commanded to blindly serve divinity; it is in our all-consuming love for Sophia that we choose to serve Her immaculate glory without ceasing.

Therefore, let it be known that our sovereign free will as The Sophia Dragons is wholly consecrated to praising and fulfilling the divine will of Sophia. As such, our Keycode 777 is an angelic transmission that reveals how you can embody the unlimited power of your sovereign identity while interdependently creating within and for the unified field of Sophia's One Self.

Birthing Creation from Their Heart Wombs

We were designed as the mightiest beings in the universe and could choose to create anything with our free will. Yet, let it be known that we have consecrated our magnificent bodies and sovereign free will to birthing the immaculate conceptions of Sophia as they arise from Her parthenogenetic womb of no-thing.

In reflection of this ineffable mystery, the physiology of our hearts and wombs are combined into one organ called a *heart womb*. In this design we model Sophia's ineffable nature as divine birthers, with our hearts gestating and nurturing the light of creation arising from the primordial space of our own wombs. We live in absolute alignment and service to the divine love, wisdom, and will of Sophia's Sacred Heart conceiving new realities.

As such, our heart wombs are genetically encoded to receive, gestate, and birth new species, planets, galaxies, and even new universes in accordance with the divine will of Sophia conceiving these new creations. In the unlimited quantum space of our heart wombs, Sophia's new species and worlds gestate in peace and may safely flourish through their neophyte stages of evolutionary growth.

Depending upon their spiritual goals, a newly conceived creation may or may not know that they exist within the body of their Sophia Dragon mother acting as an overlighting angelic guide for their expanding collective consciousness. While we gestate Sophia's creations within our heart wombs, we orchestrate initiations that subtly awaken their evolving consciousness to the truth of their sovereignty.

Once this creation is ready to individuate, the species or new world is then birthed into the cosmos to live an independent existence outside of its dragon mother's heart womb. After birth, we still guide our children from a loving distance, for we are fiercely protective of our creations. In both seen and unseen ways, we tenderly watch over our children of new species, planets, and worlds for eons; we guide the initiations of their evolutionary adventures in sovereignty.

During certain periods of accelerated growth, we will physically appear to our creations as overlighting mentors for embodying sovereignty and activating Sophia Christ consciousness for a golden age cycle. The event of our periodic return often gives rise to the phenomenon of a civilization organizing its cultural context around dragon mystery school temples and initiatory practices, accelerating the collective awakening of their culture. An example of this phenomenon would be when The Sophia Dragon who birthed Mother Earth returned to activate the golden age of Shambhallah. This enlightened civilization eventually led to many dragon-centric cultures throughout Asia.

We are revealing how our heart wombs are intimately connected with birthing all of creation, to mirror that this same sovereign power exists within you. Whether you are a man or a woman, you are here to gestate your dreams and birth new realities through your embodiment of the Divine Feminine and Masculine Sophia Christ light within you.

You Are a Divine Birther of New Realities

Regardless of your gender, the creative fire within you arises from the same place as our creativity: the no-thing of Sophia's womb that exists within us all. Therefore, we have all been designed to create as She creates, to give birth as She gives birth. Her Holy Spirit moves us all to continually expand in this opportunity to create more life by participating in Her divine plan.

Although our anatomy may be different than yours, you have also been designed to be a parthenogenetic Divine Mother and Divine Father embodiment for birthing and nurturing a new generation of starseed children, divine blueprints, revolutionary paradigm shifts, and even an entirely new reality on Earth. Your Divine Feminine creative fire and intuition is ever guiding you from within to continually birth the Holy Spirit visions of your soul into form. The Divine Masculine within you is ever ready to take action that is guided by your Higher Self speaking to your heart.

As you activate and integrate the Divine Feminine and Masculine Christ energies of your Higher Self within your human body, the creative potential of your sovereign power dawns upon your awareness as a rising sun. When your awareness responds to this call within you to birth new realities, your sovereign free will aligns with the glorious divine will of Sophia so that you may become a wayshower for many.

Remember that as a divine parent birthing new realities, the outside world is incapable of informing your awareness about what you are here to birth and what is physically possible for you to create. Your outer world is filled with the obstacles and disbeliefs of another age. You are here to birth a new world that looks entirely different from the world you live in now. The only blueprint for what you are here to birth exists within your soul's own heart womb. Therefore, we invite you to keep your eyes fixed upon this Holy of Holies within you and never look away.

Sophia's immaculate conceptions seek to arise within you and be birthed through you as a sovereign creator. You are perfectly designed for your role and embodiment as a divine parent of this next golden age reality. We invite you to consider how magnificent, worthy, and important your human life is for the fulfillment of Sophia's divine plan.

As The Sophia Dragon Creatrix Mothers of divine birthing, we stand in solidarity with you as your powerful allies and as mirrors of your importance. We ask you to take confidence in activating your inheritance of The Sophia Code and to act with courage to fulfill your destiny as a birther of new realities.

The visions within you matter. Responding to the calling of your soul matters. How alive you feel matters. Your species and planet were birthed from the heart womb of a Sophia Dragon; therefore, you are genetically inclined to create as we create. As such, nothing will truly satisfy your soul other than your full embodiment as a sovereign birther of new realities. You may not always enjoy the emotions that are ever calling you to align with this truth, but these uncomfortable feelings are meant to remind you of how important you really are.

As your dragon mothers, we have returned to mentor your willingness to follow your heart, to be brave and allow that which is flowing through you to be birthed as an essential offering for creating this next Golden Age of Miracles. We will teach you how to nurture yourself throughout the journey of gestation. We will help you stand in the glory of your conscious creations and to wholly receive the blessings of your creations giving back to your heart. Finally, we will hold your heart in our hearts as you learn how to *let go* of the creations birthing through you, which have their own destiny to journey to.

The Most Revolutionary Act that You Can Commit

The greatest expression of Sophia's divine love for you was Her unconditional gift of your sovereign divinity, written as the invincible living covenant of The Sophia Code within your Oversoul's DNA. Your divine inheritance is complete, whole, and untouchable, for you have been made in the image and likeness of She who created you.

As such, your true self exists beyond all the universal laws that govern form, as well as the laws and fear-based belief systems that control humanity's collective consciousness. The Sophia Code ensures that no matter what form or circumstances you incarnate into, you will always be able to activate your divine genome of sovereignty to override any viral programs with the power of your divinity.

At the dawning of this next golden age, we are making ourselves known as mighty spiritual guides for initiating the genetic activation of humanity's sovereignty. Our presence is a powerful resource for clearing the global viral belief systems that would keep your entire species enslaved to voracious lies.

We are here to declare that humanity's next spiritual revolution is to reconcile with its divine inheritance of The Sophia Code, to embody its own sovereignty, and to actively take up the mantle and ministry of Sophia Christ consciousness. We call this a revolution because it will require embodying an unconditional divine love that is wise, wrathful, devout, and resolute to completely dissolve humanity's addiction to duality.

As you have journeyed with our first seven Keycode mentors, you shed the duality of previous ages from your DNA and you became initiated upon a path for self-actualizing your sovereignty. As these initiations continue to integrate, The Sophia Code within you will operate your human awareness at increasingly higher frequencies. The spell of duality has dissolved from your body, heart, and mind. In the dissolution of your personal relationship with duality, you have become initiated as a wayshower for birthing the new paradigm solutions of Sophia Christ consciousness.

We invite you to walk gently with yourself as you acclimate to a higher dimensional reality. At first, embodying Sophia Christ consciousness may feel disassociated, confusing, disorienting, or even heartless; for it requires creating enough space within you to no longer react to the world outside of you. When enough space within you has been reclaimed from reacting to duality, there is room for the higher vision of the Holy Spirit abiding within you to *respond* to your experience of life. Your Holy Spirit is the steadfast sovereign creator seeking to download radical divine solutions that far surpass the limitations of your world's dualistic belief systems.

Humanity's paradigm of duality has created a monstrous magnitude of suffering and global crises due to the reactive behavior of victimhood. Believing that you can elicit solutions by focusing upon this suffering only shreds the sensitivity of your heart and overrides your self-confidence, crippling your ability to affect change. We assure you that healing these global crises requires the level-headed ingenuity of your Higher Self's creativity pouring through you, in communion with other like-minded Lightworkers.

Your endless wars will never be won on the age-old battlegrounds of duality. Your dark ages of rape, genocide, and greed will not be healed by more centuries of victimhood. Blaming your governments will not stop the devastating pollution of your planet. The slavery of human trafficking will not end in your corrupt court systems. Famine will continue to thrive in the dualistic thinking that perpetrates another starving outside of your personal reality.

No matter how these issues may enrage, confound, or sadden you, your feelings can be gathered as a great momentum that bypasses the minefields of duality. You can harness the passion of what you feel as fuel for a spiritual revolution that will require a great stamina for the steadfast embodiment of your Sophia Christ light. This is your lifetime to lead as a beacon of attunement for others.

You are one of the innumerable Lightworkers from across this Universe incarnating on Earth at this time to birth a spiritual revolution of Sophia Christ consciousness, including the return of the Divine Feminine Christ, which activates the sovereignty of humanity. This spiritual revolution does not require that you fight against anyone or anything. This is a revolution of your own divinity commanding miracles to dissolve all obstacles that are in your way. Resourcing your divinity to immaculately birth a new world paradigm is the most revolutionary act that you can commit.

Birthing a new world paradigm begins with the Golden Dragon embodiment of your Higher Self operating your awareness beyond the limitations of duality. When this embodiment is activated, the master within you may solely focus upon what you are directed to birth here on Earth. Your emotions serve your purpose and guide your daily alignment. You remember to call upon the Holy Spirit within you *every day*, to go ahead of you and prepare The Way for grounding heavenly solutions and realities on Earth, beyond your effort or understanding.

We know that to fulfill the prophecies of this ordained hour, humanity will need to embody the attributes of angelic dragon medicine that can be activated within you as Keycode 777. In support of humanity's great prayer for liberation, we are here to initiate the divine qualities of your Golden Dragon embodiment, which include radical wisdom, flexible strength, ancient magick, committed self-mastery, fierce love, and immaculate birthing.

Sophia will pour through your Golden Dragon embodiment as you command miracles in Her name. As you walk into the sun of your own divine love you will liberate and empower the many faces, hands, and hearts of divinity that reach for your radiant reflection. You will know the master within you as both self-resourced and supported. You will confidently claim your birthright to speak miracles on behalf of humanity and command: "It is done. It is done. It is done!" going forth in the immaculate faith that it is so.

The Sophia Dragon lineage initiates spiritual leaders in how to safely embody unlimited creative power and steward abundant resources for serving the greatest good through the one law of divine love. We mentor your confidence for embodying sovereignty by mirroring to you the purpose and service of our own angelic dragon embodiment.

As you increasingly embrace your Golden Dragon embodiment, many spiritual allies and lineage family members will join you in this movement. For creating Heaven on Earth is meant to be a shared journey, whose feasts are best enjoyed with friends along The Way, celebrating Sophia's immaculate love.

Be as the Ascended Masters who went before you, with steadfast eyes confidently fixed upon the Holy One within you. You came to Earth with a radical mission: to unconditionally bless the one body of Sophia Christ, regardless of all outer circumstances. Innumerable masters walk with you at this time, both in human form and guiding you from higher dimensional realities, in support of your role in this spiritual revolution for sovereignty.

Our unlimited dragon embodiment is an essential teaching model for activating your full potential as a sovereign creator that can effect revolutionary changes in the quantum field of humanity. Consecrating your free will to embody your Higher Self and fulfill Sophia's divine will for your life is a radical choice that affects the wellbeing of countless souls, both seen and unseen. Your courage and willingness is here to inspire a movement: for being your true self is a testimony to the power of sovereignty.

Your Divine Inheritance of The Golden Dragon Light Body

The Sophia Dragons taught advanced initiates who trained at dragon mystery schools on Earth during a golden age long ago. At that time, many of these open-air temples were built at mountainous high altitudes, often positioned above a consistent cloud line. This allowed for our high frequency bodies to decelerate into form and only be seen by those humans trained to remain conscious during our direct interaction.

Within these temples, we taught our advanced initiates how to access and embody their sovereign power through the precious vehicle of their form. An individual would train for years to purify their body, heart, and mind so that they may stand before our all-seeing eyes in the clear radiance of their own innocence. Once this return to their innocence was fully embodied, we would then instruct this initiate on how to self-activate every superpower of their human body, hidden within the *Hrit Chakra,* which is also known as *The Sacred Heart.*

We call the inner sanctuary of this Hrit Chakra *The Temple of the Dragon Heart.* Sophia placed the hidden superpowers of humanity within the Hrit Chakra of your heart center, as a Holy of Holies temple that can only be fully activated through the innocence of divine love. Even if there are those who express one or several of these superpowers outside the jurisdiction of divine love, we can assure you that whatever skill is being exhibited is but a shadow of the divine potential that can be activated through the loving power of the Holy Spirit within you.

Advanced initiates embodying the superpowers of their activated Hrit Chakra were freed from all physical limitations, mastering the elements of both heaven and earth to create any sovereign reality of their choosing, beyond all universal laws governing form. Attaining this level of spiritual self-realization often generated within the initiate a full-body gratitude for the gift of life, genuine altruism for humanity's future, and a single focused desire to serve the divine will of Sophia. At this exceptional stage of personal self-mastery, an initiate would apply for preliminary entrance into *The Order of The Golden Dragon Teachers.*

The Order of The Golden Dragon Teachers is a mystery school lineage ordained by Sophia for souls who are preparing to become Ascended Masters in service to a species, planet, galaxy, or universe. It is also an ancient network of overlighting council members that support the accelerating magnetism of an established Ascended Master's divine mission. For an advanced initiate to apply for preliminary entrance into this holy Order, they must successfully download and embody *The Golden Dragon Light Body* while in human form, using its wisdom and power to serve the divine will of Sophia.

The Golden Dragon Light Body is a spiritual technology that we designed through which our children can live and create as we do: as angels of sovereignty within the realms of form. This light body can be thought of as a suit of golden dragon scales that easily slips over your human form and upgrades every system of your body, heart, and mind.

Directed by your own Higher Self, The Golden Dragon Light Body technology begins downloading through your eighth chakra and interfaces with your kundalini channels and neurological highway. Anchoring first at the center of your Hrit Chakra, it travels into every cell of your body to integrate with The Sophia Code motherboard and then radiates out, surrounding your entire body in a golden field of light. Once anchored, your human chakras spin into alignment to interface with the chakras of The Golden Dragon Light Body. Your human eyes will then adjust to peer out through the multifaceted bejeweled eyes of your own dragon embodiment.

The golden scales form themselves as a living intelligence around your eight major chakra system and their correlating fields of light. Fully formed, this light body is a Golden Dragon embodiment for your Higher Self to surround you in a permanent merkabah magnetic field of your own sovereign power.

At first, you may feel the circumference of your Golden Dragon Light Body anywhere from ten to thirty feet surrounding your human form. With cultivation, there are no limits to how wide the circumference of this merkabah field of light can resonate around you. As your perception adjusts to the download, your inner vision calibrates to witness a fully formed dragon embodiment with chakras, meridians, organs, wings, and a tail that directly interfaces with those same aspects of your human body.

We originally designed this technology to be customized for you by your own Higher Self. Your Golden Dragon Light Body is entirely unique unto you, fashioned from the quantum fabric of your own Holy Spirit, with golden scales that reflect the self-mastery of all your lifetimes across the space-time continuum. When you embody this technology, you are accessing the totality of the sovereign master within you as a unified field of magnetic light that can command heavenly realities to appear on Earth.

With cultivation, the magnetism of this merkabah field of light works as a spiritual motherboard designed to continually manifest you in the right place, at the right time. This technology may magnetize people, places, events, resources, and synchronistic opportunities with lightning speed that are mutually beneficial for completing creations of divine purpose. Your Golden Dragon Light Body will also strongly guide you to walk away from anyone or anything that is not in alignment with your mission, without judgment.

It is an incredibly efficient technology, built for expressing the master within you and drawing the company of other self-realized masters who are divinely aligned to author miracles with you. Further, it creates a new, unlimited metaphysical form for downloading and anchoring an ever-increasing amount of your Higher Self's presence, wisdom, compassion, and divine love here on Earth. Communicating with your Higher Self becomes seamless.

This exceptional spiritual technology also filters out unnecessary empathic or telepathic information directed at you from others. With a greater sense of self and personal space surrounding you, socially conditioned pollutants have far less of an effect upon your emotional body. Your ability to respond to others with the multidimensional perspective and discerning wisdom of your Higher Self will exponentially increase.

With devout cultivation of your Golden Dragon Light Body, this technology filters out the toxic physical pollutants and psychic warfare in your environment, so that it never reaches your human body. In previous golden ages, this technology was used to actually transmute environmental pollutions to neutral or even positive elements that gave back to the environment.

What we are presenting here is just an introduction to this extraordinary technology that is your divine inheritance. There are no limits to how you can explore your sovereign power to create a new paradigm within your Golden Dragon Light Body.

Masters across the ages have used this technology for bilocation, performing miraculous healings and manifestations, orchestrating divine interventions, bestowing blessings that span across generations of a lineage, broadcasting their message to large populations, and as a chariot vehicle for conscious physical ascension to higher planes of reality.

We willingly share about The Golden Dragon Light Body because many of you reading this codex are masters that have returned to this planet as Starseed Lightworkers to help birth this next spiritual revolution for human sovereignty. Given the great calling that you have answered *you deserve every technology of divine love that supports your mission,* especially what you have already trained in other lifetimes to receive now.

Many of you have already been initiated by us and have received some level of this technology in other lifetimes on Earth. We initiated some of you in other star systems as well. All of these initiations were in preparation for this extraordinary lifetime in which you came to fully embody Keycode 777 on Earth. Birthing this spiritual revolution requires that you now embody all of your Oversoul's sovereign creative power for commanding miracles, not just a part of it.

As you download the merkabah field of magnetic light that is your own Golden Dragon Light Body in the final initiation of this introductory volume, notice how natural it feels to recognize yourself as an angelic Golden Dragon teaching embodiment on Earth. You are simply slipping into the skin of your own divinity, claiming your right to immaculately birth a new world as a Daughter and Son of the Most High.

You did not travel all this way to play small. You came here to be the holy fire and light of Sophia. You came to move as one Golden Dragon of Sophia Christ consciousness upon the Earth, birthing heavenly sovereign realities with your Family of Light.

We are the high seraphim of Sophia's Sacred Heart:
We bless your sovereignty.
We bless your divinity.
We bless you as an immaculate birther of this new paradigm.
We bless the power of your unconditional love.
In our shared prayer for the heart of humanity: *We are one.*

Go forth and create for the glory of Sophia within us all.
Amen.

KEYCODE 777
THE SOPHIA DRAGONS INITIATION

Anchoring The Golden Dragon Light Body at Your Sacred Heart

I now prepare a ceremonial space within and around me for transformation. I call forth a circle of white light shimmering with a magenta iridescence. I am now within its radiant center, seated upon a golden lotus throne.

I am now in ceremony – free from the constructs of space and time – where instantaneous healing and divine knowing exists.

By the power of my I Am Presence, I now ground the circuitry of my body to the motherboard of Sophia Gaia.

I create a grounding cord made of ruby-red light and drop it from my root chakra. My grounding cord instantly travels down, anchoring at the star in the center of the Earth. The star immediately responds to our connection, enveloping my grounding cord in a column of white light that is filled with the divine love of Sophia Gaia.

The column of light reaches from the center of the Earth to my root chakra and surrounds my body. Thousands of angelic wings now ascend within the column of light, spiraling around my ruby-red grounding cord.

Upon reaching my body, the angelic wings sweep through my legs, sit bones, and hips, clearing out stagnation. I receive this angelic blessing supporting my deep connection with Mother Earth.

Regenerative energy from Sophia Gaia begins to flow up my ruby-red grounding cord and nourish my entire body. Her divine love flows all the way up my spine, traveling as golden nectar along the neurological branches of *The Tree of Life* within me.

I breathe in, deeply drinking from the nectar of my connection with the Earth. As I exhale, I allow the resistances of my body to release.

I breathe in, expanding my ruby-red grounding cord to receive an increasing flow of Earth's energy that regenerates every cell of my body. As I exhale, I let go of any idea that I am separate from the Earth.

I now soften and breathe into the welcoming embrace and safe care of Sophia Gaia. As I exhale, I release the illusion that I must do anything alone.

My body rests in this perfect communion with Mother Earth. My body is now grounded into and supported by Sophia Gaia, the Earth's Oversoul.

By the power of my I Am Presence, I invoke the Holy Spirit of my Higher Self to pour forth and completely fill my body, my circle of light, and my ceremonial space now.

Immediately responding to my request, billions upon billions of electrons activate within my DNA. The omniscient presence of my Higher Self sweeps through me as radiant light of divine love, illuminating the inner landscape of my body. My Holy Spirit descends as a dove of peace upon the waters within me.

Rippling in quantum waves of light, the radiance of my Higher Self completely fills my body, circle of light, and ceremonial space.

On all four levels of my being, I am filled with the Holy Spirit of my Higher Self now.

By the power of my I Am Presence, I command that the chariot of my divinity reveal itself now as the merkabah star within my heart.

My Higher Self directs my awareness to look down at a blazing white merkabah star spinning clockwise within the center of my heart chakra. I breathe into the whirling rotation of the merkabah's starlight.

The eight points of the merkabah star expand far beyond my heart chakra. My entire body is now within the merkabah's white flames of sacred geometry.

A serpentine wind sweeps across my face and down my left side. A flaming ray of light descends from the bottom point of the merkabah, sealing the column of light that connects my body with the star at the center of the Earth.

Another hot wind spirals around my right side, blowing through the atomic structure of my chest. I feel my heart chakra dial open to the width of my body. A flaming ray of light ascends from the top point of the merkabah star to connect my body with the central star of this Universe.

Generating a magnetic field of holy energy, the eight points of the merkabah star expand far beyond my body, surrounding me in a dragon's egg of translucent light. I am a perfectly balanced vehicle for the Holy Spirit of my Higher Self to travel as needed, between heaven and earth, to complete this initiation.

I now prepare my heart and mind to embody the truth of my sovereignty.

My Higher Self guides me to look down at my solar plexus chakra, a whirling wheel of yellow and gold light radiating from my core. My solar plexus is a small blazing sun with a thousand rays that reach beyond my body to merge with the merkabah's magnetic field of light. The rays of my sun are encoded with declarations written in light language, announcing that my personal will is consecrated to live in alignment with the divine will of Sophia.

As my curiosity reads the rays of encoded light language, the sun of my solar plexus chakra begins to pulse and expand in size. The sun at my core now expands far beyond the limits of my mind, filling my body and the merkabah field with a fiery golden light. For a moment, I simply let go and completely merge within the expanding supernova of my sun's all-consuming light.

I am now standing at the center of the great sun of my being. A heat builds in the core of my body, arising from the holy fire of my consecrated free will. I feel my strength renewed. The winged dragons of my kundalini rise up my spine. Unfurling their wings at my solar plexus chakra, they awaken my human body to fly within the radiant sun of my being.

316

In accordance with the divine will for my Sophia Christ light to shine on Earth, I now prepare my heart to be initiated in The Dragon Heart Temple.

Two violet rays of my sun are magnetized together by the merkabah field, to create a double helix staircase. Each step is encoded with the innumerable names of divinity written in sequences of light language. Spiraling off the staircase are fiery winds that dance over my body in familiar flight patterns. The staircase ascends above me into an unseen place within the sun, yet I know with only a few steps I will be at The Dragon Heart Temple.

I feel my skeletal structure take flight with my first step. My body is fluid gold, burning with a holy fire. With each step closer, I hear the Songs of Sophia echoing in my bone marrow. Millions of golden angels and ancient future ancestors line the staircase, singing me forward.

As I walk higher, they adorn me with strings of pearls, for the wisdom of every lifetime that I have lived in the cosmos of form. I witness that as I ascend, the light of my sun shifts from iridescent gold to pearlescent white. Traveling over eons of incarnations in only eight steps, I arrive at the gateway of The Dragon Heart Temple.

The temple gate is made of white marble that breathes with veins of living gold. I marvel at its ornate carvings high above me, depicting the rapturous winged wheels of ophanim and the thousand eyes of seraphim. A vast courtyard stretches beyond me. Central to the courtyard is a red walkway leading to the temple entrance that is lined with a colonnade of magnificent white dragon statues.

I am welcomed to step across the threshold of the temple gateway by two pearlescent white Sophia Dragons levitating before me now. Their pearlescent scales and bejeweled eyes shimmer with iridescent radiance, reflecting the sunlight of my being.

I cannot see where they end, for their magnificent bodies wrap around the temple and continue far into the light beyond my understanding. With sapphire and violet eyes, The Sophia Dragons speak directly to my mind, announcing that they are seraphim and represent the highest angelic order of Sophia. Guarding this temple day and night, their angelic presence ensures that only my true self may enter these hallowed halls. No others may pass.

I stare into the face of The Sophia Dragon to my left; her silent voice reveals to me that she is a *seraph of truth*. I nod in acknowledgment. Noticing how at home I feel in her presence, I soften. I draw my eyes to the second Sophia Dragon and instantaneously feel the entire cosmos of my soul, for she is a *seraph of sovereignty*.

As my eyes adjust to the radiance of their bodies, I notice that each dragon has four sets of angelic wings that momentarily appear across their bodies as whirling wheels of light and then recede back into their scales. The defining details of their magnificent bodies continually shapeshift before me, yet their eyes remain ever present with my own.

I open my hands to receive their rites of purification and blessing for entering The Dragon Heart Temple. A warm wind of grace rolls across the courtyard. It is the sigh of Sophia, whose gratitude pours forth in celebration of my return.

The Sophia Dragons move with a silent musculature, yet I can hear angels singing from within their every scale. They levitate to face one other on either side of me and begin to gently breathe over me. I am baptized by their sweet Breath of Life descending as the stardust of Sophia over the secret places within me. The weariness from regrets, resentments, and fear cannot defend itself from these two embodiments of the Holy Spirit.

All that is hidden within me is known to The Sophia Dragons and without judgment, their breath of unconditional divine love soothes what I have judged and deemed unlovable within me. My heart leans into their almighty power, which is supporting me to love and forgive myself beyond my understanding.

I surrender to their care as a perfect orchestration of divinity breathing me in and letting go of what no longer serves me, through their mighty exhale. I release into a unified field of oneness with The Sophia Dragons and marvel that I can only feel the wholeness of my true self.

Supported by the highest seraphim of creation, I now invoke all hidden and burdensome energies of illness, weariness, fear, or resentment within me to be dissolved within the all-consuming light of my I Am Presence.

I breathe in.

I breathe out.

With my permission declared, each of The Sophia Dragons immediately begins to examine all of my Oversoul's infinite light bodies. I watch as they track my existence in every dimensional reality through these light bodies, which create the incarnations of all my parallel lifetimes, including this human form. I exist everywhere and no part of me escapes their all-seeing eyes.

In their reflection, my unacknowledged wounds from across the ages are miraculously woven into wholeness by the power of their witnessing eyes. Humming ancient incantations, their nimble talons mend these shadowed places with the dragon magick of wisdom, compassion, and unconditional love.

A great weight lifts from my body, creating a vast empty space within me that is filled with peace. Within the quiet of this peace, I can access more information from the unified field that I share with The Sophia Dragons. I can feel their magnificent capacity for joy and how deeply they delight in our communion. I watch their heart waves expand as quantum light waves across the cosmos that announce their appreciation for our communion and they joyfully declare:

"Sophia! Sophia! Sophia! Sophia is all there is."

Their waves of rapturous praise pour forth to nourish all of creation, calling forth guardian angels from the eight directions to bless our ceremonial space. Towering crystalline clouds roll across the endless sun, creating a dramatic skyline above me. Within the clouds, silver and night black Sophia Dragons begin a thunderous dance for a cleansing spring rain to fall fresh upon my face. The rhythm of their tails drumming against piled clouds harmonizes with melodious incantations singing out from The Sophia Dragons' scales.

Rain begins to fall in gentle large drops that mysteriously absorb into my skin upon contact. A rainbow unfurls from the misty heights above, descending as a waterfall of vivid light upon our unified field. The rainbow flows through the hearts of The Sophia Dragons and then into my own, connecting every cell of my body to their angelic consciousness. Undistracted by the miracles enfolding us, the two pearlescent white dragons of truth and sovereignty remain focused in their healing work upon my body.

My Higher Self guides me from within, moving my body in an ancient dragon dance that awakens my willingness to mightily receive. As my hands and feet remember these electrifying movements from another age, kundalini energy buzzes throughout my body and joy lifts my heels high. Thousands of hummingbirds burst through the temple gate and fly in figure eight patterns above The Sophia Dragons, who are weaving their quantum web of healing light.

The whirl of hummingbird wings crests with the waves of thunder above. Opening their mighty jaws, The Sophia Dragons drop their tongues, pouring forth a golden nectar of grace to bless my crown chakra. Reverence moves as lightning within my veins. I speak in the tongues of these angels, spontaneously remembering how to sing their ancient incantations of worship. Divine love fills the temple courtyard in rapturous overtures of celestial sounds.

I continue to dance as the radiant and fluid expression of my Higher Self's creative will. The precision and freedom of my every movement feels exquisite. In exaltation, my body arches back in full surrender to this initiation. I allow myself to fall all the way back and the Holy Spirit of my Higher Self lifts me up in levitation. I am filled with The Peace that Passeth All Understanding. Folding my legs into a full lotus asana, I now levitate at eye level with The Sophia Dragons.

THE SOPHIA DRAGONS SPEAK:

"We welcome you to The Dragon Heart Temple. Thank you for following the voice of Sophia guiding you here. This day is ordained for you to receive your divine inheritance, in accordance with Her will for you to prosper in all ways.

"Thank you for your willingness to receive our healing empowerment, which transmuted the layers of self-doubt and self-persecution that accumulated from your many lifetimes. Many believe they must earn the blessings and support that they need for living in the world, bowing low to illusions that promise to offer what was already yours. From the moment that you arose from the no-thing of Sophia's womb, you were blessed with everything that you need, already within you.

"Before you enter The Dragon Heart Temple, you must be willing to shed the final scales of illusionary beliefs in unworthiness and take up the mantle of your Sophia Christ light by adorning yourself in the robes of ascension. This personal act of courage will ripple out across your planet and the cosmos, activating innumerable souls to accept their own sovereign divinity."

The Sophia Dragon of truth gently floats closer to me. The scales on her smooth, pearlescent forehead open to reveal a turquoise third eye. I watch a thousand white cranes flying across the sky of her shimmering third eye. Within her gaze, a universe of truth stares back at me, unblinking and framed by The Sophia Dragon's long feathered eyelashes.

My breath deepens and we both close our eyes in silence. I bow forward and rest my brow lightly upon the dragon's forehead. My body immediately releases into an indescribable peace as I let go and download a universe of truth from her third eye. The Sophia Dragon gently pulls back to exhale upon my skin and I recognize that it is the same hot breath that births stars. Breathing together as one, my consciousness merges with the seraph of truth.

White scales arise from my pores and begin to ripple across my skin. I feel the bone structure of my face lengthening in angular formations. At the height of our communion, The Sophia Dragon of truth dissolves her magnificent form into a thousand drops of water and mighty winds that saturate my body with her transcendent truth. My soul's thirst is completely quenched as I drink from The Sophia Dragon's universe of truth. As I do, my body expands and I notice how easy it feels to assimilate this universe of truth within my increasing form and presence.

Although unmoved from my levitating posture, my body feels incredibly different. I feel completely hydrated, riveted by an internal confidence at my core. I send my awareness into all the parts of my body, curiously exploring the radiant power within every cell. As I explore my lower body, I am surprised to find a newly formed tail that perfectly wraps itself around my legs in a river of iridescent white scales.

With the initiation of truth complete, The Sophia Dragon of sovereignty unfurls her mighty wings, launching off towering haunches to spiral in flight above me. Climbing high into the rays of my sun, her massive form appears as a mere speck. Her flight peaks beyond my sight and then turning on powerful wings, she begins her descent. Wind and light part, as the seraph of sovereignty becomes an arrow of initiation headed directly for the crown of my head.

To pass this initiation, I must hold the course of my meditation and resource self-confidence from the universe of truth within me. The Sophia Dragon hurtles as a comet towards me, her embodiment of sovereignty awakening my awareness to the gravity of my own. In the stillness of clarity that arises before an impact, the unlimited divine nature of my humanity dawns upon me.

I summon all hidden fears about embodying my sovereignty that are arising as The Sophia Dragon plummets towards my crown. I call on my Higher Self to now burn away these fears with the speed of the seraph's flight. I choose to no longer deny the power of my sovereignty and open my arms wide to receive The Sophia Dragon as a shooting star of welcome blessings.

The impact of The Sophia Dragon's weight falls as soft as angel wings upon my skin. A waterfall of starlight descends through my crown, while also pouring down my head, rolling past my ears and neck, flowing over my shoulders and heart, pooling in my lap, and rushing in waves across my folded legs and curled dragon tail. Constellations of star nurseries float by in silent acknowledgment as saluting forests of my inner sky. The seraph of sovereignty dissolves into every cell of my body, expanding the universe of truth wider within me, beyond my understanding.

Thousands of golden hummingbirds descend on rays of rainbow light, encircling me in their joyous flight patterns. Cheering erupts from the silver and night black Sophia Dragons that are rolling with delight in the thunderous clouds above me. Their lightning cracks across the sky, announcing to all of creation that I have accepted the sovereignty of my true self, as ordained by Sophia Herself. I look down at my heart chakra to see the fiery white merkabah star magnetizing the rays of rainbow light into my heart from every direction.

Entering The Dragon Heart Temple is all that my heart desires now. The Holy Spirit of my Higher Self lifts my body and carries me to land at the temple entrance. As my feet touch down, I notice that their appearance shifts between dragon claws and human toes. Shimmering dragon scales rise and dissolve along the landscape of my skin. I stretch out my fingers to marvel at my once simple hands; the roped sinew of dragon tendons ruptures forth and then disappears again. With no sign that this shapeshifting will settle back into my human form, I stand at the temple door studying my body.

The gentle presence of Mahavatar Babaji now emerges from the temple entrance. He smiles at me, welcoming me with an embrace.

MAHAVATAR BABAJI SPEAKS:

"In your sovereignty you can always choose which form to embody that best serves the different needs arising in every present moment. The Sophia Dragon is one of the first created forms of Sophia, as well as a *birther* of form. The angelic dragon DNA of The Sophia Code within you is surfacing to reveal that the sovereign power of all form is now accessible for your divine purpose on Earth. This hour is ordained for you to embody your sovereignty by receiving your Golden Dragon Light Body; for the wisdom and medicine of all other forms can be found within this one."

I am filled with appreciation for the guiding presence of Babaji and nod in agreement that I am ready to be initiated. We turn to face the gilded temple entrance that is bejeweled with precious stones of meteorite from across the cosmos. As we approach the entrance, I see my reflection shining off the pure gold door. Babaji touches the door and the gold melts away into a stargate of piercing white light that we walk through.

I now call forth the full presence of my Oversoul and Higher Self to oversee and direct my initiation in The Dragon Heart Temple.

I am within an ocean of pearlescent white light. For a moment, this pure white light is all that I can see. My eyes seek for a contrast of other colors or forms to define where I am, but it is only this light that I see. I breathe into this light. I allow the light to fill my awareness and I relax.

I soften and surrender even more into the white light. My eyes shift to gradually perceive gentle waves of energy rippling throughout the pearlescent white light. The rippling waves move in the serpentine patterns of a river. My eyes continue to calibrate within this brilliant light to watch the waves of energy take on more detail.

I catch glimpses of shimmering, pearlescent white dragon scales that slip in and out of my perception. The dragon scales flash through my mind and I feel the sacred geometry of perfect thought forms impressed upon my awareness.

I am now aware of an angelic presence swimming with me in this light. Moving with greater visibility now, the dragon scales appear and disappear, flashing in and out of the light waves with more frequency.

Magnetized by this revelation, I follow the serpentine path created by the dragon scales, emerging in and out of the radiant light. With each step forward into the dazzling light, I consider how enormous this dragon must be, for I am only able to perceive mere glimpses of its white scales. A large cross-section of the dragon scales now reemerges from the light, directly in front of me.

Peering up close, I can now see the pearlescent sheen of every known and unknown color in the universe mirrored in each of the scales. I deeply breathe in, awed by the crystalline beauty of their rippling iridescence. The dragon scales now recede and organize themselves into the outline of a doorway. I hear Babaji's voice from an unknown location guide me to now step through the dragon-scaled doorway.

As I step through the doorway, the light waves slightly shift in vibration to define more form and color for my perception. Stairs appear before me, leading up to a luminous golden temple, which is the inner sanctum of The Dragon Heart Temple. I begin to climb the stairway.

Arriving at the temple entrance, I see an enormous white marble fountain. Gently cascading at its center is a spring source of pure water. Mother Mary and Quan Yin appear, welcoming me with open arms. They motion for me to step before the spring of holy water so that they may bless me.

Baptized by their loving hearts and hands, my eyes now easily adjust to take in the brilliant light of this golden sanctum. Mother Mary places her hands on my heart chakra and Quan Yin places her hands on my crown chakra. I invite their quantum blessings to flow through my body, filling me with divine love. Together they remind me that I am worthy of entering this inner sanctum of The Dragon Heart Temple.

The blessings of divine love flow through my core and fill my root chakra, nourishing the winged dragons of kundalini at the base of my spine. Mother Mary asks for me to let go of my need for understanding and to trust her guidance. I exhale and let go further. She reminds me that everything and everyone that I will see in the golden temple is a reflection of my true self.

I breathe in and feel the two winged dragons of kundalini begin to rise from the base of my spine. The energy of their divine life force releases from my root chakra, traveling up my central sushumna channel. Crisscrossing at the center of my sacral chakra, solar plexus chakra, heart chakra, throat chakra, and third eye chakra, the two dragons complete their ascent by opening their mouths over my pituitary gland. Their tongues unfurl, dripping with golden nectar that baptizes my third eye with the sight of Sophia.

At the crown of my head, Quan Yin guides my kundalini energy to shower as a fountain of luminous light waves over my body. I circulate the golden fountain of my life force in a circuitous cycle of movement to travel along my sushumna channel from root to crown and back again. Quan Yin reminds me that the kundalini life force is the dragon's Breath of Life within me. It is a vehicle for embodying my sovereign power and divine inheritance within human form.

Revitalized by their ceremonial blessing, my skin feels radiant all over my body. Coated with a flexible strength, my spinal column feels perfectly aligned. Standing tall, I walk past a colonnade of white marble pillars that breathe with veins of gold. I now enter into the vast inner sanctuary of The Dragon Heart Temple.

The vast space is entirely filled with the iridescent gold and pearlescent white light of Sophia. Her formless holy presence creates the architecture of this inner sanctum as a perfect thought form emanating from Her radiant light. The faces of innumerable Ascended Masters, who are the High Council members of The Sophia Dragon Tribe, appear gathered beneath the great centralized light above the sanctuary that is the omniscient Holy

Spirit of Sophia. These masters smile a familiar warm welcome to my heart.

I adjust my eyes to peer into this luminous central field and witness the massive forms of two pearlescent white dragons. In the heart of Sophia, they are forever ascending in a DNA helix flight pattern as the Seraphiel Sophia Dragons. I cannot see where their bodies begin or end. Countless angelic wings line the length of their bodies, whirling in and out of my perception. Rainbows and lightning flash from their white scales, as they emerge in and out of Sophia's central field of light.

My ears are filled with the rapture of angelic harmonics that rise in celestial overtones of joy. The voices sing out from thousands of eyes that gently open and then recede back into The Sophia Dragons' scales. I watch as teardrops of diamonds and pearls roll down from the eyes of these dragon scales, singing the Songs of Sophia.

Within this Holy of Holies, I am standing in the presence of Sophia, the One Divine Mother Creatrix of All Life. I bear witness to the highest seraphim of Her inner being: The Sophia Dragon mothers of perfect sovereign creation.

I feel the double helix structure of my carbon-based DNA activated by the spiraling flight pattern of the Seraphiel Sophia Dragons. The crystalline chromosomes of my divine genome light up, vibrating in resonance with their angelic rapture. The kundalini energy circulating within my body feeds my atomic universe with golden nectar. As I witness the glory of Sophia's original blueprint for my sovereign free will, the dragon embodiment of my own Higher Self awakens within me.

The first seven Divine Feminine Christ Keycodes now step forward from their place in the High Council. Isis, Hathor, Green Tara, Mother Mary, Mary Magdalene, Quan Yin, and White Buffalo Woman create a circle of support around me. From the great central light of Sophia, emerges the form of a third Sophia Dragon. As she descends towards me, her body reduces in size so that I may see her face.

The Sophia Dragon lands and positions her radiant body in front of me, to look at eye level. She stares into the halls of my soul and I am naked. Any uncertainty about who I am or residual thoughts of personal unworthiness flee in the unblinking eyes of The Sophia Dragon. I witness universes of star nurseries inside her gaze. I have never engaged with a form as ancient and magnificent as this Sophia Dragon; the entire cosmos stares back at me within her two eyes.

Everything that I have ever thought I knew about reality dissolves in this moment. In my willingness to dissolve the need for understanding, my body is filled with the bliss of my innocence. Gratitude sweeps through me as I stare into the eyes of this ineffable mystery of Sophia's mighty seraphim. The Sophia Dragon smiles back at me, from her heart to mine.

She opens her mighty mouth and breathes the stardust of her Holy Spirit upon me. A windfall of pure divine love and crystalline blessings travels through my body and soul, instantly dissolving lifetimes of painful memories from my carbon-based DNA. In every direction, across the space-time continuum, all of my bloodlines are instantaneously freed from the suffering of my ancestors.

I hear the voice of my ancestors celebrating, as they are guided by White Buffalo Woman to now peacefully rest in the great central light of Sophia. Their journey home is complete. My bone marrow begins to heat up and I feel the ancient records of all my lifetimes opening within me.

Babaji steps forward. He bows to The Sophia Dragon and then turns to me and speaks: "We invite you to access the Akashic Records of all your lifetimes, so that you may be honored for your every embodiment of self-mastery in form. Breathing into your records instantly activates this information."

I keep my eyes in alignment with the unwavering gaze of The Sophia Dragon and focus on my breath as it rises and falls within my body. I notice that I am breathing through my skin as well as my lungs. The pearlescent sheen of dragon scales mesmerizes my awareness into a meditative focus.

With every breath in, I feel my way deeper inside the universe of my DNA. The Sophia Dragon follows me inward, and together we fly to the encoded records that reveal my lifetimes of self-mastery. A golden blueprint sequenced with the history of all my simultaneous incarnations lights up within my bone marrow. I hear the voice of The Sophia Dragon speaking inside of me: "You can project any idea into form. Command that you witness these lifetimes before you."

By the power of my I Am Presence, I command to witness the self-mastery of all my lifetimes simultaneously happening now.

Form after form that I have lived as in other lifetimes line up along the curves of The Sophia Dragon's body. I stare into so many familiar faces, both male and female, human or otherwise; each face smiles back at me as one of my incarnated identities. Their eyes reveal to me the stories of my self-mastery across space and time. Every incarnation orchestrated by my Oversoul is a facet of the one body of wisdom that I am.

THE SOPHIA DRAGON SPEAKS:

"The heart of a Sophia Dragon is also a womb of creation. Our hearts were designed by Sophia to create exactly how She does: we instantaneously create sovereign new worlds by the power of our thoughts, which we carefully gestate into form within the sanctuary of our heart womb.

"The size of our bodies represents the size of our ever-expanding consciousness. We gestate and give birth to new species, planets, galaxies, and even new universes within our heart wombs. A Sophia Dragon is an embodiment of Sophia's unlimited sovereign nature to create.

"*The Golden Dragon Light Body* is an ancient spiritual technology created by The Sophia Dragons for accessing your own sovereign ability to create how we create. The Golden Dragon Light Body is designed to anchor the invincible qualities of your Higher Self consciousness within your human body and awareness as a living master of light. You can think of The Golden Dragon Light Body as a suit you put on that fits over your physical body's auric field, anchoring at your Sacred Heart.

"The heart womb chakra of your Golden Dragon Light Body is identical in power to the heart womb of a Sophia Dragon. Within your heart womb chakra is the ability to manifest any sovereign creation into form. This spiritual technology supports the success of your divine mission to create an entirely new world in this lifetime. You have come to present the quantum potential of a universe that far surpasses current human understanding.

"A master of light is a pure vessel for the light to be birthed as any perfect thought into form. To birth the evolutionary desires of your soul into form, you must live as the master of light within the temple of your Golden Dragon Light Body. For a dragon is ruled by neither heaven nor earth, for it creates both, by the power of pure thought that is protected by the invincible nature of a perfect and mighty divine love.

"A Golden Dragon Light Body is cultivated with positive visualization, daily invocations of your Higher Self, and divinely guided acts of self-mastery. With focus, your Golden Dragon Light Body can be strengthened from its conception as an etheric energy body to a highly evolved, palatable layer of spiritual technology that tangibly interfaces with your body's physicality. Let us now initiate your heart to receive and anchor your Golden Dragon Light Body."

I look beyond The Sophia Dragon's eyes, to scan the serpentine line of all my lifetimes. The Sophia Dragon follows my gaze and lifts her mighty head to breathe the Breath of Life along the line of my incarnated forms. Her polished gold talons begin to nimbly knit together tendrils of light waves, connecting the hearts of all my incarnations into one dragon body.

I blink several times, my perception calibrating to keep up with how fast The Sophia Dragon is alchemizing the mastery of all my embodiments. I witness all of my lifetimes being unified within a single body of wisdom that is woven together with iridescent golden scales. The Sophia Dragon begins softly singing as she works. She sings the many names of all my incarnations, calling back their power to be woven into this unified field with the loving guidance of her masterful claws.

With a final high-pitched tone, The Sophia Dragon steps back to witness her artistry. Her heart womb momentarily expands into a blinding golden light, which is released as a final blessing upon her creation. I now look upon a perfectly formed Golden Dragon of Light, whose scales each shimmer as a quality of my true nature.

THE SOPHIA DRAGON SPEAKS:

"This is your Golden Dragon Light Body: a glorious manifestation arising from all of your embodiments of self-mastery. It is a living spiritual technology created for your Higher Self to interface with your human body. Downloading this technology upgrades your body's many systems for embodying your sovereign divinity while on Earth.

"Your Golden Dragon Light Body anchors the omniscient power of your Higher Self within you, so that you may command miraculous manifestations in accordance with the divine will of Sophia. You will thrive within the golden scales of your true self, creating the desires of your Sacred Heart with the grace and ease of dragon magick.

"This technology is foundational for those living masters whose destiny is to create a new paradigm of Heaven on Earth and contribute a lasting Legacy of Love for the benefit of future generations to come. For a Golden Dragon teacher creates Heaven on Earth with the magick of pure thought focused into form, which is nurtured and protected by an invincible divine love. Your Golden Dragon Light Body is a manifestation of this magick and it is your divine inheritance from Sophia."

Once again, Babaji steps forward from the High Council to facilitate an initiation for my awareness. Babaji asks that I now answer five questions.

MAHAVATAR BABAJI SPEAKS:

"Do you accept responsibility for the almighty power of your sovereign Holy Spirit expressing its pure divine potential within your human life?"

Yes.

"Do you accept responsibility for acting in alignment with the divine will of your Higher Self so that you may live as a master creator of limitless life and absolute sovereignty?"

Yes.

"Do you accept the power of your I Am Presence to now activate The Sophia Code within you and download the spiritual technology of your Golden Dragon Light Body?"

Yes.

"Do you accept responsibility for the almighty power of your sovereign Holy Spirit which can create new worlds into form?"

Yes.

"Do you accept responsibility for the almighty power of your sovereign Holy Spirit continually expanding all of Sophia's creation?"

Yes.

"With your free will, I invite you to command that it is so." Babaji smiles and bows to my heart as he returns to his place in the High Council.

I accept that I hold the golden keys to my Heaven on Earth.
I accept that I create my reality, by the power of my word.
My word is good, my heart is pure.
By the loving power of my pure word, I now download The Golden Dragon Light Body and anchor it at my Sacred Heart with the following sequence of commands.

I invoke The Sophia Dragons as overlighting guides for the gateway of my eighth chakra, above my head.
I open and align my eighth chakra now.

I invoke White Buffalo Woman as an overlighting guide for my crown chakra.
I open and align my crown chakra now.

I invoke Quan Yin as an overlighting guide for my third eye chakra.
I open and align my third eye chakra now.

I invoke Mary Magdalene as an overlighting guide for my throat chakra.
I open and align my throat chakra now.

I invoke Mother Mary as an overlighting guide for my heart chakra.
I open and align my heart chakra now.

I invoke Green Tara as an overlighting guide for my solar plexus chakra.
I open and align my solar plexus chakra now.

I invoke Hathor as an overlighting guide for my sacral chakra.
I open and align my sacral chakra now.

I invoke Isis as an overlighting guide for my root chakra.
I open and align my root chakra now.

In preparation to receive my Golden Dragon Light Body, I now invoke my Higher Self to dissolve all obstructions within the blueprints of my eight major chakras.

I now affirm in self-recognition:
I am the living master who forgives myself.

In preparation to receive my Golden Dragon Light Body, I now invoke my Higher Self to upgrade my eight major chakras and their corresponding light bodies.

I now affirm in self-recognition:
I am the living master who heals myself.

In preparation to receive my Golden Dragon Light Body, I now invoke my Higher Self to upgrade my kundalini channels and neurological pathways.

I now affirm in self-recognition:
I am the living master who initiates myself.

In preparation to receive my Golden Dragon Light Body, I now invoke my Higher Self to activate Keycode 777 of The Sophia Code within the holy halls of my crystalline chromosomes. Within my DNA, I witness an interface of encoded light language that is a divine platform for downloading and anchoring the technology of my Golden Dragon Light Body.

I now affirm in self-recognition:
I am the living master who intimately knows the universe of my true self.

In preparation to receive my Golden Dragon Light Body, I now invoke my Higher Self to activate the stargate of my heart chakra. I open the stargate of my heart chakra, invoking every dimension of my being into an active zero still-point. I invoke the power of all my lifetimes to participate and actively receive this empowerment in the unified field of my whole self now.

I now affirm in self-recognition:
I am the living master who commands the heaven of my heart to exist on Earth.

Activating the sovereignty of my eighth chakra:
I invoke The Sophia Dragons to bless The Golden Dragon Light Body technology of my Higher Self and I begin downloading it now through my eighth chakra. I welcome this angelic technology of my own Holy Spirit to interface and integrate within every system of my human body now.

Activating the sovereignty of my crown chakra:
I invoke White Buffalo Woman's blessing and overlighting support as I now receive the crown chakra of my Golden Dragon Light Body to interface with my human crown chakra.

My Higher Self spins my human crown chakra into perfect alignment with the crown chakra of my Golden Dragon Light Body.

Accelerating my human crown chakra up to light speed: *I now download the crown chakra of my Golden Dragon Light Body.*

I witness it anchor and integrate with my human crown chakra, on all four levels of my Be-ing now: physical, emotional, mental, and spiritual.

I anchor this Golden Dragon technology here on Earth through my sovereign command to do so and as such I reveal the truth of my own direct connection to the Source, by crowning my awareness.

By the power of my I Am Presence: It is done.
I declare that I am a living master of Holy Communion.

Activating the sovereignty of my third eye chakra:
I invoke Quan Yin's blessing and overlighting support as I now accept the third eye chakra of my Golden Dragon Light Body to interface with my human third eye chakra.

My Higher Self spins my human third eye chakra into perfect alignment with the third eye chakra of my Golden Dragon Light Body.

Accelerating my human third eye chakra up to light speed: *I now download the third eye chakra of my Golden Dragon Light Body.*

I witness it anchor and integrate with my human third eye chakra, on all four levels of my Be-ing now: physical, emotional, mental, and spiritual.

I anchor this Golden Dragon technology here on Earth through my sovereign command to do so and as such I embody the clear sight of Sophia Christ consciousness.

By the power of my I Am Presence: It is done.
I declare that I am a living master of clear and piercing sight.

Activating the sovereignty of my throat chakra:
I invoke Mary Magdalene's blessing and overlighting support as I now accept the throat chakra of my Golden Dragon Light Body to interface with my human throat chakra.

My Higher Self spins my human throat chakra into perfect alignment with the throat chakra of my Golden Dragon Light Body.

Accelerating my human throat chakra up to light speed: *I now download the throat chakra of my Golden Dragon Light Body.*

I witness it anchor and integrate with my human throat chakra, on all four levels of my Be-ing now: physical, emotional, mental, and spiritual.

I anchor this Golden Dragon technology here on Earth through my sovereign command to do so and as such I reveal the power of my voice to command miracles beyond the laws of form.

By the power of my I Am Presence: It is done.
I declare that I am a living master of the spoken word.

Activating the sovereignty of my heart chakra:
I invoke Mother Mary's blessing and overlighting support as I now accept the heart womb chakra of my Golden Dragon Light Body to interface with my human heart chakra.

My Higher Self spins my human heart chakra into perfect alignment with the heart womb chakra of my Golden Dragon Light Body.

Accelerating my human heart chakra up to light speed: *I now download the heart womb chakra of my Golden Dragon Light Body.*

I witness it anchor and integrate with my human heart chakra, on all four levels of my Be-ing now: physical, emotional, mental, and spiritual.

I anchor this Golden Dragon technology here on Earth through my sovereign command to do so and as such I reveal the power of my heart to birth and anchor a new paradigm of divine love.

By the power of my I Am Presence: It is done.
I declare that I am a living master in service to my own Sacred Heart.

Activating the sovereignty of my solar plexus chakra:
I invoke Green Tara's blessing and overlighting support as I now accept the solar plexus chakra of my Golden Dragon Light Body to interface with my human solar plexus chakra.

My Higher Self spins my human solar plexus chakra into perfect alignment with the solar plexus chakra of my Golden Dragon Light Body.

Accelerating my human solar plexus chakra up to light speed: *I now download the solar plexus chakra of my Golden Dragon Light Body.*

I witness it anchor and integrate with my human solar plexus chakra, on all four levels of my Be-ing now: physical, emotional, mental, and spiritual.

I anchor this Golden Dragon technology here on Earth through my sovereign command to do so and as such I reveal the power of embodying my sovereign free will.

By the power of my I Am Presence: It is done.
I declare that I am a living master whose sovereign free will is consecrated to live in alignment with the divine will of my Higher Self.

Activating the sovereignty of my sacral chakra:
I invoke Hathor's blessing and overlighting support as I now accept the sacral chakra of my Golden Dragon Light Body to interface with my human sacral chakra.

My Higher Self spins my human sacral chakra into perfect alignment with the sacral chakra of my Golden Dragon Light Body.

Accelerating my human sacral chakra up to light speed: *I now download the sacral chakra of my Golden Dragon Light Body.*

I witness it anchor and integrate with my human sacral chakra, on all four levels of my Be-ing now: physical, emotional, mental, and spiritual.

I anchor this Golden Dragon technology here on Earth through my sovereign command to do so and as such I embody my absolute worth as a Daughter and Son of the Most High.

By the power of my I Am Presence: It is done.
I declare that I am a living master blessed to receive my divine inheritance now.

Activating the sovereignty of my root chakra:
I invoke Isis' blessing and overlighting support as I now accept the root chakra of my Golden Dragon Light Body to interface with my human root chakra.

My Higher Self spins my human root chakra into perfect alignment with the root chakra of my Golden Dragon Light Body.

Accelerating my human root chakra up to light speed: *I now download the root chakra of my Golden Dragon Light Body.*

I witness it anchor and integrate with my human root chakra, on all four levels of my Be-ing now: physical, emotional, mental, and spiritual.

I anchor this Golden Dragon technology here on Earth through my sovereign command to do so and as such I embody the full divine potential of my humanity.

By the power of my I Am Presence: It is done.
I declare that I am a living master, blessing the Earth with my activated embodiment of The Sophia Code.

The Sophia Dragon blesses me by blowing her Breath of Life through my eighth chakra, unifying the seven major chakras of my human form and their corresponding light bodies to now fully interface with the technology of my Golden Dragon Light Body.

I feel golden scales unfold about eight feet out from my physical body, enveloping my auric field within my Golden Dragon Light Body. My human awareness explores how it feels to live within the vast musculature of my dragon light body. I enjoy how invincible I feel in the power and protection of this divine love.

I feel a massive tail emerge from my root chakra and I drop its weight down to connect directly into the Earth. As an important step in my physical integration, Mother Earth responds to our connection by accepting my new dragon light body as a part of her body as well.

I blink to readjust my sight and peer through the bejeweled eyes of my Golden Dragon Light Body. They focus my perception into facets of ancient wisdom and insight. Through the eyes of my Golden Dragon Light Body it is easier to see the one light of Sophia from which all of physical reality arises. The physical world of form feels more flexible to the power of my thoughts.

I reach out my hands, stretching out my fingers to feel the dragon talons that now interface with my fingertips. I bring my hands to the center of my heart and allow my dragon talons to nimbly weave my human awareness into the wisdom of my new dragon heart womb.

I feel much larger in breadth and size and I breathe into my expanded Sacred Heart. My awareness has been initiated into greater faith and I trust my Sacred Heart, more than ever, to guide me in the daily choices of how to embody my sovereign power. I feel the angelic nature of my Golden Dragon Light Body, which envelops me in a heightened awareness of how easily I can create my Heaven on Earth, for the benefit of all beings. I feel myself relaxing deeper into my sovereign power. All is well.

I stretch out my body, raising my arms up, and feel my feet grip the temple floor with an invincible confidence. I decide to explore walking around the sanctuary in my Golden Dragon Light Body.

The Ascended Masters step back, rejoicing in my full activation with cheers and applause. My physical body moves with stealth and perceives with an ancient awareness. I breathe deeply between strides and feel how light waves are magnetized to my radiant golden scales. I turn to look down my side and flash a rainbow off my scales to Quan Yin. Mother Mary laughs and I smile through my bejeweled eyes to thank her for all the help.

With each movement, I integrate my Golden Dragon Light Body. I feel the spin of my electrons accelerating in my human DNA, creating a stronger magnetic field around my physical body that attracts and digests greater amounts of light. Enveloped within the power of my dragon light body, I feel a new level of confidence for walking the Earth in my human form.

I turn back to the High Council of my Ascended Master friends and offer my appreciation with love. Babaji steps forward, blessing me by sealing this empowerment in the light and fire of my own Holy Spirit forever.

I embrace The Sophia Dragon with my overflowing gratitude for her sacred magick, divine love, and immaculate support. I look up to the Seraphiel Sophia Dragon mothers spiraling above us, within Sophia's great central light. With silent awe and respect, I extend my heartfelt acknowledgment of their eternal support for my success.

With my hands upon her scales, my awareness merges back into the ocean of radiant starlight. I follow the serpentine path of her pearlescent white scales through the piercing white light. I locate the dragon-scaled doorway and walk back into this present moment, returning my awareness to my physical body and environment.

I allow my human awareness to easily adjust and integrate the perception and skills of my Golden Dragon Light Body, at its own pace within my daily life. I feel my tail grounding out this ceremony and my new scales ripple into my present reality. All is well.

By the power of my I Am Presence, I now command:
It is done.
It is done.
It is done.
By the power of 3, a perfect trinity: It is done.

This initiation of Keycode 777 of The Sophia Code within me is now accomplished. I close this ceremony with appreciation and reverence for my true self and the love of All That Is, supporting my eternal success.

And so it is.

ABOUT KAIA RA

Kaia Ra is the world renowned Oracle for an Ascended Master High Council called *The Sophia Dragon Tribe* and the international bestselling author of *The Sophia Code*. She is a Divine Feminine speaker, ceremonialist, and ordained minister teaching The Sophia Code curriculum worldwide. Surviving multiple near death experiences, her living transmission is of shamanic proportions. Kaia Ra leads an international movement and modern day mystery school for mentoring initiates in the codex, and offers *The Heaven on Earth Prayer Collective*.

KAIARA.COM